ULTRA
at
SEA

FICTION

We Joined The Navy
We Saw The Sea
Down The Hatch
Never Go To Sea
All The Nice Girls
HMS Leviathan
The Fighting Temeraire
One of Our Warships
Good Enough For Nelson
Aircraft Carrier
The Good Ship Venus
A Drowning War

NON-FICTION

Freedom's Battle: The War at Sea 1939–1945
The Forgotten Fleet
The Little Wonder: The Story of the Festiniog Railway
Sir Walter Raleigh
Air Power at Sea 1939–1945
Hurrah For the Life Of A Sailor: Life on the Lower Deck of the
    Victorian Navy
The Victoria Cross At Sea
War In The Pacific: Pearl Harbor to Tokyo Bay
Sink The Haguro!
Hands To Action Stations!: Naval Poetry and Verse of WW2
Find, Fix and Strike: The Fleet Air Arm at War 1939–1945
Below The Belt: Novelty, Subterfuge and Surprise in Naval
    Warfare
Jellicoe
Captains & Kings: The Royal Navy & The Royal Family 1901–1981
Convoy: The Defence of Sea Trade 1890–1980
The Death of The Scharnhorst
The Little Wonder: 150 Years of the Festiniog Railway
    (Revised edition)
Carrier Glorious: The Life & Death of an Aircraft Carrier
Air Power at Sea 1945 to Today
Warrior: The First and the Last

ULTRA
at
SEA

How Breaking the Nazi Code
Affected Allied Naval Strategy
During World War II

JOHN WINTON

WILLIAM MORROW AND COMPANY, INC.
NEW YORK

Library of Congress Cataloging-in-Publication Data

Winton, John, 1931–
    ULTRA at sea: how breaking the Nazi code affected Allied naval
strategy / John Winton.
        p.   cm.
    Includes index.
    ISBN 0-688-08546-6
    1. World War, 1939–1945—Cryptography.   2. World War, 1939–1945—
Naval operations, English.   3. World War, 1939–1945—Secret
service—Great Britain.   I. Title.
D810.C88W57   1989
940.54′5941—dc19   88-32654
                                                                              CIP

Printed in the United States of America

First U.S. Edition

1 2 3 4 5 6 7 8 9 10

CONTENTS

ILLUSTRATIONS

Nos. 8, 11, 12, 13 and 14 are reproduced by kind permission of The Imperial War Museum.

1 | EARLY PRE-ULTRA DAYS

When one player consistently knows which cards his opponent holds, how much and how often dare he go on winning before his opponent begins to suspect and changes the cards or the game? That, in essence, was the main problem – unique in the history of warfare – which the possession of Special Intelligence (later to be code-named ULTRA) posed for the Allies in World War Two.

The problem was especially acute at sea, where the Admiralty traditionally exercised only remote control, redistributing naval forces around the various commands worldwide to meet the changing needs of strategy and giving the local Commander-in-Chief all the forces and intelligence it could, but then wherever possible leaving him, as the man on the spot, to make the final decisions. Bitter experience had shown that interference from afar often led to catastrophe.

But ULTRA eventually gave the Admiralty an unprecedented overall view of the enemy's naval operations and intentions and, because only the Admiralty could know the whole picture, ULTRA forced the Admiralty to take a much closer and more active part in the day-to-day running of operations, especially in the early days and particularly in the Atlantic and Home commands.

Always a present operational gain had to be balanced against the future prospect of losing what Mr Churchill called 'the precious secret of ULTRA'. Too much success could be disastrous. Too many U-boats sunk, for instance, at their remote refuelling rendezvous might arouse the enemy's suspicions and cause him to change cyphers which had been only broken after much labour over a long period of time. Worse, it might even cause him to doubt the inviolability of the Enigma coding machine.

Therefore, in the early days, much of the intelligence provided by ULTRA could not be used, either at once or for some considerable time. Nobody knew how much could be used operationally. The

Admiralty had to gain experience gradually. But as time passed and a wider intelligence picture was revealed, as more and more jigsaw pieces slotted into place, as the significance of events and signals sometimes years in the past became apparent, so ULTRA could be used with growing confidence and in an ever wider operational capacity.

However, just as at first the operational use of ULTRA erred intentionally on the side of over-timidity, so, in the latter days of the war, as one intelligence officer later admitted, 'if there had been a turning-off of the tap of Special Intelligence, before the end of the war, and before the result was beyond any reasonable doubt, the intelligence directorates would have been hard put to it to find those capable, by a keen analytical examination of the lesser grades of intelligence, of producing an accurate forecast or estimate of the enemy's dispositions and intentions'.

So accustomed did intelligence officers eventually become to a steady and complete flow of ULTRA that other forms of intelligence, which might tend to point in another direction, were sometimes ignored. For example, the German advance in the Ardennes in December, 1944, was not foreshadowed by ULTRA because the Germans were keeping W/T silence. But excellent intelligence from photo-reconnaissance, which had revealed a considerable build-up of German forces and vehicles in the rear of the Ardennes front, was discounted.

ULTRA, though crucial, was after all only one form of intelligence. Under the general heading of Sigint, or Signal Intelligence, which was any Intelligence derived from the Signal Intelligence Service, were the 'Y' Service, as it was known in Great Britain, or Radio Intelligence Service as it was known in the United States, which was responsible for the interception and exploitation of all enemy radio transmissions which might yield intelligence, including direction finding (D/F), navigational beacons and aids, and enemy radar and infra-red transmissions. T.A., or Traffic Analysis, was the study of communications networks and the procedures, signals, callsigns, and plain language messages passing over them, coupled with the use of D/F and other technical aids. RFP was a process which filmed the type and peculiarities of a particular transmitter, while TINA was the study of the idiosyncratic morse characteristics of individual wireless operators.

Various forms of intelligence had code-words. ULTRA was the code-word for Special Intelligence, resulting from the solution of high-grade codes and cyphers. Crypt Intelligence, code-worded CIRO-PEARL, was intelligence resulting from medium grade codes and cyphers, or, code-worded PEARL, from low-grade codes and cyphers. Intelligence from Traffic Analysis, excluding D/F, was THUMB 1, while THUMB 2 was that derived from a study of D/F bearings and results from other technical aids.

But even Sigint itself was only one of the intelligence sources available. There were reports from warships visiting foreign ports, and from naval attachés accredited to foreign embassies. Returning businessmen could often provide invaluable information from their business contacts and personal observations. Photo-reconnaissance, even by the beginning of the war, was a highly developed skill. There were reports from agents or foreign nationals, interrogation of prisoners of war, those of the enemy after capture and our own after escape. A study of enemy newspapers and enemy radio was always rewarding; in the autumn of 1940 the exultant German media, rejoicing in success, provided priceless intelligence on, for example, the U-boats, the individual captains, and their crews (so much intelligence, in fact, that for the rest of the war Naval Intelligence Department resisted the strongest pressures, from the Prime Minister downwards, to provide more publicity material on the successes of Allied submarines and Allied anti-U-boat measures).

Much geographical, topographical and statistical intelligence could be gained from pre-war publications. A holiday resort brochure, or a family snapshot, could well show the width, gradient and even the texture of a possible assault landing beach. The 1938 edition of *Jane's Fighting Ships* contained a full-page advertisement for German *Schnellbootes*; thus, the Admiralty was actually urged to buy new, before the war, one of the E-boats it made such strenuous efforts to capture after the war had begun.

But ULTRA was the most highly prized intelligence jewel of all. In January, 1940, when the Admirality became aware of the potentialities of this Special Intelligence, which was from a particularly sensitive and absolutely reliable source, it warned the C-in-C Home Fleet and certain other chosen senior naval officers that it was possible they might be receiving intelligence from high-grade Sigint which would be sent to them in the Flag Officer's cypher, in special messages prefixed by the code-word HYDRO. The prefix HYDRO was used until June, 1941, when the German naval Enigma was first read currently and the barest trickle of Special Intelligence suddenly became a flood. HYDRO was then replaced by ULTRA.

The Admiralty took the strictest precautions to safeguard the ULTRA secret. It was revealed only to certain Flag and Senior Officers, and not more than three other selected members of the cypher staff. The names of these 'ULTRA-indoctrinated' officers had to be communicated to NID. NID had to be informed of any alterations to the list. When a name was to be added, it had to be reported to NID at least a month beforehand and the 'new' officer had to be briefed by the Flag or Senior Officer concerned. An ULTRA-briefed officer was not supposed to place himself in any position where he could be captured by the enemy. (This posed particular problems for the RAF, when 'indoctrinated' officers had to be restrained from returning to flying with an operational squadron.)

Messages prefixed ULTRA were encyphered on special 'one-time' pads, each having a unique combination of letter groups, which gave total security. Only one copy of an ULTRA signal was made by the recipient and it was kept locked in a separate log. Pads, signals and signal logs had to be kept separate from ordinary cyphers and cypher logs. All cypher groups and rough workings were kept locked by an ULTRA officer and burned when no longer required (by order, this was usually to be no longer than a week from the date of receipt). ULTRA messages in the log were burned when no longer required (by order, this was usually to be no longer than a month from the date of receipt).

It was forbidden to mention the word ULTRA, or to make an reference of any kind which might suggest a source of special intelligence in any other signals, or in war diaries or reports of proceedings, or to reply to an ULTRA signal with the prefix ULTRA REPLY. If information first transmitted in an ULTRA signal had to be passed on in another signal, it had to be paraphrased and so worded that, if captured or intercepted by the enemy, any reference to enemy intelligence could not be traced back to ULTRA alone. Any reference to the name of an enemy ship had to be avoided and any positions given in an ULTRA signal had to be given in a different way.

Any operations undertaken as a result of ULTRA had to have a 'cover story' – some corroborative information such as naval or air reconnaissance, or a source such as 'Y', to account for the presence of Allied forces at the scene. It was very easy, through an excess of zeal, to make mistakes over this requirement. As Group Captain R. H. Humphreys, Head of 'U' Air Intelligence Section at the Government Code and Cypher School at Bletchley Park, wrote after the war, there was 'always a danger that – in order to exploit a good opportunity – extremely thin corroborative information would be viewed through rose-coloured glasses and be construed into the cast-iron alibi required. My own maxim was that the alibi must contain more information, of the kind which MIGHT induce a NORMAL operation, than the original item from "U", and that I must not assume that, in the event of a security investigation, the enemy would automatically dismiss the possibility of a "U" leakage, merely because there had been another source. You can't fool all of the people all of the time.'

By the outbreak of the war it was known at the Government Code and Cypher School (GC & CS) at Bletchley Park that the German Navy, Army and Air Force were all using cyphers based upon the Enigma machine, which was an electro-mechanical wired encyphering machine with a series of drums or wheels, first available on the European commercial market in the 1920s. The arrangements and settings of the drums or wheels on the Enigma machine could be changed as often as every 24 hours. Anyone not in possession of the correct settings was then confronted by the problem of choosing between one hundred and fifty million, million, million solutions. So, clearly, GC & CS would have to mount a massive co-ordinated cryptanalytical offensive upon the Enigma cyphers of all three German armed services.

Successes against the German naval Enigma were not achieved until March and April, 1941, and then only in fits and starts. Thus Special Intelligence played no part in the early events of the war at sea.

There was no warning from Special Intelligence (nor indeed from any other naval intelligence) of Kapitan Leutnant Gunther Prien's sortie into Scapa Flow in *U–47* early on 14 October, 1939, when he sank the battleship *Royal Oak* at anchor. The German pocket battleship *Admiral Graf Spee* sailed unremarked from Wilhelmshaven on 21 August, 1939. The Admiralty disposed hunting groups of warships world-wide to intercept her. But when, having already sunk eight merchant vessels of 49,383 tons in the Atlantic and one of 706 tons in the Indian Ocean, *Admiral Graf Spee* met the cruisers *Exeter*, *Ajax* and *Achilles* off the River Plate on 13 December, 1939, the encounter was brought about by Commodore Henry Harwood's own interpretation of *Admiral Graf Spee*'s likely intentions and not by any prompting from intelligence.

Intelligence contributed nothing when the pocket battleship *Deutschland* sailed from Wilhelmshaven on 23 August, 1939, sank two ships of 6,962 tons in the Atlantic and sent the captured *City of Flint* (4,963 tons) to Tromso, and returned to Gdynia on 17 November. Similarly, the German battlecruisers *Scharnhorst* and *Gneisenau* sailed from Wilhelmshaven on 21 November, 1939. They sank the armed merchant cruiser HMS *Rawalpindi* in the North Atlantic two days later and returned unscathed on 26 November. On 18 February, 1940, these two ships sailed again with the heavy cruiser *Admiral Hipper* but turned back after a chance sighting by an aircraft of Bomber Command off the Shetland Isles.

It was very fortunate that these early sorties by heavy German warships did so little damage to Allied shipping. But intelligence could take no credit for that. The Home Fleet did sail, with intelligence information, on more than one occasion in 1939, but on false trails.

On 12 February, 1940, *U–33* was sunk by the minesweeper HMS

Gleaner whilst attempting to lay mines in the Clyde estuary and three Enigma wheels were recovered from the crew. The German patrol boat *VP2623* was captured on passage from Germany to Narvik on 26 April, 1940. Papers were taken from her which enabled GC & CS to read, retrospectively in May, the naval Enigma for six days in April. More cypher material might have been recovered, but the vessel was looted before she could be properly searched. From these snippets, such as they were, GC & CS did succeed in establishing that every German warship, even the smallest, relied entirely on Enigma machine codes.

GC & CS also confirmed that German surface ships and U-boats both used two main Enigma keys, the Home and the Foreign, changing to the Foreign in distant waters. Thus, some 95 per cent of German naval traffic was encyphered in the Home Enigma key. Even the meagre amount of information they had managed to get was still enough to show GC & CS the magnitude of the task they faced in breaking into the German naval Enigma. (Only a further five days' Home Enigma traffic, for dates in April and May, 1940, had been broken by February, 1941.)

The Foreign Enigma Key, used by the pocket battleships and the auxiliary cruisers, was never broken. Special Intelligence therefore revealed nothing about further sorties by German commerce raiders in 1940 and early 1941. The heavy cruiser *Admiral Scheer* sailed from Gdynia on 23 October, 1940, and, in a cruise which lasted until her arrival at Kiel on 1 April, 1940, sank or captured seventeen ships of 113,233 tons, including the armed merchant cruiser HMS *Jervis Bay*.

GC & CS had broken into one German Air Force Enigma key, used for operational and administrative communications, in May, 1940, and continued to read it until the end of the war. This, the first German Enigma key to be decisively broken over a long period, revealed that *Admiral Hipper* was to make a reconnaissance sortie into the Barents Sea in September, 1940.

But the German Navy Enigma was still inviolate and there was no further Enigma information when *Admiral Hipper* sailed for two more sorties late in 1940 and early in 1941. Leaving Kiel on 5 December, she sank one ship of 6,078 tons on the 24th and then attacked the large troop convoy WS.5A some 700 miles west of Finisterre on Christmas Day. Two ships in the convoy and the cruiser HMS *Berwick* were damaged before *Hipper* retired, arriving in Brest on 27 December. On 1 February *Hipper* sailed again and sank eight ships, including seven from one convoy SLS 64 on the 12th, totalling 34,042 tons, before returning to Brest on the 15th.

Scharnhorst and *Gneisenau* sailed from Kiel on 22 January, 1941, for ʌn extended cruise. Although sighted more than once by ships and aircraft, they were not intercepted and together sank or captured twenty-two ships of 115,623 tons before they arrived at Brest on 22 March.

German commerce raiders, which were merchant ships converted into warships with concealed armament, did tremendous damage to Allied shipping. Of the 'First Wave' of six, Schiff 16 *Atlantis* sailed on 31 March, 1940, and the sixth, Schiff 45 *Komet*, on 9 July. Assisted by an almost total lack of intelligence about them or their movements, by November, 1941, these six raiders had sunk eighty-eight ships, of 538,000 tons. Two were sunk: Schiff 33 *Pinguin* by the cruiser HMS *Cornwall* on 8 May, 1941, and *Atlantis* by the cruiser HMS *Devonshire* on 22 November.

In April, 1940, GC & CS broke into the Enigma key the Germans were using in Norway. HYDRO signals about German naval movements, based on these decryptions, were sent to Admiral Sir Charles Forbes, the C-in-C Home Fleet. But they were of no immediate operational value. Ignorance about the movements of German ships was almost complete. As Sir Charles complained, 'It is most galling that the enemy should know just where our ships ... always are, whereas we generally learn where his major forces are when they sink one or more of our ships.' Certainly, there had been intelligence indications before the sailing of *Scharnhorst* and *Gneisenau* on 4 June, 1940, but the correct inferences were not drawn and the sinking by these two ships of the aircraft carrier HMS *Glorious* and her destroyer escorts HMS *Acasta* and HMS *Ardent*, in a brisk gun action off northern Norway on the afternoon of 8 June, came as a shattering surprise.

Sir Charles was nearer the truth than perhaps he knew. In fact, German naval intelligence had been reading the main British naval cypher to a limited but significant extent since 1938 and, except for a short 'black-out' after the outbreak of war, were reading as much as thirty per cent of British naval traffic by the beginning of the Norwegian campaign in April, 1940. They continued to do so until the end of August, 1940, when the cyphers were modified.

The balance of decrypting success lay with the Germans throughout the first eighteen months of the battle of the Atlantic. At first the U-boats were hampered by their own lack of numbers, the relative inexperience of U-boat captains and crews, by the Germans' observance of certain legal and political restrictions on submarine warfare, and the fact that, although the Admiralty had instituted convoy immediately at the outbreak of war, many escorts were detached from convoy duties to patrol the Narrow Seas against a possible invasion of the United Kingdom.

But in August Hitler threw off all shackles from the U-boats, removed all restrictions and declared a total blockade of the British Isles. The U-boats forsook their previous tactics of attacking at periscope depth by day. Instead, they remained on the surface and attacked by night, thus being able both to evade the asdic search for submerged submarines and to use their own great surface speed (compared to the escorts). Furthermore, the fall of France allowed U-boats to operate from ports in Brittany, several hundred miles nearer the Atlantic than their German bases, which allowed them to stay longer on patrol or to patrol much further afield. June to October, 1940, was what the U-boat commanders called their 'happy time'.

This might have continued, but in November, 1940, many of the escorts guarding against invasion were restored to convoy duties and more Coastal Command aircraft were transferred to anti-submarine patrols. Nevertheless, by the spring of 1941, the numbers of U-boats had increased and the U-boat arm was preparing for a renewed offensive in the Atlantic, using 'wolfpack tactics' on a quite unprecedented scale.

The new offensive might have been decisive. But, in the spring of 1941, the German Naval Enigma at last began to yield to cryptanalytical attack. However, before ULTRA, as it was soon to be named, could play any major part in the Atlantic, it first made possible a smashing tactical victory in another theatre – the Mediterranean.

2 | THE MEDITERRANEAN AND MATAPAN
March, 1941

'Intelligence about Italy was sparse,' said Admiral Cunningham, Commander-in-Chief of the Mediterranean Fleet, at the outbreak of war; 'we had no subterranean access to Italian secret documents or decisions.' In fact, a very high proportion of Italian codes had been broken and were being read regularly at Bletchley Park for some years before the war. The Italian Navy's most secret high-grade cypher, and its general naval code book, were both being largely read as early as 1937 onwards. So, too, was one of the two codes used by Italian naval attachés at embassies abroad. Other high-grade cyphers, used by the Italian Air Force in East Africa and in the Mediterranean, by the Italian Army in Libya, and by Italian diplomatic missions and intelligence in Spain, were also being read fairly easily.

There were other, discreet, sources. According to Cunningham's Chief-of-Staff, Commodore Willis, at the outbreak of war between Great Britain and Germany in September, 1939, the British and Italian naval staffs in the Mediterranean came to an arrangement, 'to avoid incidents', whereby the Italians 'informed us of the movements of their submarines and provided surface escorts'. The only condition, said Willis, 'was that we shouldn't let the Germans know. This was very reasonable.'

This arrangement worked, to the mutual satisfaction of both sides, for some time, until MEIC (Middle East Intelligence Centre) in Cairo referred to it in their 'magazine of titbits', which had a wide circulation. The High Commissioner in Egypt 'blurted it out' to King Farouk, whose entourage was full of Italians, whence it got back to Rome, who made 'a well-justified complaint' through the British Ambassador. 'My remarks to the Head of MEIC (Colonel Cawthorne),' said Willis, 'were unprintable.'

Nevertheless, from this and other sources, but chiefly from Sigint, the British had, by June, 1940, a good knowledge of the Italian Navy and its workings, strengths and weaknesses. This level of intelligence was maintained, for a very short time, after the beginning of hostilities against Italy on 11 June.

The Mediterranean Operational Intelligence Centre (OIC) had a great deal of up-to-date information on the whereabouts of Italian submarines, their patrol areas, their numbers and order of battle. As a result, no less than nine Italian submarines were sunk or captured by the end of June. On 19 June, in the Red Sea, *Galileo Galilei* surrendered after an attack by the trawler HMS *Moonstone* and was towed by her into Aden. (Pictures of *Moonstone* entering harbour, looking extremely pleased with herself, and the story that other ships had signalled her 'Is That Your First Today?' appeared in the British press – understandably, from a publicity point of view but, from the intelligence angle, most reprehensibly.)

Documents captured from *Galileo Galilei* revealed the sailing orders and patrol areas of four more submarines, three of which were sunk, and cypher books upon which a special section of Mediterranean OIC, staffed from Bletchley Park, set to work. On 29 June, west of Crete, the destroyers *Dainty* and *Ilex* sank another Italian U-boat, *Uebi Scebeli*, and recovered the new code book, with recyphering tables, which the Italian Navy was about to introduce in July.

For the British surface fleet, too, the war began well enough, and events seemed to convince the Italian Navy that their opponents' intelligence was better than it actually was. The 2nd Destroyer Flotilla was at sea, on a sweep for Italian submarines on their way to their war stations, when war was declared, and *Dainty* attacked a submarine two hours before hostilities officially began. When, on 11 June, within only a few hours of Italy entering the war, Cunningham took his main fleet to sea for a sweep of the central Mediterranean, to attack any enemy forces which might be encountered, he did so without any specific intelligence and nothing was found.

However, D/F in Alexandria had revealed Italian ships, including the cruiser *Garibaldi*, north of Derna and actually very close to Cunningham's fleet. To Cunningham's extreme annoyance, the vital signal was received in his flagship *Warspite* too late for any action to be taken. Signalling procedures were improved. D/F signals were given a much higher priority. When Cunningham took his fleet to sea on 7 July for a sortie which resulted in an engagement with the main Italian battle fleet off the coast of Calabria on the 9th, he had the benefit of D/F intelligence as well as useful information from decoded signals in the Italian Fleet code, and some signals in plain language.

Thus, at one point in the action, Cunningham was shown a signal from the Italian cruiser admiral requesting permission to return to harbour. He remarked 'Reply – Approved!' More importantly, intelligence betrayed the intention of the Italian fleet commander Admiral Riccardi (who had actually been Cunningham's friend and guest before the war) to lure Cunningham's ships into a submarine and aircraft ambush close in to the Italian coast.

In the event *Warspite*'s main 15" guns scored a hit on the Italian flagship at the prodigious range of 13 miles – an important psychological success. The Italian fleet hauled off and never again willingly faced up to a British battleship's fire. When Cunningham finally broke off, when there was in any case no chance of engaging the enemy again before they passed through the Straits of Messina, his fleet was only 25 miles from the Calabrian coast. But, both before and after retiring, Cunningham's ships were subjected to hundreds of bombing attacks by aircraft of the Regia Aeronautica. *Warspite* and the carrier *Eagle* were picked out as special targets. Although only the cruiser *Gloucester* was hit, several others were near-missed, and the accuracy and intensity of the attacks were an ominous portent for the future.

More than once it must have appeared to the Italians that Cunningham had the assistance of more intelligence than in fact he had. On 18 July two Italian cruisers steaming eastward, bound for a shipping raid in the Aegean, were intercepted off the northern coast of Crete by the Australian cruiser HMAS *Sydney* and five destroyers. After a long running pursuit and gunnery duel, the Italian cruiser *Bartolomeo Colleoni* was sunk. This encounter must have seemed not to have been pure accident, but, in fact, it came about as a result of a chance sighting by one of the destroyers.

From mid-July, 1940, the British intelligence situation, so far as knowledge of the Italian Navy was concerned, deteriorated drastically, and permanently. During that month the Italians overhauled the high-grade cypher systems for all three armed services. On 5 July the Italians brought in a separate cypher system for their submarines who, until then, had used the general fleet code book, which was being largely read. On 17 July the Italians introduced new cypher tables for surface ships. Later, in October, they brought in new tables for their most secret naval cypher. They also changed the lower-grade codes for all three services, which made them much more difficult to read, and tightened up on general security, such as the transmission of plain language messages.

The new Italian Army and Air Force book cyphers were broken again reasonably quickly and continued to be read for quite long periods. But the main naval book cyphers, used by the Italian Fleet for most of its important signal traffic, were never read again after July, 1940, except for very brief 'fitful gleams of light' from captured documents.

This intelligence 'black-out', after a long period when Sigint about the Italian Navy had been comparatively plentiful, was a very severe operational disadvantage. For the next nine months Cunningham's fleet based at Alexandria in the east, and Force H under Admiral Sir James Somerville at Gibraltar in the west, both had to rely almost entirely upon D/F, low-grade Sigint, traffic analysis, photo-reconnaissance and such scraps as could be gleaned from the Italian Army, Air Force and diplomatic Enigmas.

During this period photo-reconnaissance (PR) by flying boats from Alexandria and Gibraltar and (from September, 1940) by Glenn Martin Marylands based at Malta was by far the most immediately valuable source of intelligence, although there were not nearly enough PR aircraft in those early days to provide consistent information about the movements of the main Italian fleet, or about the routes and timings of convoys sailing between Italy and Libya, or preparations for sailings in Italian ports and in Italian bases in Libya.

However, PR provided invaluable up-to-date information for the attack by *Eagle*'s aircraft at Tobruk harbour on 6 July, and for the torpedo strike by Fleet Air Arm Swordfish at Bomba on 22 August. The latter operation, which had some Sigint assistance, was even more successful than its participants knew. The Italian depot ship *Monte Gargano* and the submarine *Iride* were sunk and the torpedo boat *Calypso* was badly damaged. *Iride* actually had on board 'human torpedoes' intended for an attack upon Cunningham's ships in Alexandria harbour on 25/26 August.

The greatest triumph of PR at that stage of the war was the attack upon the main Italian fleet at Taranto. It had been originally planned for Trafalgar Day, 21 October, but was postponed because of damage to *Eagle*'s aircraft fuelling system (caused by near-misses from the often-derided Italian high-level bombing), and because of a fire in the hangar of the newly-arrived *Illustrious*.

On 10 November newly-arrived Glenn Martin Marylands flew PR sorties from Malta which revealed the positions of major units of the Italian battle fleet at Taranto and, just as important, recent changes there in the dispositions of balloons and anti-submarine nets. These vital photographs were flown out to *Illustrious* who was by then actually on her way to the flying-off position.

The strike, on the night of 11 November, was carried out by twenty-one Swordfish from *Illustrious*, with additional aircraft and crews loaned from *Eagle*. Flying in two waves and armed with torpedoes or bombs, and flares, the Swordfish achieved complete surprise and sank three Italian battleships at their moorings, thus dramatically changing the balance of capital ship power in the Mediterranean, literally overnight. Two Swordfish were lost; the crew of one became prisoners of war.

To reap full benefit, it was essential to obtain accurate information of the damage actually done. A decoded message to the Italian Naval Attaché in Peking gave some details, but there were many contradictory and inaccurate reports from a variety of sources. Photographs from the PR Glenn Martins again gave the best answers.

Taranto was a heavy defeat, and yet another shattering psychological blow for the Italian Navy. This was just as well for the Allies, because, on the intelligence front in the Mediterranean theatre, the balance of success still lay very much with the Italians. The Taranto raid, for example, actually forestalled an Italian plan to bombard Suda Bay of which the British had no advance intelligence information.

Meanwhile, their own good intelligence service enabled the Italians to time and route their convoys to Libya so as almost completely to avoid British forces. Between June and December, 1940, the Italian Navy passed 690,000 tons of shipping in fast convoys to Libya, with losses of less than two per cent. Even as late as October, 1940, when the Italians were advancing towards Sidi Barrani and it was urgent that their convoys should be intercepted, only one such convoy had been sighted, and it was still not known whether the convoys were being routed inshore via Tripoli or directly across to Cyrenaica.

British forces in Malta, both air and surface, were very weak, largely because the weight of air attack which the Italians could bring to bear on Malta had been greatly overestimated before the war. It had been generally conceded, at least by the Army and the RAF, that Malta would be untenable in time of war and it would be a waste to maintain large forces there. When war did come, the weakness of the British forces at Malta, especially the shortage of aircraft, meant that there was a serious lack of air reconnaissance at a time when other intelligence was also lacking.

But if Cunningham's ships failed to get to grips with their enemy, it was not for want of trying. Cunningham believed in keeping his enemy in a state of permanent apprehension, always afraid that if he did venture out, he would at once be attacked. Between June and October, 1940, ships of the Mediterranean Fleet put to sea no less than sixteen times. But, short of intelligence, they sighted the enemy on only three occasions.

More often than not Cunningham's ships were fumbling in the dark, or were actually misled by such intelligence as there was. With the main Italian naval codes still unbroken (as they were to remain), traffic analysis was virtually the only source of advance information about the Italian fleet. But TA 'was at best inadequate and on occasions led to quite false conclusions'.

There were other confusions. In November, 1940, the 7th Cruiser Squadron sortied into the Adriatic and successfully intercepted one of the regular Italian convoys to Albania. They had already sunk four ships when a message was received, originating from the Naval Attaché in Ankara, that the Italian fleet was about to put to sea to bombard Corfu. The cruisers thereupon broke off their attack and prepared for action with the Italian fleet. But the message proved to be utterly false.

On 27 November, when Force H engaged the Italian fleet off Cape Spartivento, Admiral Somerville was given no prior warning whatsoever from intelligence. The sightings by *Ark Royal*'s aircraft that day were, in fact, the first information Somerville had had of the Italian fleet for fifteen days.

In the New Year of 1941, it was the enemy's turn to surprise Cunningham. Early in January the first elements of Fliegerkorps X, the Luftwaffe's specialist anti-shipping force, began to arrive in Sicily. The build-up was extremely rapid; only seven bombers had arrived by 5 January, but within a week there were almost a hundred, and by the end of the month the total of long-range bombers, dive-bombers and fighters had risen to over 200.

The Air Ministry had reported the arrival of Luftwaffe units in Sicily to the Chiefs of Staff on 9 January, but took no further steps to warn the Admiralty of any special danger. The Admiralty, for its part, appears to have assumed that Cunningham's and Somerville's ships already had considerable experience of the Regia Aeronautica and would be expecting heavy raids in any case and therefore, it seems, decided that the news of the arrival of the Luftwaffe would be of no particular value to the fleet. For whatever reason, the information was not forwarded either to the Mediterranean Fleet or to Force H.

Thus the first appearance of the newcomers on 10 January, 1941, was a most unpleasant shock for the ships concerned and for Middle East intelligence. The Mediterranean Fleet and Force H were both at sea, carrying out a complicated east–west operation (EXCESS), involving warships and merchant ships, and including an important convoy for Malta. Cunningham flew his flag in *Warspite*, with *Illustrious* in company.

On the afternoon of the 10th convoy and escort were some miles to the west of Malta, covered by *Warspite*, *Valiant*, *Illustrious* and five destroyers. An attack by two Savoia SM.79 torpedo bombers was driven off by *Illustrious'* Fulmar fighters who, unfortunately, were still

14

at low altitude when large formations of Junkers Ju.87 Stukas and Junkers Ju.88s were sighted approaching from the north.

Warspite's 'Y' Officer had given an hour's warning of the attack, but its severity and accuracy still came as a surprise to everyone, not least to Cunningham, who was professionally interested in watching what he called 'this new form of dive-bombing attack'. He had no doubt he was watching 'complete experts' and 'could not but admire the skill and precision of it all'.

The bombers concentrated upon *Illustrious*, although *Warspite* was also hit, and pressed home their attacks to very close range. *Illustrious* was hit by six 500 kg bombs. Her armoured flight deck was pierced and her steering gear crippled, both aircraft lifts were put out of action, and there were many casualties among her people. Steering by main engines, *Illustrious* reached Malta. Despite frequent heavy air attacks, she was repaired sufficiently to be able to sail on 23 January and, eventually, to reach the United States.

After such setbacks, a victory was, as John Jervis said in an earlier war in the Mediterranean, 'very essential to England at this moment'. The transport of British troops in special convoys to the Piraeus (Operation LUSTRE) to take part in the campaign in Greece had begun on 6 March, 1941. Soon the Germans began to exert pressure upon their Italian allies to take some action against these convoys. By mid-March the Italians were planning a major offensive by a force of cruisers, accompanied by a battleship covering force, which was to penetrate into the waters south of Crete and intercept the troop convoys.

GC & CS had obtained one success against an Italian naval machine cypher. The Italians had used a version of the Enigma somewhat carelessly during the Spanish Civil War, which had given GC & CS a toehold in the cypher. The Italians brought into use an improved version for the Navy in 1940. This was broken in September of that year. But unfortunately it only carried one or two messages a day until the summer of 1941, when it was withdrawn from the Navy and used solely for Italian Secret Service traffic. However, it was the intercepts from this source in March which gave the first hints of the impending Italian naval offensive.

The first ULTRA (so called here, although the code name was not introduced until June, 1941) signal in the sequence was sent on 17 March from the Admiralty to the C-in-C Mediterranean, Vice Admiral Malta, Flag Officer Force H, and other addressees, informing them that ten motorised S.S. ferries, forty *Landungsflossfaehre* (landing ferries on floats), one landing battalion and one *Trossengeraat* (windlass apparatus) were to be made available from German sources in the central Mediterranean on 26 March. A second ULTRA, on the 21st, said that these ferries and landing troops were going to be used for supplying German air and military forces along the North African coast.

On 25 March the Admiralty sent two ULTRA signals. The first, from a German Air Force Enigma intercept, was at 0915: available heavy German fighters were being flown from North Africa to Palermo a.m. on the 25th for a special operation. The second, from an Italian naval Enigma, at 1705: Rome informed Rhodes that today, 25 March, is D-Day minus 3. An ULTRA of 0820 on 26th, which began 'following presumably refers to my signal 1705/25', revealed that there was to be air reconnaissance of Alexandria and Suda Bay and traffic routes on D-2 and D-1, attacks on Cretan aerodromes on the night of D-1, intensive reconnaissance between Crete and Athens from dawn to noon on D-Day itself, with attacks on Cretan aerodromes at dawn on D-Day and further reconnaissances of traffic routes between Crete and Alexandria.

A second ULTRA on that day, timed 1007, gave very much more detail for D-Day: intensive reconnaissance over an area bounded by the coast of Crete, the east coast of Greece, the Gulf of Athens, and the line Kea–Milo–Cape Sidero from dawn to noon, dawn reconnaissance of routes from Gavdos to Alexandria and Caso to Alexandria, and a dawn attack on Cretan aerodromes. The third ULTRA, of the 26th, at 1244, confirmed that the instructions given in the 820 ULTRA emanated from the Italian General Staff and referred to the 1705 ULTRA of the 25th.

In a signal of 1728 on the 26th to his Vice Admiral Light Forces (Vice-Admiral H. D. Pridham-Wippell), Cunningham summarized these ULTRAs and added his own appreciation, that 'operation is either a large-scale air attack on convoys or else a surface raid into Aegean. I consider that if we now move out (large?) forces these movements will only be delayed until fuel obliges return to base, My intention therefore is to clear area concerned and so endeavour to make enemy strike into thin air whilst taking all action possible damaging him whilst he is doing so.'

D-Day, 28 March, could and should have been an excellent choice of date for the Italians. The Mediterranean Fleet had put to sea on the 20th, to cover a convoy to Malta. The ships had returned to Alexandria on the 24th and might have been expected to stay there at least for several days. There would have been two convoys in the area of operations on the 28th: AG.9, of troopships on their way from Alexandria to the Piraeus, and convoy GA.8, returning from the Piraeus to Alexandria. Both convoys would have been escorted by forces very much inferior to the striking force the Italian Navy planned to use.

Furthermore, Italian MAS one-man torpedo boats raided Suda Bay on 26 March, with no prior warning from British intelligence. They torpedoed an oiler and the cruiser HMS *York*, damaging her so badly she became a total loss. Thus, had the operation taken place as intended, British forces at Suda Bay should have been unable, and those at Alexandria would have been too far away, to intervene.

Forewarned by ULTRA, Cunningham made his preparations. There was no longer any question of the Italian Navy being able to descend with greatly superior force upon weakly escorted and surprised troop convoys, nor was Suda Bay so disorganized by the attack on *York* as the Italians may have hoped. Cunningham began to mobilize naval and air forces over the whole of the eastern Mediterranean.

At 1814 on the evening of 26 March Cunningham signalled his intentions to Pridham-Wippell and to the Admiralty. Force B, of the 7th Cruiser Squadron, of HMS *Orion* (wearing Pridham-Wippell's flag), HMS *Ajax* and HMAS *Perth*, with a fourth cruiser, HMS *Gloucester*, and destroyers, was to complete with fuel and sail p.m. the next day, 27 March, from the Piraeus. Force B was to rendezvous at 0630 on the 28th in a position 30 miles south of Gavdo (a rocky island 20 miles south of Crete) with Force C, the five destroyers *Nubian*, *Mohawk*, *Havock*, *Hotspur* and *Greyhound*, who would sail from Alexandria p.m. on the 27th. Two more destroyers, HMS *Hereward* and HMAS *Vendetta*, would be ordered to Suda Bay, to join Pridham-Wippell on the 27th, while the destroyers HMS *Juno*, *Jaguar* and *Defender* would be kept at immediate notice at Piraeus.

Precautions were taken over the convoys. AG.9 was to carry on until after dusk on the 27th and then turn back for Alexandria. The southbound convoy GA.9 was to be held in harbour until the situation became clearer.

As for Suda Bay, the anti-aircraft cruiser HMS *Carlisle* was also ordered there to reinforce the air defences, because intense air activity was expected, and the Senior Base Naval Officer was ordered to withdraw patrol craft under the defences of Suda Bay. Meanwhile, the Greeks were to be warned to keep the area clear of shipping and would be asked to keep their destroyers at short notice for steam. The Fairey Swordfish of 815 Squadron, Fleet Air Arm, at Maleme in Crete, were to stand by to be airborne from dawn on the 27th. The RAF were asked for maximum air reconnaissance to westward of the Kithera Channel.

Pridham-Wippell was told 'your action must depend on circumstances. Your dawn position (on the 28th) has been selected to enable you to withdraw in face of an unreasonably superior force or to intercept force as it returns'. All authorities were warned 'to stand by for trouble'.

Meanwhile the Admiralty had been studying the possible implications of the earlier signals, having at first concluded that the Italians
intended only attacks by surface ships on the convoys. However, it
was possible, as signalled to Cunningham in another ULTRA at 0025
on 27 March, that military forces were also to be employed, because
some of those Enigma intercepts had been signed by a high official in
the Italian War Office. There was also the information about the ferries
and the landing forces, which might still mean something. The only
point the Admiralty could not fit into this general picture was the
concentration of German heavy fighters at Palermo.

At 0846 on the 27th the Admiralty followed with another ULTRA:
Rome (the same Enigma source as before) had informed Rhodes at
1200 on 26 March that the presumed situation of the British fleet at
that time was: two battleships, one aircraft carrier and the 7th Cruiser
Division at sea off Crete; convoy between Suda and Piraeus; one
battleship, one aircraft carrier at Alexandria. (A later Italian report, of
1900 on 27 March, put three battleships and one aircraft carrier certainly
at Alexandria, which was correct, and at least one battleship and one
aircraft carrier at sea, which was incorrect. But this report was not
decrypted and sent to Cunningham until 1410 on the 28th, when it
was too late to affect the outcome.)

Cunningham considered the situation during the forenoon of 27
March and at 1131 he signalled the Admiralty that 'our appreciation
is much the same' as in the ULTRA of early that morning; and that,
in addition to his intentions signalled at 1814 the day before, he now
also intended that his battleships and the carrier HMS *Formidable*
(who had recently come through the Suez Canal, arriving in
Alexandria on 10 March) would be south of Crete by dawn on Friday,
28 March.

Cunningham also signalled that forenoon to Pridham-Wippell to
tell him of the change of plan: the 1st Battle Squadron (*Warspite*,
Valiant and *Barham*) and *Formidable* were now going to sail after dark
that night, Thursday, 27 March, and proceed westward south of Crete;
Force C, of five destroyers, would be needed to screen the battle fleet
and would not now be joining Pridham-Wippell: convoy AG.9 would
be turned back only sufficiently to be to the eastward of the battle fleet
at dawn, and would then resume its passage; if there were no further
developments, Pridham-Wippell was to rendezvous with the Commander-in-Chief at a position (given) south of Crete at 1700 the next
day, Friday, 28 March.

The final ULTRA in that pre-operational sequence was at 1510 on
27 March, to Cunningham, to Vice Admiral Malta and to the Chief
of Intelligence Staff, Alexandria: at 2000 on 26 March the same Enigma

source in Rome had informed Rhodes, Tripoli and Valona that from W/T analysis the disposition of British forces at 1800 on 26th was two or three battleships and an aircraft carrier in the Mersa Matruh area, two convoys in an area 80 miles south of Gavdos, one cruiser and three destroyers at Suda, some units located by D/F in the area of the Piraeus and north of Naxos, a convoy arriving in the Piraeus, and, finally, Force H in the Atlantic.

It was now time for Admiral Cunningham to carry out a 'cover plan' of his own, to defeat enemy intelligence. He was a keen golfer. So, too, was the Japanese consul in Alexandria, who was on the links most afternoons where, as Cunningham said, he was 'unmistakeable, indeed a remarkable sight, short and squat, with a southern aspect of such vast and elephantine proportions when he bent over to putt' that Cunningham's Chief of Staff, Commodore Willis, dubbed him 'the blunt end of the Axis'.

That afternoon Cunningham himself went ashore with his golf clubs and an ostentatiously large suitcase, obviously intending to spend the night ashore. That evening Cunningham quietly retrieved his suitcase and returned on board *Warspite*. The fleet sailed at 7 p.m. 'What the Japanese consul thought and did when he saw the empty harbour next morning,' said Cunningham, 'was no affair of mine.'

During the morning of the 27th a Sunderland from Malta had reported three Italian cruisers and a destroyer some 80 miles east of the south-eastern corner of Sicily and steering south-eastward. This seemed to suggest that Italian heavy ships were also at sea and, judging by the course the Italian ships were steering, heading for the convoys to Greece. The Italian reconnaissance aircraft which flew over Alexandria at midday on the 27th and again in the afternoon would have seen and reported (as indeed they did) the British battle fleet and an aircraft carrier still in harbour.

Cunningham himself was not entirely convinced that the Italians were coming out. In spite of the Sunderland's sighting report, in spite of increased and persistent Italian air reconnaissance over Alexandria in the previous few days, in spite of what he himself described in his memoirs as 'some unusual Italian wireless activity, which finally decided us to go to sea after dark', he still thought that the Italians would not dare 'to try anything'. He bet his Staff Officer (Operations), Commander Manley L. Power, ten shillings that they would see nothing of the enemy.

In fact the main Italian Fleet was at sea. The Italian fleet commander, Admiral Angelo Iachino, flying his flag in the new, fast (30 knot) and powerful (nine 15″ guns) battleship *Vittorio Veneto* had sailed from Naples at 2100 on 26 March. He was joined on passage south by the

10,000 ton 8" gun cruisers *Trieste*, *Trento* and *Bolzano* and the 8,000 ton 6" gun cruisers *Abruzzi* and *Garibaldi*, all from Brindisi, and three 10,000 ton 8" gun cruisers *Zara*, *Fiume* and *Pola*, from Taranto.

Iachino disposed his ships in three main groups: Force Y, the flagship and four destroyers; Force X, of the three *Triestes* and three destroyers; and Force Z, of the three *Zaras* and the two *Abruzzis*, escorted by six destroyers.

At 1225 on 27 March *Trieste* signalled Iachino that she been sighted by a Sunderland. Iachino soon received the decyphered report and was relieved to see that the Sunderland had reported only three cruisers and a destroyer. Mist had fortunately hidden the main body of the Italian fleet. Later in the afternoon Iachino had the reconnaissance aircraft's report of three battleships, two aircraft carriers and some cruisers, still in Alexandria. Iachino later complained bitterly of inadequate or misleading air reconnaissance, but, certainly in the early stages, he did have adequate information which all tended to suggest that the Italian plans were about to be successful and he himself might be on the verge of a smashing victory against the Allied convoys to Greece.

At dawn on 28 March Iachino's three groups were some 60 miles south of Crete, steaming south-east. *Vittorio Veneto*'s Meridionali Ro.43 reconnaissance seaplane was launched and at 0643 reported four cruisers and four destroyers, only 50 miles away. These were Pridham-Wippell's ships, who realized they had been sighted and turned away. *Trieste* sighted cruisers just before 0800 and a short and inconclusive cruiser gun action followed, in which no ship was hit. By 0900 the Italian ships had turned back to the north-west, being shadowed from a cautious distance by Pridham-Wippell's ships.

At 0900 on the 28th Iachino received an important signal from Rhodes: 'At 0745 No. 1 aircraft of the Aegean strategic reconnaissance sighted one carrier two battleships nine cruisers 14 destroyers in sector 3836/0 course 165 degrees 20 knots'. As Iachino's force had been in that area at the time, he assumed it was his own ships which had been sighted and he replied to Rhodes that a gross blunder had been committed. In fact, with hindsight, it seems that Iachino should at least have considered the possibility that the ships referred to might be the enemy. Ironically, it was Iachino himself who was to commit the grossest blunder of all that day, by persistently discounting reasonable evidence, from more than one source, that the British battle fleet was at sea.

But one of Iachino's main complaints, that he was shadowed and harassed by enemy aircraft for much of the day, with very little assistance from Axis aircraft, was justified. His ships were sighted and reported early on the 28th by *Formidable's* aircraft. In the afternoon they were brilliantly shadowed by *Warspite's* Swordfish and, during the course of that day, they suffered eight air attacks, by Swordfish, Albacores and Fulmars from *Formidable*, by Swordfish from Maleme, and by RAF Blenheims of 84 and 113 Squadrons.

At first these attacks did not appear to have any serious effect. *Vittorio Veneto* was hit aft by one torpedo, which decreased her speed considerably and allowed Cunningham, approaching from the south-west, to hope that the enemy battleship might be delivered into his hands. But *Vittorio Veneto* was able to pick up speed again, draw away and eventually escape.

But during the last attack of the day, at dusk, an Albacore from *Formidable* hit the cruiser *Pola* with one torpedo, which stopped her dead in the water. Iachino, still unaware that Cunningham's battle fleet was at sea, detached *Zara* and *Fiume* to assist *Pola*. That night all three cruisers were surprised and overwhelmed in a short but murderous action at very close range by the guns of *Warspite*, *Valiant* and *Barham*. During a wild night of destroyer action, two Italian destroyers were also sunk.

Thus, with the help of ULTRA, Cunningham achieved a smashing victory over the Italian Navy. There were no more attempts to disrupt the convoy to and from Greece, and indeed no further appearance by main units of the Italian fleet for another year.

3 | BISMARCK

At the beginning of 1941 GC & CS had still made very little progress in breaking the German Navy's Enigma. By February, 1941, only five more days traffic in the Home Key (in which 95% of German naval traffic was encyphered) had been broken and those were for dates months earlier, in April and May, 1940. But, in the spring of 1941, like a stubborn log-jam at last breaking up, the trickle of decryptions suddenly surged and then developed into a steady flow.

It began in the obvious way, by physically capturing machines and cyphers from the enemy. As a result of planning beforehand, the German armed trawler *Krebs* was captured during the raid on the Lofoten Islands on 4 March 1941. The Commanding Officer was killed, the Enigma machine and cyphers thrown overboard, and the ship was abandoned. But spare Enigma wheels were recovered, with enough material to enable GC & CS to read the whole of the traffic for February, 1941, comparatively quickly (i.e., at various dates from 10 March onwards).

Generally speaking, every time cypher traffic is broken, it becomes easier to break further traffic in the same cypher. With this success behind them, GC & CS were able, by cryptanalytical methods, to break (again, comparatively quickly, between 22 April and 10 May) the whole of the traffic for April, 1941, and to go on to break the May traffic, reading much of it with delays of between only three and seven days.

These successes led to more. Study of the decrypted February and April traffic showed that the Germans were maintaining two weather ships, one north of Iceland, the other in mid-Atlantic. This information might not have had any obvious operational significance, but the study also showed that although the weather reports were in a weather cypher and were outwardly different from Enigma signals, the ships did carry the Naval Enigma. Therefore, the capture of one of these remote and isolated weather ships might yield a complete Enigma machine and its cyphers.

Two special 'cutting-out' operations were mounted. By the beginning of May D/F reports had shown that the weather-reporting ship *Muenchen* had already been on her station east of Iceland for some time. Since she had been there so long, she might be planning to stay and would have on board Enigma settings for some time to come. In the first operation, codenamed E.B., on 7 May, 1941, *Muenchen* was captured by the cruiser HMS *Edinburgh* and the destroyer HMS *Somali*. Her crew were taken on board *Edinburgh* and *Somali* with no casualties, while *Muenchen* herself was taken in tow to Thorsavn. She had made an enemy sighting report, so it was later announced that she had scuttled herself before anybody could board her.

In fact, as the 'Hush Most Secret' signal reporting the operation described it, 'Captain Haines [of *Edinburgh*] has important document'. This was the German naval 'Home Waters' Enigma key for June, 1941.

Before the second operation was carried out, chance and quick-thinking brought about a stunning intelligence success for the Allies. Two days after E.B., on 9 May, *U–110* (commanded by a notable 'ace', Kapitan Leutnant Julius Lemp) attacked Convoy OB318, outward bound from Liverpool, and sank two ships with a salvo of three torpedoes. The U-boat was itself counter-attacked with depth-charges by the convoy's escort, the destroyers HMS *Bulldog* (Commander A. J. Baker-Cresswell) and *Broadway*, and the corvette HMS *Aubretia*, and driven to the surface where the crew abandoned ship. The survivors (Lemp was not among them) were picked up by *Aubretia*.

Baker-Cresswell was quick-witted enough to realize that the U-boat's crew would assume their boat had been sunk. Their Captain was certainly dead. The U-boat men were hustled below decks. They saw, and were told, nothing. The other ships of the convoy sailed onwards and out of sight. Meanwhile the U-boat was boarded by a party from *Bulldog* who descended into the control room and methodically stripped the boat of all the equipment they could remove. *U–110* was taken in tow but, to everybody's great disapointment, sank by the stern after some hours.

However, the cryptanalytical gains from *U–110* were beyond price. They included, amongst other items, the Enigma machine with that day's settings still on it, the special code settings for high-security 'Offizierte' (officer only) traffic, and the current code book for U-boats' short-signal (*Kurzsignale*) sighting reports. These two types of traffic could now be read and later versions of them could be cryptanalytically reconstructed. The 'Home Waters' (German '*Heimisch*', code-named 'Dolphin' by GC & CS) Enigma settings from *U–110* were for April

23

and June (also taken from *Muenchen*). The settings for May had been destroyed.

The Germans continued to believe that *U–110* had been sunk with all hands. Therefore its capture, as HM King George VI said when he was investing one of the boarding party, *Bulldog*'s Engineer Officer Lieutenant-Commander G. E. Dodds, with his well-earned DSC, was perhaps the most important single event in the whole war at sea. '*Heimisch*' (renamed '*Hydra*' on 1 January, 1943) was the key used by ships and authorities in home waters and the Baltic, and by all U-boats (until the Atlantic U-boats changed to '*Shark*' on 1 February, 1942). From 1 August, 1941, '*Heimisch*' was read virtually continuously and currently until the end of the war.

The first result of this success was the revelation of a small armada of tankers and supply ships which the Germans were sending to sea to support an extended raid on the Atlantic shipping routes by the giant battleship *Bismarck* and the heavy cruiser *Prinz Eugen*. But before action could be taken against these minor players, ULTRA was to play a crucial part, along with Naval Attaché's reports, photo-reconnaissance and D/F, in the tremendous dramas of the main protagonists.

By the second week of May, 1941, it was clear that German reconnaissance aircraft were paying more attention than usual to Scapa Flow and to the area between Jan Mayen Island and Greenland. This might indicate a possible German attack on Jan Mayen Island, or a break-out by warships through the Denmark Strait. On 14 May an ice report by Flag Officer Commanding Iceland seemed to discount any attack on Jan Mayen. In the same week the German Air Force Enigma revealed that Focke Wulf Fw 200 long-range Kondors had been carrying out reconnaissance of the ice conditions between Jan Mayen and Greenland. On 18 May the Admiralty signalled to the C-in-C Home Fleet, Admiral Sir John Tovey, 'German aircraft carried out ice reconnaissance north and west of Iceland during night 17th–18th May'.

At that time intelligence was still unable to provide any reliable information on the whereabouts, the readiness for sea (or even the exact size and armaments) of major German naval units, but Tovey now began to make some preparations. He ordered the cruiser HMS *Suffolk*, on patrol in the Denmark Strait, to pay particular attention to the edge of the ice pack. Tovey also ordered her sister ship HMS *Norfolk*, wearing the flag of Rear Admiral Wake-Walker, commanding the 1st Cruiser Squadron, to sail from Iceland and take over the patrol, so that *Suffolk* could refuel at Hvalfjord. Both cruisers would then have replenished with fuel.

Bismarck and *Prinz Eugen* sailed from Gdynia at 0200 on 19 May. A prisoner later said that *Bismarck* was sighted by the Swedish cruiser *Gotland* off Bornholm in the forenoon of the 19th, but the first definite information of this encounter came from the pilot of one of *Gotland*'s seaplanes, who sighted the German ships a day later, on the afternoon of 20 May. This vital news was passed to Captain Henry Denham, the British Naval Attaché in Stockholm, through one of his diplomatic contacts, Colonel Roscher Lund, the Norwegian Military Attaché.

At 2058 that evening of 20 May Denham signalled to the Admiralty that during the morning of 20 May eleven German merchant ships passed northbound through the Kattegat and that at 1500 on 20 May two large warships, escorted by three destroyers, five escort craft and ten or twelve aircraft passed Marstrand (in the Kattegat) on a north-westerly course. Denham classified his signal B-3, showing that he was not very sure of its reliability (messages were graded A to E, to denote the reliability of the source, from A, completely reliable, to E, reliability unknown, and by the numbers 1 to 5 to show the reliability of the message, from 1, completely reliable, to 5, reliability unknown. Thus, for example, A-1 was a completely reliable report from an utterly reliable source, while D-4 would be a doubtful message from a dubious source.)

According to the testimony of prisoners of war, *Bismarck*'s mine-sweeper escort parted company at 1345 on 20 May. War watches were set at 2030 and the first British air reconnaissance was said to have been sighted at 2242. There was an air raid alarm at 0230 on the morning of 21 May. *Bismarck*'s ship's company went to action stations, expecting an attack at dawn. But there was none. At 1115 on 21 May *Bismarck* entered a fjord south of Bergen and anchored close (600–700 yards) to the shore.

Meanwhile, acting on Denham's report, the Admiralty asked for photo-reconnaissance. Two Spitfires of No. 1 PRU at Wick flew over the Norwegian fjords. At 1330 on 21 May one Spitfire photographed what were later pronounced to be a battleship (795 feet × 105), presumed to be *Bismarck*, with three merchant vessels (actually secured alongside her as torpedo defences) five miles south-south-west of Bergen, and one cruiser (670' × 75'), presumed *Hipper* Class, with one destroyer (415'), six merchant vessels (200'–400'), and six smaller craft, ten miles west by north of Bergen.

Air reconnaissance was to yield nothing further for another 29 hours. But at this point ULTRA provided a vital piece of corroborative information. Although, by May, 1941, the German naval Enigma was on the way to being broken, there were still lengthy delays in decoding. On 19 May GC & CS delivered to the Operational Intelligence Centre (OIC) in the Admiralty some material dated 24 April. It had nothing

25

which had any bearing on *Bismarck*. But further material of the same date, delivered two days later, came like a flash of light to the OIC. At 1828 on 21 May the Admiralty signalled Tovey and a wide range of addressees: 'Immediate "Bismarck" embarked five prize crews with necessary charts at end of April and has been carrying out practises in the Baltic with "Prinz Eugen".' This information was now nearly a month old, but it had come from the German W/T traffic of the tugs serving *Bismarck* and it gave a priceless clue to the enemy's intentions, so that the Admiralty could add the comment: 'One "Bismarck" and one "Prince Eugen" class reported by reconnaissance at Bergen on 21 May. It is evident that these ships intend to carry out a raid on trade routes.'

Tovey, flying his flag in the battleship HMS *King George V* at Scapa Flow, was not entirely convinced, and asked for the date of origin of this information. He himself did not think it likely that the German admiral would be so foolish as to pause at a place so convenient for air reconnaissance as Bergen. *Bismarck*'s sortie might imply the possibility of an attack on east Iceland, either as a separate operation, or as part of the operation of passing *Bismarck* out into the Atlantic. There had been a recent but unreliable report of a U-boat north of Iceland and, possibly more significant, a Luftwaffe attack on the W/T station at Thorshavn in the Faeroes.

However, Tovey made his dispositions on the basis that the German ships were heading for the trade routes. The new battleship HMS *Prince of Wales* and the veteran battlecruiser HMS *Hood* with destroyer screen, sailed on 21 May to patrol the Iceland–Faeroes passage, or, if *Bismarck* were reported still in harbour, to take the chance to refuel at Hvalfjord. The cruisers HMS *Birmingham* and *Manchester*, already patrolling the Iceland–Faeroes passage, were ordered to refuel at Skaalefjord in Iceland and resume their patrol. *Suffolk* was to rejoin *Norfolk*. The cruiser HMS *Arethusa*, about to leave Hvalfjord for Reykjavik, was ordered to stay. The submarines *P.31* and the Free French *Minerve* were sent on patrol. The battlecruiser *Repulse* sailed from the Clyde to rejoin the flag at Scapa, where *King George V*, cruisers and destroyers, and the aircraft carrier *Victorious*, came to short notice for steam. Tovey wanted to keep his flagship in harbour until the last possible moment, so that he would have at least one battleship fully topped up with fuel, and he would also be able to discuss the latest situation over the telephone to the Admiralty.

Bismarck and *Prinz Eugen* sailed from Bergen at 1945 on 21 May, six hours after the PRU Spitfire had photographed them and about an hour after the Admiralty had signalled its appreciation of their intentions. There was still a delay of between three and seven days in reading

26

the German naval Enigma, so that ULTRA contributed nothing more at this time. Air reconnaissance of the area from Trondheim to Kristiansand was carried out from first light on 22 May, but visibility was bad in fog and low cloud, and the results of the reconnaissance were inconclusive. No ships were seen, but that did not mean they were not there.

Acting on his own initiative, Captain St.J. Fancourt, commanding HMS *Sparrowhawk*, the Royal Naval Air Station at Hatston in the Orkneys, organized a reconnaissance flight to see if the German ships were still there, and if so, to mount an attack. The aircraft was a Martin Maryland, flown by the CO of 771 Squadron, Lieutenant (A) Noel Goddard RNVR. His observer was Commander G. E. ('Hank') Rotherham, who was actually the Executive Officer and Second-in-Command at Hatston, and not borne for flying duties, but was a very experienced Fleet Air Arm observer.

Flying as low over the sea as Goddard dared in the poor visibility, the Maryland made a perfect landfall on the Norwegian coast. 'It was one of those days,' Rotherham said, 'when all one's errors cancel each other out and we hit it dead on.' They made one low-level run over Bergen fjord and harbour, before escaping to seaward pursued by a storm of anti-aircraft fire. Goddard's Telegraphist Air Gunner was unable to raise anybody on the Coastal Command frequency on the flight back, so made his emergency signal on the Hatston Target Towing frequency, and passed to the C-in-C and the Admiralty by telephone. At 2200 on 22 May Tovey received the vital information: Bergen harbour, and the Korsfjord leading up to it, were empty.

When Tovey himself sailed that night, he did not know whether *Bismarck* would steer for the Iceland–Faeroes passage or the Denmark Strait. To cover both, he had *Norfolk* and *Suffolk* patrolling the Strait, with *Prince of Wales* and *Hood* steaming north to support them, while *Manchester*, *Birmingham* and *Arethusa* were covering the Iceland–Faeroes passage, with *King George V*, *Repulse*, *Victorious*, four cruisers and ten destroyers in support to the south.

The German Admiral, Gunther Lutjens, flying his flag in *Bismarck*, had actually chosen the Denmark Strait. His ships were already well on their way. A prisoner's diary showed that at 2100 on 22 May *Bismarck* was north of the Arctic Circle, making 24 knots and heading for the Strait which she entered during the forenoon of 23 May.

At 1932 that evening *Bismarck* was sighted in the Denmark Strait by *Suffolk* who hastily retreated into the nearest fogbank, fortunately without being fired on. She continued to shadow the enemy by R.D/F, whilst sending off enemy sighting reports, none of which were received. Tovey's first knowledge of the enemy was from *Norfolk*,

27

who was fired on, and sent an enemy sighting report at 2032. Both cruisers then settled down to shadow the enemy from astern throughout that night.

The cruisers' reports gave *Hood*, wearing the flag of Vice Admiral L. E. Holland, and *Prince of Wales* the chance to intercept. The enemy was sighted at 0535 on the morning of 24 May. The gun action began at 0553 and, as usual, the initial German gunnery ranging and shooting were excellent. At 0600, after a short exchange of salvoes, *Hood* suffered a hit amidships which started a major fire on her upper deck.

Watchers in both the British and the German ships saw a bright pulsing glow on *Hood*'s deck and then a great tongue of vivid flame soar up to the sky, followed by a column of black and grey smoke, as *Hood* disintegrated before their horrified and amazed eyes. *Prince of Wales* had also been damaged, with some casualties, and, at 0613, broke off the action and turned away under smoke. She had scored two hits on *Bismarck*, which were to have later consequences, but the honours of the encounter had clearly gone to the German ships. The senior surviving British officer, Rear Admiral Wake-Walker in *Norfolk*, decided not to attack again but to continue to shadow by visual sighting and R.D/F.

At first *Bismarck* tried to shake off her pursuers, but towards midday on 24th Lutjens appeared to give up the attempt and altered course from south-west to south. *Bismarck* had also slowed to 24 knots, because of damage forward from one of *Prince of Wales'* hits. This was good news for Tovey, who had been concerned that his enemy would steer west away from all his ships, towards Greenland, possibly to rendezvous with an oiler.

Tovey himself was still over 300 miles away. At 1600 he detached the carrier *Victorious*, with four cruisers, to launch a torpedo-bomber attack from a position about 100 miles from the enemy. Nine Swordfish of 825 Squadron, led by their CO, Lieutenant-Commander Esmonde, took off shortly after 220. The weather had deteriorated, there was a gigantic swell running from the north-west, and the flight deck was hidden in sheets of rain and spray. Many who watched the Swordfish go wondered whether they would ever be seen again.

Visibility was very poor, but the Swordfish were fitted with a new ASV (Air to Surface Vessel Radar) which at 2357 revealed a contact. Esmonde's Swordfish flew down to attack but discovered that their 'target' was the US Coast Guard vessel *Modoc*, with Bismarck herself in sight six miles away. All surprise had been lost, but the Swordfish carried on with their attack, through heavy anti-aircraft fire, and scored one hit amidships. Miraculously, all nine Swordfish landed safely on *Victorious* who helpfully shone searchlights and navigation lights, despite the risk of U-boats, to assist them.

In those high latitudes at that time of year, it did not get dark until well after midnight. At 0140 on 25 May, in gathering darkness, *Suffolk* was ordered to shadow independently by R.D/F. She continued to zigzag, finding that although she lost *Bismarck* on the outward leg, she could pick her up again on the inward beat. But perhaps success made *Suffolk* over-confident, for when she swung back on one inward leg her quarry had gone. The last R.D/F contact had been at 0306.

Intelligence had played no direct part while Tovey's ships were in visual or R.D/F contact. From the time of *Norfolk*'s first sighting on the evening of 23 May until *Suffolk* lost contact early on 25th, *Bismarck* had transmitted no fewer than twenty-two signals. At 0855 on 25 May the Admiralty signalled to Tovey: 'During the period shortly after the torpedo-bomber attack until 0258/25, *Bismarck* made a series of signals, some very long, and a fair inference is that owing to damage received enemy has recast his plan.'

Bismarck evidently did not realize for some time that her shadowers had lost contact. Lutjens may also have been misled by a Luftwaffe reconnaissance report of 22 May that battleships and possibly an aircraft carrier were still in Scapa Flow (although this was later drastically amended to 'one light cruiser and six destroyers'). *Bismarck* continued to transmit lengthily another three signals, the first at 0854 fully half an hour long, and the third at 1054.

Although these signals were not broken until 28 May, too late to be of any assistance to Tovey, *Bismarck*'s transmissions were all detected by D/F and their bearings plotted in the OIC against the enemy positions reported by *Norfolk* and *Suffolk*. Also, the RFP section at Flowerdown kept watch on *Bismarck*'s frequencies and obtained reliable 'signatures' of her W/T operators from RFP and from TINA.

At 0927 on 25 May the Admiralty sent Tovey a signal giving the D/F bearings of *Bismarck*'s 0854 signal and followed with more bearings at 1030 and 1054. At that time the Admiralty only transmitted the raw D/F bearings and not the positions worked out by the OIC. The bearings were wrongly plotted in the flagship. Although the Admiralty's plotting staff noticed the discrepancy between OIC's position and the more northerly and westerly position of *Bismarck* which Tovey signalled to his fleet at 1047, the Admiralty did not point it out to Tovey, because they were not absolutely certain of their own fix, and because Tovey might have later and closer bearings from another source such as one of his destroyers.

After contact with *Bismarck* had been lost, the D/F receivers at Scarborough were kept trained in the direction signals were expected, so that even the briefest transmission could be detected. But meanwhile the problem remained: what were *Bismarck*'s intentions now? She could go westward, to meet a tanker. She might return to Norway. She might head south for Brest.

On 24 May OIC reported that the usual W/T control station for *Bismarck*'s radio frequency had been transferred from Wilhelmshaven to Paris. In fact, *Bismarck* was ordered to shift to the Paris control at midday on 24 May.

Throughout 25 May opinion at sea and in the Admiralty hardened in favour of Brest. Wake-Walker in *Norfolk* signalled at 0616 that when contact was lost the enemy had either steered west or turned east and cut under the shadowing cruisers' sterns. Wake-Walker himself searched to the west and by 1057 had made up his mind the enemy was steering for Brest. The Admiralty signalled at 1023 to Force H, steaming up to the Bay of Biscay, to proceed on the assumption that the enemy had turned towards Brest at 0300, and at 1158 to the battleship HMS *Rodney*, who had been on her way to America, to assume that the enemy was proceeding towards a Bay of Biscay port.

The value of continuing to monitor signals, even though they did not appear of immediate value, was shown that forenoon of 25 May. At 1057 the Admiralty informed Tovey that 'Radio finger-prints (RFP) indicate that the ship which transmitted at 0854/25 in a position to the eastward of the last known position of the "Bismarck" is the same ship that transmitted a number of messages after the torpedo-bomber attack last night.' This message, indicating an eastward movement by *Bismarck*, confirmed that the position plotted in Tovey's flagship was too far to the north.

But there was one further hesitation that afternoon, when the Admiralty interpreted a transmission from a U-boat (on a U-boat frequency) as originating from a surface ship, and instructed *Rodney* that the enemy was proceeding to Norway through the passage between Scotland and the Faeroes.

All doubts were finally resolved by ULTRA. Answering an enquiry about *Bismarck* from the Luftwaffe Chief of Staff, who was in Athens in connection with the invasion of Crete, the Luftwaffe authorities in Berlin used a Luftwaffe Enigma cypher, which was being read by GC & CS. Thus, at 1812 on 25 May the Admiralty was able to signal: 'Information received graded A1 that intention of "Bismarck" is to make for the west coast of France.'

In fact Tovey had already made up his mind. At 1548 he had altered course from 055 to 113 but had altered to 080 (a course from his position heading straight for Scapa Flow) 24 minutes later. At 1621 he asked the Admiralty (in the light of their signal to *Rodney*): 'Do you consider enemy making for Faroes?' But at 1821 on the 25th Tovey made the decisive alteration of course to 117.

Bismarck was belatedly keeping radio silence, but the hunt for her now began to move towards its climax, like the events in a noble tragedy. Now that it was certain *Bismarck* was heading for France, air reconnaissance was concentrated in that direction. *Bismarck* was sighted by a Catalina at 1030 on 26 May and by a Swordfish from *Ark Royal* three-quarters of an hour later.

Tovey was now embarrassed by shortage of fuel. He decided that unless the enemy's speed could be reduced by air attack, *King George V* would have to give up the chase at midnight on 26th. At 1550 *Ark Royal* flew off a Swordfish strike force which mistakenly attacked the cruiser *Sheffield.* A second strike, flown off at 1915, successfully attacked *Bismarck* between 2055 and 2125 and obtained two hits, one of them right aft, jamming *Bismarck*'s rudder. At 2130 she suddenly turned north and thereafter seemed to be steaming in a wide circle.

While *Bismarck*'s crew worked frantically, and unavailingly, to free the rudder, Lutjens made a last signal to Hitler just before midnight which, from the ship's company's viewpoint, might have been better put: 'We fight to the last in our belief in you, my Führer, and in the firm faith in Germany's victory.'

Sheffield was fired on briefly, and at 2140 had turned away and lost touch. However, she made contact with Captain P. R. Vian in *Cossack* with his 4th Destroyer Flotilla, who found *Bismarck* again and shadowed, making several unsuccessful torpedo attacks on her, through the night of 26/27 May.

King George V closed *Bismarck* on the evening of the 26th, but, with the light bad, Tovey hauled off again, to the NNE, intending to engage from the west at daylight, when *Bismarck* would be silhouetted against the dawn. During the night *King George V* was joined by *Rodney.* Dawn was at 0600 and at 0723 both battleships steered towards the enemy. They sighted *Bismarck* at 0843 on 27 May and opened fire at a range of $12\frac{1}{2}$ miles. An hour and a half later *Bismarck* had been reduced to a blazing helpless wreck, but was still afloat. The battleships ceased fire at 1021. The cruiser *Dorsetshire* was ordered to administer the coup de grâce with torpedoes. *Bismarck* sank at 1037 on 27 May. Of more than 2,000 men on board her, 102 were picked up by British ships, three by *U–74* and two by the German weather ship *Sachsenwald.*

The hunt for *Bismarck* contained some intelligence lessons. It had showed that D/F bearings taken while the enemy was still in sight could be valuable once contact had been lost. It showed that the approximate fixes obtained by OIC from D/F bearings should be sent as well as the raw D/F bearings. This was done henceforward. ULTRA had made two very important contributions, revealing first that *Bismarck* had taken on prize crews, and then that she was making for France. Nevertheless, it had been demonstrated, once again, that ULTRA was still only an auxiliary to other forms of intelligence.

4 | THE SLAUGHTER OF *BISMARCK*'S TANKERS AND SUPPLY SHIPS

Between 6 p.m. and 7 p.m. on 24 May *Bismarck* had reduced speed and fought a brief gun action with her shadowers. This was almost certainly to create a diversion to allow *Prinz Eugen* to part company. *Prinz Eugen* steered south-west and then south, refuelling at sea from the tanker *Spichern* on the evening of 25 May and from *Esso Hamburg* on the morning of the 27th. She was to have fuelled from *Spichern* again, and from another tanker, *Friedrich Breme*, some time after 30 May, presumably before resuming her raid on Allied shipping routes. But she developed engine defects and headed for Brest, where she had arrived by 1 June and where she was located by a PR aircraft on the 4th.

Spichern, *Esso Hamburg* and *Breme* were all part of the elaborate arrangements which the Germans had made to support *Bismarck*, *Prinz Eugen*, armed merchant raiders and U-boats on patrol. As many as twenty-one weather ships, tankers and supply ships were involved, either at sea or in harbour ready to sail. The seizure of *Muenchen* on 7 May had yielded the keys for June, so that the German Naval Enigma was being read virtually currently from 1 June. A comprehensive picture of the movements and intentions of these support vessels soon emerged. It was, as somebody said, like overhearing all their conversations. The Admiralty could plan a wholesale slaughter.

By 25 May OIC estimated that seven tankers and the motor vessel *Babitonga* were at sea in the Atlantic or en route. Another thirteen tankers, supply ships or weather reporting ships were either in harbour or their whereabouts were unknown. The tanker *Belchen* supplied two U-boats in her rendezvous area on 28 May. On 29 May, as a result of information from Enigma, the Admiralty signalled to the cruiser *Suffolk* to search for an enemy supply ship (which was *Belchen*) in the appropriate area (given in the signal) if she had enough fuel. If *Suffolk* was short of fuel, the cruisers HMS *Aurora* and *Kenya* were already on their way to the area and would do the necessary. Despite foul weather, *Kenya's* Walrus found *Belchen* without much difficulty. She was still loitering in her rendezvous area, with two U-boats in the vicinity, on the morning of 3 June, and she was sunk by *Aurora* and *Kenya*. *U–93* rescued forty-nine survivors.

Through the Enigma decrypts the OIC could follow the German ships around the Atlantic and choose the proper time, and a suitable means, of execution. After fuelling *Prinz Eugen*, *Esso Hamburg* was ordered south on 28 May to meet the tanker *Egerland* and transfer torpedoes. Early on 1 June *Esso Hamburg*, who had clearly been intended to meet *Prinz Eugen* again, signalled that she had no more room for prisoners. She was brusquely told that she must make room and that her proposed meeting with M/V *Babitonga* was to go ahead as planned. For good measure, ULTRA revealed that *U–38* was ordered to receive supplies from *Egerland* on 6 June, in a position given (which was also *Esso Hamburg's* allotted rendezvous station).

Thus it was now only a question of waiting for the appropriate time when *Esso Hamburg*, *Babitonga* and *Egerland* should all assemble at the place appointed for execution. On 30 May the Admiralty signalled to the C-in-C, South Atlantic, that D/F (the 'cover' for ULTRA) indicated with a 'high degree of accuracy' a rendezvous for submarines and oilers at a position given and ordered the cruiser HMS *Cumberland* and a destroyer to be at this rendezvous by 0800 on 3 June.

At that time *Cumberland* was some distance to the south searching for a merchant raider and although C-in-C, South Atlantic, signalled on 31 May that *Cumberland* would keep the appointment, it was in fact the cruiser HMS *London*, with the destroyer HMS *Brilliant*, who caught the 9,849 ton *Esso Hamburg*, who scuttled herself, on the evening of 4 June, and sank the 9,798 ton *Egerland* on the following morning, both ships within a few miles of their appointed rendezvous off the coast of West Africa. *Babitonga*, 4,422 tons, did not appear on 4 June, but was safely gathered in, scuttling herself after an encounter with *London* just north of the Equator on 21 June.

The 'cover story' for these sinkings was that the ships had been revealed by W/T D/F bearings and cruisers were then ordered to operational patrol areas. But clearly there would be a risk of compromising ULTRA if as many as eight ships were all sunk in a short space of time and all in the same circumstances. To minimize the risk, the First Sea Lord, Admiral Sir Dudley Pound, ordered that two ships, the 8,923 ton tanker *Gedania* and the patrol ship *Gonzenheim*, 4,000 tons, were to be spared.

But even the stars in their courses seemed to fight against the German ships. On 4 June the armed merchant cruiser HMS *Esperance Bay* sighted a German merchant ship steering west but at extreme range and was unable to intercept. Shortly afterwards, aircraft from HMS *Victorious* sighted two enemy merchant vessels steering north-west. The positions of most of the German ships were known to OIC but there were still a number of possibilities about the identities of these particular ships.

All doubts were removed at 1556 on 4 June when *Gonzenheim* signalled that she was being attacked by an armed merchant cruiser. At 2010 she further reported that she was being attacked by a battleship. Twenty minutes later HMS *Nelson* signalled that *Gonzenheim* had scuttled herself. *Gonzenheim*'s crew set fire to their ship, and it was the cruiser HMS *Neptune* who administered the coup de grâce with one torpedo.

At 2100 that evening the destroyer HMS *Marsdale* reported that she had captured *Gedania*, whose crew abandoned her in a panic when they sighted the warship. These two encounters came about purely by chance and after the First Sea Lord had forbidden any action to be taken. There was no doubt that they added greatly to the risk of compromising ULTRA.

Sometimes the German ships assisted in their own destruction. On 3 June the 10,397 ton tanker *Friedrich Breme* was ordered to return home, but, on the afternoon of the next day, was told to go to another position, to fuel a U-boat and take fifty men on board. On the 8th she was again ordered home, passing through certain given positions. On the 10th she was warned of areas believed to be dangerous. The next day she was informed she might expect to meet M/V *Elbe* along the latitude of 45° N. In fact the 9,179 ton *Elbe*, a blockade runner, had already scuttled herself near the Azores on 6 June, after being bombed by aircraft from HMS *Eagle*, and had then broadcast the fact of her suicide in plain language.

The message was picked up by *Eagle* but not, apparently, by the Germans, who obligingly informed *Elbe* on the 11th that *Friedrich Breme* was returning home along latitude 45° N. The cruiser HMS *Sheffield* made an accurate interception and sank *Breme* in position 44° 48′ N 24° W on the evening of 12 June.

The tanker *Lothringen*, whose operating area was south of Greenland, had been sent south to assist *Prinz Eugen*. But when it became clear that the cruiser's repairs were going to take longer than expected, *Lothringen* returned to her original area. On 12 June she was ordered south again to refuel U-boats operating off Freetown. But her race was now run. Acting on ULTRA, at 1631 on 13 June the Admiralty

35

ordered C-in-C, South Atlantic, to sail *London* so that she could be in a position some 17 miles east of where *Lothringen* had been told to take up her station and where *Lothringen* herself had said she would arrive on 17 June.

London was ordered to lie in wait for 48 hours. But she was not needed. Aircraft from *Eagle* found *Lothringen* on 15 June and prevented her from scuttling herself until the cruiser HMS *Dunedin* could arrive and seize her by boarding.

All the group of eight ships which OIC had estimated on 25 May to be at sea had now been accounted for, except the tanker *Spichern* who, having refuelled *Prinz Eugen*, was told on 28 May to meet *Esso Hamburg*. But she was stopped and told to return to her original area. On 2 June she was ordered home and, although the Enigma revealed her movements fairly closely, she succeeded in reaching St Nazaire under air cover on 8 June. The other seven were sunk by 21 June, all as a result of ULTRA, except *Gedania* whose movements had been revealed by the Enigma but whose sinking came about by chance.

Of the second group, those who were reported on 25 May to be in port, or whose whereabouts were unknown, *Gonzenheim* and *Elbe* had scuttled themselves. The 3,039 ton supply and prison ship *Alstertor*, returning from supporting armed merchant raiders and warships in the Indian Ocean, was intercepted by *Marsdale* and the 8th Destroyer Flotilla on 23 June, 200 miles off Cape Finisterre, and she also scuttled herself.

Late in June, a second special operation was mounted to seize another weather reporting ship, the 344 ton *Lauenburg* (WBS 2), whose operating area and routine had been revealed by the Enigma and who was confidently expected to have Enigma keys for June and July on board. The cruiser HMS *Nigeria*, with three destroyers, searched for *Lauenburg* in foggy conditions off Jan Mayen Island. She was detected on 28 June by D/F bearing (again, the ULTRA 'cover') by the destroyer HMS *Bedouin*.

All four ships closed at speed, *Nigeria* firing 6″ practice projectiles to frighten rather than damage her target. *Lauenburg*'s crew took to their single boat after the second salvo, leaving their vessel afloat and intact. The destroyer HMS *Tartar* went alongside and put a boarding party across who searched *Lauenburg* thoroughly with the guidance of a NID wireless officer. They came away with another priceless haul of intelligence documents and cypher material. *Lauenburg*, like *Muenchen*, was then sunk.

The Germans were slow to realize the extent of their losses. They continued to signal to *Egerland* for days after she was gone. On 18

June, three days after *Lothringen* had been captured, *U–103* was still signalling that she expected to meet her on the 20th. Amended orders were sent to *Lothringen* on the 19th. It was not until 21 June, when *U–103* reported that she had failed to find *Lothringen*, that the Germans appeared to suspect that something was wrong. Even then, as late as 22 June, *Lothringen* was still being told to report her position.

Other ships were sunk in isolated incidents. The 3,290 ton blockade runner *Lech*, returning from Rio de Janeiro, encountered a British warship on 28 May and scuttled herself. The weather reporting ships, *August Wriedt* and *Heinrich Freese*, were sunk in the next two days. On 10 July, north of St Paul's Rocks in the South Atlantic, the German M/V *Hermes*, 7,209 tons, scuttled herself when approached by the armed merchant cruiser HMS *Canton*. Thus, between 7 May and 11 July, 1941, fifteen German supply, weather-reporting and merchant ships, of 91,000 tons, had been sunk or captured, and eight – *Muenchen*, *Belchen*, *Lothringen*, *Esso Hamburg*, *Friedrich Breme*, *Babitonga*, *Egerland*, and *Lauenburg* – were as a result of ULTRA.

Besides *Spichern*, another of *Prinz Eugen*'s supply ships, *Kota Penang*, reached harbour safely. But she only survived until October, when she sailed from Bordeaux to support armed raiders and U-boats in the South Atlantic and the Indian Ocean. Her movements were revealed by the Enigma and *Kenya* searched for and sank her, north of the Azores, some 750 miles off the coast of Spain, on 3 October.

The Enigma not only betrayed the raiders' supply ships but the raiders themselves. The armed merchant raider *Atlantis* (Schiff 16) sailed from Germany on 31 March, 1940, and in the next twenty months sank or captured twenty-two ships of 145,697 tons, steamed 102,000 miles and circumnavigated the globe. In November, 1941, when she had been 620 days at sea, she was ordered to refuel U-boats off the Cape of Good Hope.

The instructions to *Atlantis* could not be read because they were in the '*Ausserheimisch*' key (named 'Pike' at GC & CS) which was never broken. But the U-boats were using '*Heimisch*' ('Dolphin'), even though they were operating so far away from home waters. This was the Enigma code which had been taken from *Muenchen* and *Lauenburg* and which was being read virtually currently. Thus, when *Atlantis* was ordered to refuel *U–126* at a rendezvous just south of the Equator, the Admiralty signalled at 2004 on 21 November to the cruiser HMS *Devonshire* to intercept.

The 'cover story' was that *Atlantis* was found by *Devonshire*'s aircraft (which was indeed launched on the morning of 22 November and did sight a suspicious vessel). It was *Atlantis*, with *U–126* alongside her.

When the three-funnelled British cruiser was sighted on the horizon,

37

the U-boat hurriedly let go wires and dived. *Atlantis'* captain, a very experienced and wily officer, Bernhard Rogge, recognizing a much more powerful adversary who outgunned him, transmitted alarm signals and pretended to be the British merchant ship *Polyphemus*. No doubt Rogge hoped to lure an unsuspecting opponent within range of his own guns and torpedoes.

Devonshire's Commanding Officer, Captain R. D. Oliver, kept his ship at long range while he signalled to the C-in-C, South Atlantic, for confirmation. When the C-in-C replied that the strange ship could not possibly be *Polyphemus*, *Devonshire* opened fire and quickly sank the raider.

Rogge and about 100 of his ship's company were picked up by *U–126* and later transferred to the U-boat supply ship *Python*. But she too was intercepted by *Devonshire's* sister ship *Dorsetshire*, south-west of St Helena, only a week later, on 1 December. The two U-boats in company dived, but *Python* scuttled herself.

There were now 414 survivors, from both ships. The U-boats each took some men on board. The remainder, in ten lifeboats, were taken in tow. Other U-boats were sent to assist. All the survivors reached ports in France, a distance of more than 5,000 miles, after 360 men had been in tow in open boats for ten days and sixty had been towed for twenty days.

It must have occurred to some experienced German intelligence officer, taking a long-term overall view of these events, that the circumstances of the loss of so many ships, at various rendezvous, in incidents thousands of miles apart, were at least worth some investigation. Fifteen ships, amounting to over 90,000 tons, was nothing less than a massacre – and it had all happened in a few weeks. Surely it might be possible there was some sinister connecting link. It was even possible, though almost unthinkable, that the Enigma code might have been compromised in some way.

The German DNI did indeed investigate the losses of *Bismarck* and her supply ships. As time went by it was the losses of the supply ships which preoccupied the German DNI more. There were two main investigations, the first in July, 1941, when the events of Operation RHEINUEBUNG, the codename for *Bismarck's* sortie, were still fresh, and the second in July, 1942, when interrogation of British prisoners of war from the boarding vessel *Malvernian* gave the Germans their first information of the capture of *Gedania* on 4 June, 1941.

But in both investigations, as in later ones, the Germans seemed to start from the premise that the Enigma must be inviolate. Then, as always, they looked for solutions elsewhere. In particular, they searched for evidence of treachery and betrayal.

The investigators had available to them the testimony of the *Malvernian* PoWs, the contents of the documents which it must now be assumed had been taken from *Gedania*, *Prinz Eugen*'s log and *Bismarck*'s signals during RHEINUEBUNG, reports from *Prinz Eugen*'s officers, intercepts of British signals by *Prinz Eugen* and by the B Dienst Service (the Germans' own cryptanalytical organisation) stations ashore, and the accounts released by the Admiralty of the way *Bismarck* had been tracked down and sunk.

There were, of course, some factors known to them which the German investigators could have taken into account: that the marked increase of Luftwaffe reconnaissance flights over Scapa Flow and the Denmark Strait in the days immediately prior to RHEINUEBUNG could hardly have gone unnoticed by the enemy; that *Prinz Eugen* had signalled so intensively to her support ships in the three days after she had detached from *Bismarck* that even her captain noted in the log for 27 May: 'It should be mentioned here that the unnecessary signalling, since bearings would have been taken, would certainly have given our position away.'

But, in the end, the investigators attributed the calamity to shore-watchers who reported the passage of the German big ships through the Kattegat; the Swedish sea-plane carrier *Gotland* who had been in company for a short time; the British Secret Service; British telephone-tapping; Norwegian agents, very probably, for the losses of *Muenchen* and *Heinrich Freese*; documents from *Gedania* for the losses of *Egerland* and *Esso Hamburg*; *Gedania*'s documents again, and aircraft patrols, for the loss of *Lothringen*; the enemy's dispositions of his ships, including a battleship, in the search for *Prinz Eugen*, for the losses of *Gonzenheim* and *Friedrich Breme*; aircraft patrols, searching for *Bismarck*, for the loss of *Belchen*, and causes unknown, but possibly aircraft patrols, for the losses of *Babitonga* and *Alstertor*.

In the case of *Bismarck*, German Intelligence concluded that 'the possibility of the enemy's being able to read signals by deciphering them has been unanimously discounted by all the experts'. In fact, none of the signals sent by or to *Bismarck* or *Prinz Eugen* during RHEINUEBUNG was broken. As for the holocaust of June, 1941, among the supply vessels, the conclusion was that although analysis of the causes of the losses had shown connections between five of the cases, 'for the remaining seven ships unlucky circumstances, encounters with convoy escorts, reinforced patrolling of the approaches to the Bay of Biscay must be taken into account; and it is not necessary to put the blame on a breach of security as regards the code and cipher tables'.

5 | THE 'CHANNEL DASH'

February, 1942

'Vice Admiral Ciliax has succeeded where the Duke of Medina Sidonia failed; with trifling losses he has sailed a hostile fleet from an Atlantic harbour up the English Channel, and through the Straits of Dover to safe anchorage in a North Sea port. Nothing more mortifying to the pride of sea-power has happened in home waters since the seventeenth century.'

So thundered *The Times* leader on 14 February, 1942. The news that *Scharnhorst, Gneisenau* and *Prinz Eugen* had left Brest and escaped back to Germany on 12 February, actually passing through the Straits of Dover in daylight, sent an electric tremor of indignation and outrage throughout the country. It was the first time since 1690, when the French Admiral Tourville defeated an Anglo-Dutch force off the Isle of Wight, that major enemy warships had approached so close to the English coast – and had apparently done so with impunity.

The Times leader reflected a national feeling. In the Commons the episode was called 'The war's greatest blunder'. Mr Churchill, evidently responding to the sentiments of House and country, set up a board of enquiry under Mr Justice Bucknill. This was clearly a political move, to try and disarm or at least preempt criticism. For Mr Churchill, of all people, with his knowledge of ULTRA, must have known that things were not as they seemed.

It was Hitler himself, obsessed as he was by his fear that the Allies were planning to invade Norway, who insisted against Raeder's advice that the German squadron at Brest return to Germany and should do so by what he called a 'surprise break through the Channel'. As late as 12 January, 1942, Hitler was still stressing the importance of defending Norway and of bringing back the ships at Brest, who were, he said, like 'a patient with cancer who is doomed unless he submits to an operation'.

The Allies were not privy to Hitler's private pronouncements, but

40

the break-out of the German big ships in February, 1942, did not come as a surprise. On the contrary, the date and time of the escape, and the precise route the ships would take, were all accurately revealed beforehand by the Enigma. The only surprise, a crucial one in the event, was that the German ships chose to make the passage of the English Channel in daylight. However, there were other deficiencies, and a measure of bad luck. In the end, the best intelligence in the world has to be translated into timely and effective action against the enemy. As has been said, 'the battle is the pay-off'.

Scharnhorst and *Gneisenau* had arrived at Brest, after their successful anti-shipping cruise, on 22 March, 1941. From the moment they were located there on the 28th they were prime targets both for photo-reconnaissance (729 PR sorties were flown between 28 March, 1941, and 12 February, 1942, with the loss of nine PR Spitfires) and for attack. Torpedo-carrying Beauforts of 22 Squadron, Coastal Command, raided Brest on 6 April, 1941. One torpedo hit *Gneisenau* aft and did considerable damage, causing her to go into dock. The Beaufort responsible was shot down by the intense anti-aircraft fire but its pilot, Flight Lieutenant K. Campbell, RAFVR, was awarded a posthumous Victoria Cross.

Gneisenau was hit by four bombs during a night raid on 10/11 April. Two more bombs exploded on the dockside nearby. Serious damage was done by blast and by subsequent fires, with fifty dead and over ninety injured. *Prinz Eugen* was hit during a raid on the night of 1 July. One bomb exploded on the starboard side forward, killing fifty-one and injuring thirty-two.

Scharnhorst sailed to La Pallice for engine trials and gunnery and torpedo firing practices between 21 and 26 July, 1941. She was discovered at La Pallice and attacked on 24 July by fifteen bombers who scored five bomb hits which badly damaged C turret, the engine rooms and the starboard propeller shaft. One bomb penetrated the bottom of the hull and caused extensive flooding. *Scharnhorst* took on some 3,000 tons of water and a list of six degrees and was out of action for the rest of the year. The Admiralty had confirmation of the serious damage done to *Gneisenau* by the end of April and by October had reports from PR and from the Secret Service that all three ships had been damaged.

On 17 and 19 December, 1941, the Enigma provided some valuable information: between 1 and 14 December guns' crews from *Scharnhorst* and *Gneisenau* were carrying out gunnery firing practice in *Admiral Scheer* in the Baltic. Guns' crews from *Prinz Eugen* were also practising in *Admiral Hipper*. *Scharnhorst*'s guns' crews carried out further practice in *Admiral Scheer* between 19 and 23 January.

41

PR revealed on 16 December that *Prinz Eugen* had undocked. *Gneisenau* suffered more damage from blast on 18 December, when several bombs fell in the dock beside her. But PR revealed that she was out of dock and alongside a jetty by 23 December. On 24 December the Admiralty warned all air commands that a breakout from Brest could happen at any time.

Further air attacks were made in December, 1941, and January, 1942, but only *Gneisenau*, the unluckiest of ships, was badly damaged again on 6 January, when a bomb detonated between her hull and the dockside, tearing open several compartments and causing more flooding. This damage took until 25 January to repair. She carried out engine trials and gunnery shoots in Brest roads on 27 January. Throughout January evidence had continued to accumulate that the ships were making their preparations for a break-out. PR during the month showed them in and out of dock, but all three definitely out of dock on 31 January.

In mid-January, 1942, the Enigma revealed that *Tirpitz* had moved to Trondheim. It was possible that *Tirpitz*, sailing from Norway, and the three ships at Brest might join together to make up the most formidable raiding task force the war had yet seen. But OIC assessed the situation as regards the German capital ships on 19 January and reported that 'in view of the high degree of efficiency demanded by the Germans before their warships undertake operational war cruises, it is possible that these vessels on leaving Brest will endeavour to avoid detection by, and engagement with, British naval forces, and make for an area in which they can work up with comparative immunity'. The only such area was the Baltic. In other words, all the activity at Brest pointed, not to a sortie into the Atlantic, but a break for home.

By 1 February, 1942, both PR and the Enigma had shown that the two battlecruisers were going outside the harbour at nights and returning in the mornings. OIC concluded that 'the ships at Brest are carrying out steaming trials at night, probably in Douarnenez Bay. This, taken in conjunction with the recent assembly of two destroyers, five torpedo-boats and eight minesweepers, indicates that their departure from Brest is near at hand.'

On 3 February OIC was able to summarize the German naval units which had reached the Channel in the previous ten days and estimated the German forces between Brest and the Hook of Holland as seven destroyers, ten torpedo-boats, twenty 'M' Class minesweepers, twenty-five MTBs (between Boulogne and the Hook), about six Sperrbrechers, and a number of minor war vessels. On 5 February OIC reported several recent exercises by the battlecruisers. These exercises, and the hoisting in *Scnarnhorst* of the flag of Admiral Commanding Battleships

(Admiral Otto Ciliax), were 'indications of an impending departure'. On 8 and 9 February *Scharnhorst* was seen to be in dock again. But on the 11th all three heavy ships were out of dock. Six destroyers had been seen in the harbour, but the torpedo booms were still in place and there had been no signs of an unusual concentration of fighters.

Nevertheless, it was as certain as anything could ever be in the world of intelligence that the German ships were just about to sail. The question remained: which direction would they take?

The possibility that the German ships might try to escape up Channel had been foreseen as early as 29 April, 1941, when the Air Ministry issued a plan of action, Operation FULLER, in which one of the main points made was the 'strong probability that the enemy ships would seek to pass the Narrows at Dover under cover of darkness'.

OIC already had captured charts which showed the German swept routes and lines of reference through minefields off the coasts of northern Europe. The Enigma had revealed that minesweepers in the Bight had been sweeping a new route, and had also given its position and direction. On 3 February the Admiralty summed up in a 'Hush Most Secret' message: 'Admiralty appreciate most probable course of action of enemy ships now in Brest will be to break eastward up the Channel and so to their home ports. C-in-C Portsmouth is requested to operate *Manxman* [fast minelayer] as he thinks best and to sail *Welshman* [fast minelayer] for Portsmouth complete with mines as soon as possible. *Welshman* to be placed under operational orders of V. A. Dover.'

'C-in-C Nore is requested to arrange for 6 destroyers with torpedo armament to be at 4 hours' notice in the Thames Estuary ready to operate as ordered by V. A. Dover. The additional risk to trade convoys on the east coast must be accepted. The C-in-C is further requested to hold up to 6 MTBs available for operations as ordered by V. A. Dover.'

On receiving the Admiralty's appreciation of 3 February, the C-in-Cs of Coastal, Bomber and Fighter Commands alerted their groups and put Operation FULLER into action. Coastal Command established three night reconnaissance patrols covering the area between Brest and Boulogne. Of three squadrons of Beaufort torpedo-bombers, No. 86 Squadron was held ready at St Eval in Cornwall and No. 217 Squadron was divided, three of its aircraft being at St Eval and seven at Thorney Island. The third, No. 42 Squadron, based at Leuchars in Scotland, was ordered on 8 February to fly to North Coates in Norfolk (and then, because of snow on the runways, was diverted to Coltishall).

Some 300 available aircraft of Bomber Command were allocated to stand by at two hours' notice as a striking force for FULLER each day from 4 February onwards. On 7 February the acting AOC-in-C Bomber Command, Air Vice Marshal 'Jackie' Baldwin, having decided that night bombing raids were more important than a break-out by German ships which might or might not take place, asked the Air Ministry to release these aircraft from FULLER. When the Air Ministry passed this request to the Admiralty, the reply was that a break-out was imminent and the destruction of the German ships would have a far greater effect on the war than night raids on Germany.

However, without informing the Admiralty, Fighter Command or Coastal Command, Bomber Command stood down 200 of the aircraft from FULLER and reverted the remaining 100 to the normal four hours' notice.

On 4 February Fighter Command detailed No. 11 Group to co-ordinate fighter cover with No. 10 Group to co-operate as necessary. Two-hourly daylight fighter patrols, known as 'Jim Crows', were flown between Fécamp and Ostend.

Besides the movements of fast minelayers, destroyers and MTBs, the Admiralty also flew six Fairey Swordfish torpedo-bombers of 825 Squadron, Fleet Air Arm, from Lee-on-Solent to Manston in Kent. Two old training submarines, HMS/Ms *H.50* and *H.34* (who broke down and was replaced by *H.43*) were taken from their normal duties and sent on patrol off Brest. They were joined on 3rd by HMS/M *Sealion*.

The Admiralty was later criticized for not doing more. The explanation given on 18 February, 1942, by the First Sea Lord, Admiral Sir Dudley Pound, was that naval forces in the Home Commands had necessarily to be kept at a bare minimum to enable the Navy to meet its very heavy commitments overseas.

Even so, those overseas commitments were only being partially met. *Tirpitz* was at Trondheim and ready for sea, 'an ever-present and overwhelming threat to the Russian convoys. A WS troop convoy of twenty-six troopships was due to leave the Clyde for Sierra Leone on 26 February. These two commitments alone meant that the bulk of the Home Fleet, including the battleship *King George V*, the battlecruiser *Renown*, the carrier *Victorious*, five cruisers and ten destroyers, had to be kept in readiness between the United Kingdom and Iceland. At the same time the battleship HMS *Rodney* had to be detached from the Home Fleet, and the battleship HMS *Malaya* and the cruiser HMS *Hermione* had to be sailed from Gibraltar to the Clyde, to escort the WS convoy.

Although the Admiralty's own appreciation was that the German ships would head up Channel, the Admiralty still had to make dispositions to cover all the other alternatives open to the enemy. Thus, the special naval dispositions made to meet the German threat from Brest were small but they were the maximum available. In short, as Pound said, 'Our world-wide naval commitments made it impossible to concentrate an adequate naval force to dispute the passage of the German battle-cruisers up the Channel.' But in the event this unavoidable inadequacy was compounded by some errors, some bad weather and bad luck, and one misjudgement – that the German ships would time their sailing from Brest so as to pass through the Narrows in darkness.

On 8 February Coastal Command issued an appreciation that the ships were likely to leave any time after 10 February, and this opinion was shared by OIC. But it could not be confirmed. There had been some decrypted information in recent days about fresh minesweeping activity on the new passage through minefields in the Bight, and at 1800 on 11 February further decrypts were obtained which enabled OIC to plot the whole of this new route.

So the information was complete, except for the vital detail of the enemy's timing, on which the Enigma decrypts gave no further hints. By ill luck daily German naval Enigma traffic for 10, 11 and 12 February was not decrypted until the 15th. It was most unfortunate that ULTRA faltered thus at a critical moment.

Operation FULLER did not, of course, rely solely upon forewarning from ULTRA, but it so happened that the other means of getting early warning of the enemy's departure also suffered from operational mishaps and misfortunes.

Before sailing, the submarine *Sealion* had been provided with the latest information obtained from the Enigma on enemy minefields and swept channels off Brest (although, of course, her CO, Lieutenant-Commander G. R. Colvin, was not informed of the source). On 6 February Colvin was given discretion by the Admiralty 'to penetrate inside Brest roads, to try to catch the German ships in the enclosed waters where they had been seen to carry out their trials and exercises'.

On the afternoon of 11 February *Sealion* entered Brest roads, saw nothing and retired at 2035 to charge batteries. The PR flight that day, the first the weather had permitted since 9 February, showed that the ships were all out of dock but still in harbour, with the torpedo booms still shut, at 1615.

It seems almost certain that the German decision to sail on the night of 11/12 February was clinched by the approach of a warm front from Iceland which reached the British Isles at 1400 on the 11th, bringing thick low cloud, strong winds and rain. It was ideal weather for a break-out and the German ships intended to take advantage of it. In fact they were preparing to sail at 1930, but were delayed by an air raid alert (a raid which had actually been mounted as a result of that day's PR). They sailed at 2245 on the 11th, screened by six destroyers and accompanied by five M-Class minesweepers. They would have been seen by *Sealion*, but she had already withdrawn.

The submarine may have missed the ships, but there were still the special air patrols being flown by Coastal Command. The most westerly, code-named 'Stopper', between Brest and Ushant, was flown by 224 Squadron from St Eval, one of whose ASV-radar equipped Hudsons took off at 1827 on the 11th. Its radar was switched off during a brush with a Ju.88 night fighter at 1917 and, unfortunately, it would not function properly when it was switched on again. This Hudson therefore went off patrol at 1940.

Because of difficulties at St Eval, a replacement Hudson did not arrive over Brest until 2238. Nevertheless, this aircraft could still have detected the German ships, which had not yet passed out of the 'Stopper' patrol area. But its ASV set, although in working order, showed no echo. (At that stage of their development, the ASV sets were only 50% reliable.)

The next patrol, 'Line SE', also flown by 224, was from Ushant to the Ile de Bréhat, at the north-eastern corner of Brittany. The first Hudson reached is patrol position at 2015 on the 11th, but at 2055 it reported that its ASV was defective. It was ordered to return. Unhappily it was not replaced and 'Line SE' was therefore unwatched when the German ships passed through the area at 0050 on 12 February.

The third patrol, 'Habo', flown from Le Havre to Boulogne until dawn, was carried out by 223 Squadron from Thorney Island. Their first Hudson arrived at 0032 on 12 February and left at 0554. A second Hudson arrived at 0355 and should have patrolled until 0715 but, because of mist which was forecast to turn into thicker fog, it was recalled early and went off patrol at 0613, when the German ships were still to the westward, and had not yet arrived in the patrol area.

There was still a chance that the routine Fighter Command 'Jim Crow' patrols by Spitfires, flown daily at first light between Ostend and the mouth of the River Somme, might retrieve the situation. But when this patrol ended just before 1000 on 12 February, the German ships were still some distance to the west and hidden behind a bank of cloud almost down to sea-level. Had the weather been clearer, one of the Spitfires must surely have spotted the enemy force. Furthermore, and to complete a history of frustration and failure, low clouds and a smoke screen hid the German ships' departure from the PR flight over Brest at dawn on 12 February.

Thus, by a most unfortunate combination of bad weather, material failures and mistaken (with hindsight) decisions by Coastal Command, the German ships passed undetected through all three patrol areas. Worse still, Vice Admiral Dover, Admiral Ramsay, and his staff were never told that some patrols had been curtailed or not flown at all. Naturally they assumed, lacking information to the contrary, that all patrols had been carried out in full and that nothing had been seen.

With hindsight, it could be said that Coastal Command should have drawn attention to these deficiencies in their patrols, just as Admiral Ramsay's staff should have checked. Equally, it could be said that more attention should have been paid to radar contacts, that there should have been a greater readiness to break radio silence in view of the seriousness of the impending situation, and that all those who were charged with watching the channel and preparing for the enemy ships should have been very much more alert.

In fact, there was no particular reason why anybody should be more alert on that day than on any other. The Admiralty and Coastal Command, with the benefit of ULTRA, might issue their forecasts of imminent break-out, but these were certainly not passed down to those who would have to take action, to the captains of ships and submarines, the COs of RAF stations and squadrons, the commanders of shore batteries and radar installations, still less to squadron air controllers and the pilots of individual aircraft. All these had known for months that the German ships were at Brest and some day, some time, might break out. But there was nothing so far to indicate that 12 February was the day. Once again, the best intelligence in the world is wasted if it is not passed in time to those who can use it.

The first indication was provided by the Luftwaffe, who mounted special fighter patrols over the German ships as they steamed up Channel. From 0825 that morning of 12 February, radar stations along the south coast had begun to detect radar echoes of aircraft. By 0959 they had plotted four groups, all circling over a small area north of Le Havre. Enemy jamming had begun at about 0920 (the start having been delayed that morning so as not to arouse Allied suspicions).

But such radar contacts were not so uncommon as to cause undue concern, and the radar plotters continued to track them as they headed up Channel. It was not until about 1000, when the enemy force was already off Dieppe, that No. 11 Group, Fighter Command, awoke to the possible significance of the plots. Those four groups clearly had a common purpose. In fact, as it was suddenly realized, they were all moving steadily north-east at a speed of between 20 and 25 knots.

Two Spitfires of 91 Squadron, flown by the CO and a Sergeant pilot, took off at 1020 from Hawkinge near Manston to investigate. By then radar stations from Beachy Head to Dover were beginning to plot echoes of surface vessels. At 1016 the radar station at Swingate near Dover had three large echoes, off Boulogne, at a range of about 56 miles. At 1052 a radar station near Newhaven reported 'two fairly large ships' off Le Touquet.

The two Spitfires did sight ships but did not report them because they were keeping radio silence. The pilots did not know that Operation FULLER had been initiated, nor would the code-word have meant anything to them if they had.

The Spitfires landed at 1050 and the pilots reported that they had seen a convoy of twenty to thirty ships off Boulogne, escorted by five destroyers. They also sighted a group of nine E-boats. Considering the weather conditions, this was a very accurate summary of the actual situation. But it was the Sergeant pilot who mentioned, at the very end of his debriefing, when the information he and his CO had given was already being rushed to No. 11 Group and to Flag Officer, Dover, that he had also seen one ship with a tripod mast and massive super-structure. When shown a copy of *Jane's Fighting Ships*, he confirmed that he could have seen *Scharnhorst* or *Gneisenau*.

Meanwhile two other Spitfires carrying out a sweep which had nothing to do with FULLER had also sighted the German ships. They too were keeping radio silence. They landed at 1109 to report that they had sighted the German ships at 1042, 16 miles west of Le Touquet. Fighter 'Command broadcast this sighting report at 1125. As so often, there had by then been a common awakening. Several officers, from the radar station commander at Swingate to the air liaison officer on Ramsay's staff at Dover and including the air controller at Biggin Hill, had by then guessed the truth – the German ships were out.

It was, in fact, the air liaison officer on Ramsay's staff who acted on his own interpretation of the radar plot and rang up Manston at 1045 to warn Esmonde, the CO of 825, to bring his Swordfish to immediate readiness, setting torpedoes to run deep (i.e. against major warships). Briefing was at 1130. The squadron was to be airborne at 1220 and to attack at 1245. Five squadrons of fighters were to rendezvous with Esmonde and cover his attack. Ten Spitfires of 72 Squadron had arrived by 1228. Esmonde, already late, decided not to wait and set course for the target at once.

Two more Spitfire squadrons (401 and 411, both Canadian) did sight the enemy ships and engaged German fighters. The Spitfires did their best, and were credited with two German fighters, but it was not enough to save Esmonde and his six Swordfish. They were intercepted by the German Me.109s when they were only ten miles out to seaward of Ramsgate and still some 12 miles from the enemy. Of Esmonde's flight of three Swordfish, Esmonde's own aircraft was shot down, when it had probably reached a range of only 3,000 yards from

Prinz Eugen. Esmonde and his two aircrew were lost. The other two Swordfish were also shot down. One air-gunner was killed; the other five in the crews were picked up by MTBs.

The three Swordfish in the second flight, led by Lieutenant J. C. Thompson, were last seen crossing the destroyer screen and taking violent evasive action under fighter attack. All three were lost, with their entire crews. Nothing more was ever seen or heard of them.

'In my opinion,' Admiral Ramsay signalled the Admiralty, 'the gallant sortie of these six Swordfish constitutes one of the finest exhibitions of self-sacrifice and devotion to duty that the war has yet witnessed.' Esmonde was awarded a posthumous Victoria Cross. His body was recovered from the Medway two months later.

Fighter Command flew 398 sorties during the day, and lost seventeen aircraft. They made 102 attacks on various naval vessels: one 600-ton ship and one E-boat were destroyed, with another eight escort vessels claimed damaged. Sixteen enemy aircraft were destroyed, with three probables and seventeen damaged.

Five MTBs and two MGBs cleared Dover harbour at 1155, steered east-south-east at 36 knots, and sighted the enemy at 1223. The leading four MTBs, attacking through fog and smoke, fired their torpedoes from outside the E-boat screen, at ranges of 4,000 to 5,000 yards. The fifth MTB suffered an engine defect and fell behind the rest, but managed to slip round behind the E-boat screen and fire one torpedo at *Prinz Eugen*, at a range of about 3,000 yards. None of these torpedoes hit. Three MTBs from Ramsgate cleared harbour at 1225 and one of them sighted destroyers and E-boats at 1318. They did not see the big ships and withdrew.

The twin-engined Beaufort torpedo-bombers of Coastal Command had always seemed the most likely weapons to be effective against the German big ships. They were comparatively modern, fast (*very* fast compared with the Swordfish), and their crews had been trained in the specialist task of attacking ships. But on the day they were too widely dispersed at different airfields to make a coordinated attack. There were failures of communication, in the air – and in the briefings. None of the pilots knew of FULLER. Some thought they were supposed to be attacking a convoy. Few actually knew that their targets were the ships from Brest.

In the circumstances the Beauforts did very much better than could have been expected, in unfavourable attacking conditions of poor visibility and low cloud, with a winter dusk coming on, which made ship identification, never easy, doubly difficult. Of the thirty-six Beauforts technically available, twenty-eight took part, with some Hudsons and Beaufighters.

Some lost their way hopelessly and had to return. But sixteen Beauforts did find and attack the enemy: five at about 1540, nine at about 1605, one at 1710 and the last at 1800. Another twelve Beauforts sighted small craft but failed to find the main targets. Thirteen tor-pedoes were released (three of them were aimed, unfortunately, at the British destroyer HMS *Campbell*, in error), but no hits were obtained. Three Beauforts were lost.

Campbell was one of six elderly First World War vintage destroyers from Harwich (*Campbell*, *Vivacious* and *Worcester* of the 21st Destroyer Flotilla, and *Mackay*, *Whitshed* and *Walpole* of the 16th Flotilla), who were already at sea for exercises on 12 February – fortunately, for they could never otherwise have left harbour in time to reach the enemy's position. The senior officer, Captain C. T. M. Pizey (Captain of the 21st Destroyer Flotilla), in *Campbell*, had the message that the enemy ships were coming up the Channel at 1156.

The first estimate of the German squadron's speed was 20 knots and Pizey's plan was to pass through the swept channel in the southern end of the East Coast mine barrier and intercept the enemy in the vicinity of the West Hinder Buoy, off the Belgian coast. But the broadcast reports from Dover of the enemy's progress showed that their actual speed was 27 knots. Pizey decided he must cut across the mine barrier, as though going for the corner flag, and meet the enemy much further to the east, off the Maas River. At 1318 he signalled to his ships to steer east and increase to 28 knots, and boldly led the way himself across the minefield. At the edge of the minefield *Walpole* had to turn back because of an engine defect, but the other five pressed on.

Pizey expected to encounter the enemy at about 1530. At 1517, just after *Worcester* had been bombed and near-missed by a British bomber, *Campbell*'s radar picked up two large echoes and, two minutes later, a third. At 1543, the enemy was in sight, range four miles. The destroyers closed the enemy at 28 knots and at 1546 *Mackay* turned and fired torpedoes. *Campbell* and *Vivacious* fired a minute later and *Whitshed* at 1549, all at ranges of about 3,000 yards. *Worcester* pressed even closer, and fired at 2,500 yards, but was hit by heavy shells. In the next ten minutes, lying stopped while the German squadron steamed by, she was hit again and again, and badly damaged. It was while *Campbell* was coming to *Worcester*'s assistance that she was attacked by friendly torpedo bombers. *Worcester* was eventually able to reach Harwich under her own steam, at six knots.

Westland Whirlwinds were supposed to have covered Pizey's destroyers but could not find them. Four Whirlwinds were lost. All the destroyers' torpedoes missed.

There remained Bomber Command, who received the report of the detection of the German ships at 1127. But, because their aircraft had reverted to 4 hours' notice, it was some time before Bomber Command mounted any sorties. Of 310 aircraft operationally available, 242 were eventually dispatched, in three waves, attacking between 1445 and 1700. Very few of the pilots had had any training in bombing ship targets. There was broken cloud at 1,500 feet, so it was not surprising that 188 bombers failed to find the enemy, or were unable to attack because of low cloud. Thirty-nine bombers did find the German squadron. No ship was hit but the torpedo boats *T.13* and *Jaguar* were damaged by splinters from near-misses and had to put into Rotterdam.

But it was through Bomber Command that ULTRA was able to achieve one last success, just when it seemed that the German ships were going to escape unscathed. As a result of the 'Hush Most Secret' message of 3 February, in which the Admiralty appreciation was that 'the most probable course of action of enemy ships in Brest will be to break eastwards up the Channel and so to their home ports', and using captured German charts, Bomber Command laid seventy mines on 6 February and twenty-five more, all by daylight, on 7 February.

On 10 February an OIC Special Summary stated that 'With reference to C.B. [Confidential Book] 04137 (German swept channel charts) there is evidence that a new route is being introduced in the Bight area. This route commences at Point Red 01A [53° 36′ N, 05° 15′ E] and runs to a point at 54° 00′ N, 06° 03.5′ E thence eastwards along the southern crossroute'. As a result of this summary, Bomber Command laid four more mines near the key point Red 01A on 11 February.

At 1848 on 11 February further information from the Enigma was received in OIC which, after research that night and during the next day, made it possible to plot the new channel exactly. The route was promulgated on the 12th. Bomber Command laid more mines that evening, again with special attention to Red 01A.

At 1530 on 12 February *Scharnhorst*, who was then the leading ship, struck a mine in 51° 36′ N. 03° 00′ E (off the Schelde), lost way and came to a stop. Ciliax ('Black Otto', who was not a particularly lucky or popular admiral) decided to transfer his flag to *Z.29*. But while he was crossing to the destroyer, he had the mortification of seeing *Scharnhorst* get under way again and steam past him, while he was still sitting in his boat.

The first mine was too early, and too far to the west, to be one of those laid as a result of ULTRA. But at 1955 that evening *Gneisenau* also struck a mine, off Vlieland, at 53° 29′ N, 05° 00′ E. This was ten miles from the key point Red 01A and in the direct line of approach to it. *Gneisenau* too came to a stop but was able to get under way again and work up to 25 knots. She and *Prinz Eugen* reached Brunsbuttel, at the western end of the Kiel Canal, at 0700 on 13 February.

At 2247 on the 12th *Scharnhorst* struck a second mine at 53° 37' N, 05° 15' E, which was only two miles from Red 01A and on the 'probable route' promulgated by OIC. At first *Scharnhorst* requested tugs but these were later cancelled. *Scharnhorst* got under way for the second time and by midnight was making 14 knots. She reached Wilhelmshaven on the morning of 13 February.

The mine damage done to both ships was directly attributable to ULTRA, which had so accurately revealed their route. For *Gneisenau*, the war was over. Much later, the Admiralty learned that she suffered further damage, while in the floating dock at Kiel, from two heavy bombs dropped during a Bomber Command raid on the night of 26/27 February, 1942. Her refit was abandoned in January, 1943.

The Enigma, which had betrayed the German ships, also revealed their mine damage. In view of the indignation that was sweeping the country and the criticisms being levelled at the Navy, the Admiralty must have been greatly tempted to release the news, to show that at least the enemy ships had not escaped entirely scot-free. But because the Germans withheld the news, and it was not available from any other source than ULTRA, the Admiralty could not publish for some time.

The German heavy ships were, of course, much less of a threat to Allied convoy routes at home in Germany than they had been in Brest. Admiral Raeder was quite right to describe the passage of the German squadron up Channel as 'a tactical victory but a strategic defeat'. But, in a way, it had also been a partial victory for ULTRA.

6 | _TIRPITZ_ IN THE NORTH

Tirpitz was the 'Big Bad Wolf' of the war in home waters. All by herself she constituted a 'fleet in being' and, while she still floated, she remained a potential threat. She did not need actually to go to sea. In fact, it was better that she did not. At sea, she was one capital ship, albeit very large and very powerful, but with a ship's company and guns' crews badly in need of sea-time and practice, given only patchy air cover and, as often as not, a destroyer escort as in need of sea-time as she was. She fired her main armament in earnest only once, and then against a paltry shore target not worth a battleship's notice. But while she stayed in harbour, the mere knowledge of her presence lying up in some northern fastness cast a long shadow over the convoys to Russia and affected the movements of Allied warships all over the world. All _Tirpitz_ had to do was, like Mount Everest, to be there.

Never was a ship encompassed about with a greater cloud of witnesses than was _Tirpitz_. Every stage of her building and her trials was the subject of anxious scrutiny and conjecture. She was laid down as _Schlachtschiff_ G at Wilhelmshaven on 24 October, 1936, and launched as _Tirpitz_ on 1 April, 1939, by Frau von Hassel, grand-daughter of the great Admiral von Tirpitz. Her first Captain, Kapitan zur See Karl Topp, took command on 25 January, 1941. She was completed in February and began a long series of trials in the Baltic in March.

Tirpitz made two trips to the eastern Baltic at the end of May and the beginning of June, 1941. She then returned to Kiel for a considerable period and was sighted by PR in the floating dock there on 12, 20 and 25 June. When Germany invaded Russia on 21 June the Baltic became a war zone, although the Russian Navy was never seriously to challenge the German Navy. By September, 1941, there were signs of impending activity by units of the German fleet in the Baltic. _Tirpitz_ left Kiel on 15 September and was due to arrive at Sassnitz between the 20th and 25th, with _Admiral Scheer_ and the cruisers _Koln, Emden, Nurnberg_ and

Leipzig. Between the 23rd and 26th she was at sea with the cruisers, supporting a naval bombardment of the Soerve peninsula, to the south of Saare Maa.

Sources graded B2 reported *Tirpitz* as part of a naval squadron which was sighted at intervals between 15 and 26 September moving from the entrance to the Gulf of Bothnia and Sassnitz and Trelleberg. In fact, the German Baltic Fleet of *Tirpitz, Admiral Scheer* and the four cruisers, with destroyers, torpedo-boats and minesweepers, was indeed waiting off the Aland Islands in two groups, Northern and Southern, for any attempt by the Russian fleet to interfere with the seaward flank of the German army's advance in Estonia. In the event the Russian ships stayed in harbour.

Tirpitz herself carried on with her work-up: torpedo trials in the western Baltic between 10 and 18 October, 1941, followed by fleet exercises with *Koln* and *Nurnberg*, before returning to Kiel at the end of October. She took part in more fleet exercises with *Admiral Hipper* and *Leipzig* in the central Baltic between 13 and 20 December. After degaussing off Hel on 28 December, her trials were deemed complete on 6 January, 1942. After an inspection by the C-in-C Navy, Admiral Raeder, she was finally ready for operations on 10 January. At 50,000 tons full load, with eight 38 cm (15") guns, twelve 15 cm (5.9"), sixteen 10.5 cm (4.1") and AA armament, a maximum speed of 31 knots, armour up to a foot thick, and a complement of more than 2,400 officers and men, she was the most formidable battleship in the western hemisphere.

In the years to come *Tirpitz* was attacked many times, and by a variety of arms, from the Norwegian resistance to the Fleet Air Arm, from Russian bombers to midget submarines. She almost certainly took up more staff time and thought, more space in OIC Special Intelligence Summaries, and more text in ULTRA signals, than any other single ship. In the end, ULTRA was to play a major role in her life and death.

Early in 1942 there were indications from the Enigma that *Tirpitz* was almost ready for operations and was about to move. This was likely to be the first movement by a major German warship since *Bismarck*. The information provided by the Enigma, although not always strictly in chronological order, and the inferences drawn from it by OIC and promulgated by ULTRA signal provide an excellent example of the influence ULTRA was able to exert on naval affairs and the insights it provided.

The Enigma had revealed on 3 January, 1942, that *Tirpitz* was due to berth in Gdynia on the 6th. This information was sent by the Admiralty by ULTRA signal of 1630 that same day to the C-in-C

Home Fleet, Admiral Sir John Tovey, and to a wide range of addresses all over the world, indicating the importance attached to *Tirpitz*'s movements. The Enigma for 3 and 4 January was not available in OIC until 7 January, but decoded signals then revealed that *Tirpitz* was to be inspected by the C-in-C Navy on the 7th and she would start taking on stores and victuals the same day.

Clearly some movement was imminent. But it could not be before 10 January because (such was the intimate detail of *Tirpitz*'s life revealed to OIC) that *Tirpitz* had asked for certain spare parts to be sent from Kiel 'by 9 January at the latest'. An ULTRA of 1925 on 7 January stated that *Tirpitz* would be ready to operate from the 10th, but was likely to remain at Gdynia at least until the 9th.

Tirpitz sailed from Gdynia westbound at 0800 on 11 January. That same day a signal from Wilhelmshaven dockyard informed her that repairs could not be finished before 14 January. An ULTRA of 1204 on 15 January therefore said: 'Repairs to "Tirpitz" are being undertaken at Wilhelmshaven from 14 January, 1942.' As a result, photographic reconnaissance of Wilhelmshaven was flown at 1545 on 15 January but no large ship was seen.

In fact the destination was Kiel, not Wilhelmshaven. Small pieces of evidence of what was likely to happen were accumulating from the Enigma in a manner which was beginning to become familiar to OIC: a weather forecast for *Tirpitz* of the western Skagerrak; patrol vessels in the Kattegat detailed for a 'special task' and signs that the repairs at Wilhelmshaven were due to be done on some equipment and not on *Tirpitz* herself. An ULTRA signal of 0850 on 17 January warned the C-in-C Home Fleet and other addressees in home waters that, from the number of signals being passed to *Tirpitz*, the OIC appreciation was that she was at sea and had probably passed the Skaw (northbound) early on 16 January.

A W/T message of 15 January to the two U-boats informed them that German warships passing along the west coast of Norway were bound for Trondheim. An 'Immediate' ULTRA of 1005 on the 17th passed this information to Tovey and the same addressees.

Because of chronological gaps in the Enigma available, it was not possible to reconstruct *Tirpitz*'s movements and their exact timings until later. But *Tirpitz* had indeed sailed. She left the Arkona area at 1700 on 12 January and reached Holtenau (Kiel) at 0700 on the 13th. She passed through the Kiel Canal (because the Germans wished to avoid their heavy ships making the passage of the Kattegat in daylight, where they could be seen and reported) early on 14 January and sailed from Wilhelmshaven on the night of 14/15 January.

At 1642 on 17 January the Enigma confirmed that *Tirpitz* and four destroyers had arrived at Trondheim on the night of the 16th. But air reconnaissance did not actually sight her in Foettenfjord, an arm of the main Trondheim fjord, until 23 January. However, by the 18th the Enigma was once more being read concurrently and the evidence was that *Tirpitz* was still at Trondheim, albeit apparently keeping radio silence. But, as it happened, the four destroyers returned to Kiel on 19 January, which effectively meant that, with no escort, *Tirpitz* would have to stay where she was.

The weather prevented any more flights for some days and *Tirpitz* was not seen again until 19 January, when she was in the same berth as on the 23rd. Bomber Command made a strike on the night of 29/30 January which was aborted by the bad weather. Regular air reconnaissance early in February showed *Tirpitz* still at Trondheim and apparently inactive, although on the 17th the Enigma revealed that she was due to carry out firing practices between 17 and 20 February.

Meanwhile, on 13 February, the Enigma had revealed that the Luftwaffe in south-west Norway was shortly to be reinforced by about 300 aircraft from France and Holland. Tovey and the other addressees were informed of this by ULTRA signal of 1630 on the 13th. The transfer could be purely defensive, or it could hint at a movement of more German big ships to Norway, and OIC promulgated this possibility by ULTRA at 1901 on 18 February, adding that so far as was known the ships involved might be *Prinz Eugen*, *Koln* and *Admiral Scheer*.

There were other tell-tale signs: for instance three torpedo boats of the 2nd Flotilla were ordered to leave Heligoland on 16 February and, after refuelling in Bergen, to continue to Trondheim 'to patrol the entry channel for the formation'. From this and other Enigma revelations, OIC sent an ULTRA to Tovey, at 1020 on 20 February, that 'all indications point to a very early passage, possibly today, of a unit or units from Germany to Trondheim'. Tovey, flying his flag in *King George V* with *Victorious*, the cruiser *Berwick* and seven destroyers, had sailed from Hvalfjord in Iceland at 0600 on 19 February.

Traffic Analysis on 20 February showed that the ships had already begun to leave Germany. As a result, reconnaissances were flown, one of which sighted two large warships (actually *Prinz Eugen* and *Admiral Scheer*) off Jutland at 1100 that day. Bad weather prevented the aircraft keeping contact, but its report fitted in with information from the Enigma.

There were still frequent delays in breaking the Enigma but by January, 1942, the average delay was down to about 32 hours. But it varied. From February, 1942, onwards, signals were often read currently, but at other times were still too late to be of operational use. In this case there were a great many signals but about half of them were in the 'Offizierte' (officer only) cypher, which was not being read on this occasion. However, enough could be deduced to show that by early on 21 February Admiral Commanding Battleships, Otto Ciliax, was once more at sea with a force of at least two cruisers, three destroyers and a number of torpedo boats. Good estimates could be made of their course (north-west) and speed (24 knots). It seems that Ciliax's ships returned to the Elbe after being sighted by aircraft, but according to an ULTRA of 2211 on the 21st, 'Two cruisers and five destroyers had entered Skadenesfjord and their onward passage to Trondheim would probably be carried out on the night of 22/23 February.

Some of the German ships were sighted from the air twice on 22 February and ineffective air attacks were launched. *Admiral Scheer, Prince Eugen* and the destroyers *Friedrich Ihn, Richard Beitzen, Paul Jacobi, Herman Schoemann* and *Z.25* left Bergen on the 22nd and arrived at Trondheim on the 23rd. Torpedo-carrying Albacores from *Victorious* looked for them early on the 23rd, but were baulked by snow-storms.

Thus it proved impossible to stop the German ships reaching Trondheim. But ULTRA had provided enough information for an ambush to be laid, and, in the end, ULTRA struck one last blow by enabling Flag Officer Submarines to place four submarines on patrol in the likeliest area off Trondheim. One, HMS/M *Trident*, was ordered on 19 February to take up a patrol position which proved to be only a mile and a half off the enemy ships' mean line of advance. At 0602 on 23 February *Trident*'s Captain, Commander G. M. Slayden, sighted the cruisers off Stadlandet and fired three torpedoes, claiming one hit on a pocket battleship.

At 0811 *Prinz Eugen* reported that she had been mined. In fact a torpedo from *Trident* had hit her aft, damaging her rudder and blowing away some ten metres of her stern (the Enigma revealed the precise extent of her damage on the afternoon of the 24th). *Prinz Eugen* was stopped for a time, but was able to reach Lofjord under her own power later that day and was sighted there by a PR flight on the 24th.

Prinz Eugen, being damaged, took no part in operations during her stay in Norway. But in March, 1942, *Tirpitz* made one of her very rare sorties, against the Russian convoy PQ12. Once again ULTRA was instrumental in bringing the enemy to action. But, once again, the final outcome of ULTRA depended upon success at sea, and in this case the weapon, a squadron of Albacores, failed in its task.

The convoys to Russia had begun with DERVISH in August, 1941, and for some months were scarcely molested by the enemy. By the end of February, 1942, a few ships had turned back because of the weather, but 157 merchant ships had sailed to and from north Russia, for the loss of the destroyer *Matabele* and one merchant ship, and a second merchant ship torpedoed but towed home.

Information from the Enigma was more or less continuous and normally read currently, with a maximum delay of only 36 hours. With so much intelligence from ULTRA about U-boat dispositions in the Arctic, it was possible to route convoys evasively. The southernmost limits of the polar ice north of the North Cape prevented convoys being drastically rerouted, but at least ULTRA could ensure that convoys passed through the most dangerous area at the safest times.

But by the spring of 1942 the seasonal drifting of the ice forced the convoys to pass south of Bear Island and nearer to Norway, while the rapidly lengthening days added to the danger from U-boats and the capital ships now in Norway.

To make maximum use of the warships available, PQ12 from Reykjavik and the return convoy QP8 from Murmansk were sailed on the same day, 1 March, 1942. Tovey sent his second-in-command, Vice Admiral A. T. B. Curteis, in the battlecruiser *Renown*, with the battleship *Duke of York* and an escort of six destroyers, to sea to cover the convoys. He himself would have preferred to stay at Scapa Flow, because he wanted to insure against the chances that the enemy might break out into the Atlantic and that *Scharnhorst* and *Gneisenau* might join the squadron already in Norway, and, lastly (a reason understandably omitted from his report of proceedings) because he wished to continue to have the latest intelligence over the telephone from OIC. But, in a signal of 0136 on 3 March, the Admiralty overruled Tovey, accepting the responsibility for any break-out. Tovey sailed in *King George V*, with *Victorious*, *Berwick* and six destroyers to rendezvous with *Renown* and *Duke of York* about 200 miles east of Jan Mayen Island at 1030 on 6 March.

Meanwhile the Enigma had revealed that Ciliax had once again hoisted his flag in *Tirpitz* and on 2 March provided Tovey with summaries of the positions of seventeen U-boats and enemy aircraft dispositions in Norway, in what was to become a steady stream of intelligence. The Luftwaffe sighted and reported PQ12 at 1300 on 5 March and, on the same evening, the submarine HMS/M *Seawolf* on patrol off Trondheim signalled that she had sighted 'one battleship or 8″ cruiser'.

In fact *Tirpitz* sailed from Trondheim, with a destroyer escort but without *Admiral Scheer*, at 1200 on 6 March, steering north-west, intending to intercept a convoy at 72° 00′ N, 08° 00′ E at approximately 1600 on 7 March (an accurate forecast of PQ 112 for position, if not for time). The objectives then would be the destruction of the cruiser and escorts, an engagement by the destroyer escort against British destroyers and, ultimately, the destruction of the convoy. The Germans considered their chances to be good: a probable westbound convoy had been sighted in Iokanskie Road, in north Russia, on 4 March.

PQ12 altered to the south-east to avoid ice on the evening of 6 March, resuming its north-easterly course next morning. PQ12 passed QP8 on almost reciprocal courses at noon on 7th, and steamed on towards Bear Island, 200 miles to the north-east. *Tirpitz* had already detached her three destroyers to search to the north on an almost parallel course to herself. At that time she and her destroyers were all to the south of the two convoys and not far off. *Tirpitz*, steering north-west, passed close astern of PQ12 and ahead of QP8, which had become badly scattered by gales but in fact suffered only one casualty. The Russian straggler mv *Ijora* was sunk by *Friedrich Ihn* at about 1630 on 7 March. She was the only ship of either convoy to be sunk. (*Ijora*, if *Tirpitz* ever did see her, would have been the only Allied ship *Tirpitz* sighted in her entire existence.)

Tovey intended to fly a search to the east on the evening of 7 March which would almost certainly have found *Tirpitz*, but it was cancelled because of the weather. In a confused situation, when neither Admiral had definite information of the other's whereabouts, Tovey nevertheless had a continual flow of intelligence: details of the enemy's air reconnaissance on the 7th (this actually from information sent to Ciliax); a complete set of U-boat dispositions for 6 March; and the note that, at 2000 on the 6th 'the enemy was apparently not aware that the Home Fleet was at sea'.

The three German destroyers rejoined *Tirpitz* after the sinking of *Ijora*. *Tirpitz* carried out what was almost a square search, to the north-east and then back to the south-east before finally steering east to search for the convoy. First, *Friedrich Ihn* and then the other two destroyers were detached during the night to Tromso to refuel, the weather being too bad to fuel from *Tirpitz* herself, who went on alone.

Ijora's distress signal was picked up by Captain M. Denny, senior officer of PQ12's escort, in the cruiser HMS *Kenya*, who at once steered his charges further away to the north, and by the C-in-C, who deduced from the D/F strength and bearing that the enemy was some 200 miles to the north-east of him and would very probably now make for home. Tovey therefore steered south-east to intercept. He also sent six destroyers to sweep further out to the south-east, but they found nothing. Tovey then decided he had missed his quarry and swung away to the south-west, believing that his enemy was by now out of reach.

In fact *Tirpitz* was still searching to the north, up towards Bear Island. PQ12, which had again turned south-east because of ice at noon on 8 March, was at one point steering towards the enemy. But eventually *Tirpitz* passed well to the southward, steering south-west until 6 p.m. on the 8th, when she did break off and head south for Trondheim.

It was here that ULTRA gave Tovey's ships another chance – a very great opportunity, as it turned out. From the Enigma the Admiralty learned Ciliax's own estimates of the convoy's position at 0700 on 8 and 9 March, and also that he had been ordered to return to Trondheim 'if convoy not found by nightfall on 9th'. This was passed to Tovey by Admiralty signal of 1500 on 8 March and he at once hauled round to the north-east again.

That night the Admiralty gave Tovey details of a rendezvous *Tirpitz* intended to keep with her refuelled destroyers at 0700 on 9 March, and details of her plans to search for the convoy, which the Germans now thought might have been delayed, south of Bear Island. But the Germans changed their minds, having decided not to risk *Tirpitz*, with or without destroyers, so far east. In three signals in the early hours of 9 March, and as a result of brilliantly accurate and timely intelligence, the Admiralty informed Tovey of the enemy's change of plan, ordered him to steer south-east at full speed, and gave him *Tirpitz*'s route home to Fro Havet. At 0249 on 9 March Tovey set course for the Lofoten Islands. The chase was on, and there was now a very good chance of interception in the morning.

The enemy's progress was nicely judged. Six reconnaissance Albacores were flown off *Victorious* at 0640, followed fifty minutes later by twelve Albacores of 832 Squadron armed with torpedoes, sped on their way by a signal from Tovey: 'A wonderful chance which may achieve most valuable results. God be with you'.

Tirpitz was sighted at 0802, with *Friedrich Ihn* in company, 80 miles from the fleet. The strike leader, Lieutenant-Commander Lucas, the CO of 832, himself sighted the enemy at 0842 and gave the order 'Dive to attack' at about 0915. But the attacks were not well carried out. Valuable height was lost prematurely. Approaches were made from astern and to leeward of the target. Torpedoes were dropped at too great ranges, and all missed. Two Albacores were lost.

There were some mitigating circumstances. 832 Squadron were not properly worked up for torpedo attacks. Lucas himself had only recently joined the ship and had never even flown with his squadron before. Nevertheless, the hard truth was that the first and (though nobody could know that) the only chance of ever bringing *Tirpitz* to action had been irretrievably lost.

Tovey could go no nearer the coast; the Luftwaffe's fighters far outperformed the Albacores. His destroyers had not rejoined. He hoped to mount another air search that night, 9 March, but was delayed by an attack on his ships by three Junkers Ju.88s, and then the weather closed in again. Bitterly disappointed, knowing what a great chance had gone, Tovey had to set course for Scapa Flow, while *Tirpitz* headed for Vest Fjord.

Even now ULTRA provided one last chance, by disclosing that *Tirpitz* was in Narvik and would move to Trondheim as soon as conditions permitted. Submarines lay in wait across her likely route from 9 March onwards, and destroyers left Scapa on the 11th to intercept her. *Tirpitz* sailed early on 13 March but unfortunately the Enigma did not reveal her sailing until some days later, and when she did come south, she was hidden by thick driving snow squalls. Nobody sighted her, although she did pass close to *Trident*. She reached Trondheim at 9 p.m. that evening.

Whatever the political and material justifications for the Russian convoys, as naval undertakings they were always fundamentally unsound. Convoys and escorts had to pass to and from north Russian ports along routes often restricted by polar ice and always within range of the enemy's aircraft, U-boats and surface ships, and where Allied heavy ships could not properly protect them.

Almost every convoy from March until June, 1942, was attacked either by the Luftwaffe or by U-boats, or German destroyers, or by combinations of all three. Twenty-one ships and the cruisers *Edinburgh* and *Trinidad* were lost, but another 124 ships arrived safely. Two U-boats and the destroyer *Z.26* were sunk.

As the ice receded convoys could be routed north of Bear Island and thus further from enemy air bases, but, likewise, the longer hours of daylight increased the danger of attack from heavy surface ships, of which the enemy was building up a powerful force in northern Norway. On 21 March *Tirpitz* was joined at Trondheim by *Admiral Hipper* and three destroyers. *Prinz Eugen* left on 17 May and reached Kiel on the 19th. But the pocket battleship *Lutzow* and three destroyers had arrived at Narvik by 25 May. So, by 29 June, 1942, the enemy had, in the Trondheim area, *Tirpitz*, the 8″ gun cruiser *Admiral Hipper* and five destroyers, and, in the Narvik area, the two pocket battleships *Admiral Scheer* and *Lutzow*, and six destroyers.

Convoy PQ17, of thirty-six ships, sailed from Reykjavik on 27 June. Convoy QP13 sailed in two sections, of twelve ships from Archangel on 26 June, and eleven ships from Murmansk a day later. Two ships of PQ17 turned back, but by 30 June the remaining thirty-three ships and an oiler were some 100 miles south-south-west of Jan

Mayen Island, with a close escort of six destroyers, four corvettes, two submarines and two anti-aircraft ships.

There was also a 'Support Force' of four cruisers, *London* (flag of Rear Admiral L. H. K. ('Turtle') Hamilton, commanding First Cruiser Squadron), *Norfolk*, and the American USS *Tuscaloosa* and *Wichita*, with three destroyers, to give close cover as far as Bear Island. In the deep field, north-east of Jan Mayen Island, was a distant 'Covering Force' of *Duke of York* (wearing Tovey's flag), the battleship USS *Washington* (flag of Rear Admiral R. C. Giffen, USN), *Victorious*, cruisers *Nigeria* and *Cumberland*, and fourteen destroyers.

Intelligence from the Enigma was once again good, giving full details of the Luftwaffe's arrangements for finding and shadowing PQ17, and reassurance, albeit from negative evidence, that there had been no recent movements of German heavy units. Shadowing aircraft were sighted on 1 July and the first U-boats were detected and attacked by the escorts. U-boats in a patrol line south-east of Jan Mayen found the convoy and continued to shadow: in fact, PQ17 was to be shadowed almost continuously from now on, and the enemy always had a good idea of the convoy's position.

However, with the timely aid of ULTRA, PQ17 was proving itself a very capable and, to begin with, even a lucky convoy. PQ17 and QP13 passed each other, north-east of Jan Mayen Island, on the afternoon of 2 July. The Enigma disclosed that the enemy had deduced where the convoys would pass. The enemy had originally intended to attack with heavy units at that point but in the event did not go ahead with the plan. The Enigma also revealed the facts that the enemy had sighted both convoys and planned a torpedo-bomber attack on PQ17 on the evening of 2 July.

The attack duly arrived at about 1800 and was beaten off, with one aircraft shot down. Almost at once the convoy ran into welcome fog which protected it until the next morning, when the convoy threw shadowing aircraft off the scent by altering to the east so as to pass north of Bear Island and on into the Barents Sea.

Admiral Hamilton's cruisers had caught the convoy up on 2 July and were steering on a parallel course, but out of sight about 40 miles to the north. Hamilton believed that *Tirpitz* might attack QP13 to draw the Home Fleet's battleships to the southward, while *Lutzow* and *Admiral Scheer* went for PQ17. He therefore stayed out of sight to the north, hoping thereby to have a better chance of luring the German pocket battleships into action.

Late that evening of 2 July, the Admiralty signalled: 'No direct indications of movements of enemy main units but the interest in the whereabouts of Home Fleet and fighter readiness on Norwegian coast may be significant.' But this reassuring situation was already changing. The enemy had assessed the air attacks of March, 1942, and concluded that *Tirpitz* had been very fortunate to escape damage, or worse. Hitler had imposed crippling restrictions on the future deployment of the heavy ships. He insisted that no sortie could be made unless the Home Fleet's aircraft carrier had been definitely located at a safe enough distance away. The only feasible course of action open to Raeder now was to get early reconnaissance information of an eastbound convoy, move his heavy units up to the far north and then, having first obtained Hitler's permission, sally out for a short sharp action against the convoy with as many of the heavy ships as could be got to the scene, but keeping them all as far from both Tovey's and Hamilton's ships as possible.

The restrictions imposed by Hitler were, of course, not known to the Admiralty when, on 3 July, they informed Tovey that the enemy heavy units were on the move. Enigma information for the period between noon on 1 July and noon on the 3rd became available at 0515 on the 3rd. At 0810 the Admiralty informed Tovey by ULTRA signal that: '1. Shadowing aircraft were still in contact with PQ17 at 0200/3rd. Germans stated weather conditions made it doubtful whether it would be possible to continue shadowing. 2. At 2104/2nd British Battlefleet had not been located since 2100/1st. Unverified report had been received of a Skua 60 miles west of Trondheim at 1630/2nd, which led Germans to suggest that a carrier was possible off Trondheim. 3. At 0300/2nd AOC Lofoten reported that close air escort for operation CONCERT would probably not be possible on account of weather. 4. GAF intentions for 3 July were: renewed reconnaissance for convoy, and Operation Rosselssprung (Knight's Move). Comment: CONCERT and KNIGHT'S MOVE are probably concerned with enemy main units.' (CONCERT was indeed the codename for *Tirpitz*'s move from Trondheim to Altenfjord, KNIGHT'S MOVE for the sortie against PQ17.

The Admiralty followed with a further ULTRA at 0950; 'At 0440/3rd July Admiral Commanding Cruisers [Kummetz] reported 'LUTZOW detached, remainder of formation at 0500 at Green 30.' Comment: Position of Green 30 not known but probably in vicinity of Arstad or Adnfjord'. In fact *Lutzow* and *Admiral Scheer*, with six destroyers, left Narvik for Altenfjord just after midnight, but *Lutzow* ran aground early on the 3rd, hence the reference to her being 'detached', and took no further part. A later ULTRA signal referred to her apparently not being in company with Kummetz, but her grounding was not definitely known from the Enigma until 8 July.

Soon ULTRA gave news of the other German Squadron, in a signal to Tovey at 1017: '1. Following signals were made in *Offizier* – At 2303/2 From Gruppe Nord to C-in-C Fleet Admiral Commanding Battleships. At 0326/3 From Admiral Commanding Cruisers to Admiral Commanding Northern Waters, C-in-C Fleet and *Gruppe Nord*. Comment: This indicates TIRPITZ was at sea at 2303/2 possibly operation CONCERT'. *Tirpitz, Admiral Hipper,* and four destroyers had sailed from Trondheim at 2000 on the 2nd. Three of the destroyers ran aground, but the two big ships and the surviving destroyer anchored at Gimsoy, near Narvik, in the forenoon of the 3rd. They stayed there only four hours before sailing again, this time for Altenfjord, where they had joined *Admiral Scheer* and her destroyers by 1030 on 4 July. The German heavy units were now assembled and ready to strike. All that was needed now was Hitler's permission.

Meanwhile, throughout 3 July, Tovey was being kept up to date by ULTRA: at 1408, that German aircraft had maintained contact from 0210–0430 on 3 July with a naval formation in a position given (which corresponded to Tovey's own at the time). At 1422 the Germans had also estimated PQ17's position at midnight on the 3rd with fair accuracy; U-boats were ordered to search eastward along latitude 74 North, which suggested they had lost contact (although they soon regained it). An ULTRA of 1754 informed Tovey that the Luftwaffe had reported two cruisers (actually two of Hamilton's) at 0715 on 3 July north-west of Bear Island.

Hamilton had actually closed to within 30 miles of the convoy, which had altered to the northwards, by 2215 on 3 July. At that time Tovey's ships were steering for an area 150–200 miles to the west of Bear Island, from where *Victorious'* aircraft could reach the convoy on the 4th.

The comment appended to the ULTRA signal of 1754/3rd was: 'It appears certain SCHEER has moved northwards from Narvik, probably accompanied by destroyers. Movement of LUTZOW is uncertain but she was independent of SCHEER. TIRPITZ and HIPPER may have left Trondheim area since 0001/3rd.' Later that evening of 3 July Tovey received confirmation from reconnaissance reports that *Tirpitz* and *Hipper* had left Trondheim.

At 2.40 a.m. on 4 July Tovey was warned by ULTRA that since the previous afternoon there had been an unusual sequence of enemy signals encoded in a cypher with special settings. These, Tovey was told, might relate to a special operation by German main units, and messages to the main units might not be read. On the evening of 4 July an ominous ULTRA signal of 1918 hinted that the worst was about to happen: 'C-in-C Fleet in TIRPITZ arrived Altenfjord 0900/4th July. Destroyers and torpedo boats ordered to complete with fuel at once. ADMIRAL SCHEER was already present at Altenfjord'. The obvious inference was that, as soon as their escorts had refuelled, *Tirpitz*, *Admiral Scheer*, *Admiral Hipper*, and possibly even *Lutzow*, would set out to look for PQ17.

This very inference was being drawn at about that same time by Pound in London. He had just received an Enigma intercept, timed 0740 on that morning 4 July. Considering the effect it was to have, it was not a particularly dramatically worded signal: 'FROM C in C FLEET [Admiral Schniewind] TO: ADMIRAL COMMANDING CRUISERS [Kummetz] IMMEDIATE. ARRIVING ALTA 0900. YOU ARE TO ALLOT ANCHORAGES TIRPITZ OUTER VAGFJORD (AS RECEIVED). NEWLY ARRIVING DESTROYERS AND TORPEDO BOATS TO COMPLETE WITH FUEL AT ONCE'.

To Pound the implications of the signal were obvious. Even as he stood there, holding that piece of paper in his hand, a 50,000 ton battleship, at least one and possibly two pocket battleships, and an 8" gun cruiser were closing PQ17 at 28 knots and could now be only a matter of hours away. The danger of overwhelming attack by surface ships blotted out every other consideration. With Pound's personality and the knowledge he already had from ULTRA, the stage was now set for a very great tragedy.

7 | Disaster and Triumph in the Arctic – From PQ17 to the North Cape

Somebody once said of Dudley Pound, 'He is the most even-tempered of men – he is always angry.' Certainly Pound was a difficult man to serve. He was, too often, brutally rude to his subordinates. He would administer lengthy reproofs out of all proportion to the gravity of an offence and deliver tirades of sarcastic admonishment for comparatively minor omissions. In mitigation, he was himself under constant and almost crushing mental and physical pressure. He drove himself relentlessly, working eighteen hours a day for months on end, with only the occasional few hours fishing to relieve his tensions. He acted as the Navy's buffer and mediator against the overwhelming will-power and sledge-hammer personality of Winston Churchill. He performed this service for the Navy through four years of war, and it eventually helped to break his health.

On that evening of 4 July Pound knew that PQ17 still had thirty ships but they were already east of the meridian of 27° 00′ E and beyond the point where Tovey could give them any protection. The convoy was already threatened by U-boats and aircraft. If it was allowed to continue on its way to Murmansk, it would still be menaced by U-boats and aircraft, but also, very probably, by as many as four heavy ships from Alta. Those ships could reach PQ17, which by then would only have the protection of its close anti-submarine escort, in some ten hours' steaming. Pound was evidently convinced that the convoy stood in greater danger from the surface ships than from U-boats and the Luftwaffe. To minimize what he considered the greater risk, he decided to order the convoy to scatter.

This drastic and irrevocable tactic had been successful earlier in the war: on the afternoon of 5 November, 1940, in the North Atlantic, convoy HX84 was threatened by the pocket battleship *Admiral Scheer* and ordered to scatter by the escort commander, the captain of the armed merchant cruiser HMS *Jervis Bay* who, outranged and out-gunned, nevertheless went on to attack *Admiral Scheer* single-handed and win a posthumous VC. But such a decision is best left, as in HX84's case, to the commander on the spot. To give the order from a distance is to invite disaster.

Nor was Pound's decision a sudden one. He appears to have made up his mind some time beforehand that if certain events happened he would order the convoy to scatter. He had even discussed the possibility with Tovey who was horrified and prophesied a bloody outcome if it were ever done. Pound had been very impressed by a signal of 18 June from Captain Henry Denham, the British Naval Attaché in Sweden, who had invaluable contacts and excellent sources of intelligence. Denham had correctly informed the Admiralty of *Bismarck*'s break-out a year earlier, so his appreciation of a situation was to be respected. When events seemed to be following the pattern forecast so accurately in Denham's signal – a convoy at sea, sighted from the air, German heavy ships moving up to northern Norway – all this, with the addition of the Enigma intercepts, made it seem to Pound certain that the final piece of the pattern – an attack on the convoy by those heavy ships – must be imminent.

Meanwhile PQ17, convoy and escort, had justifiable cause to be pleased with themselves. When the fog lifted, it was seen that the convoy had carried out an exemplary piece of station-keeping: all the ships were in their right columns and the columns were the proper distance apart, all in good order and perfect harmony.

At about 3 a.m. a Heinkel 'dropped through a hole in the low cloud' and torpedoed the American freighter *Christopher Newport*. But the rest of the American ships in the convoy marked Independence Day by hoisting newer and larger Stars and Stripes. The convoy was generally in good spirits. 'In the event of an attack,' one of the submarines had signalled Commander Broome, the close escort com-mander, 'intend to remain on the surface'. 'So do I,' replied Broome. Away on the northern flank Hamilton signalled his congratulations on the 4th of July to *Wichita*, who replied 'Independence Day always requires large fireworks. I trust you will not disappoint us'.

Wichita was not to be disappointed. Two major air attacks developed during the day. The first somewhat indecisive attack was beaten off by the combined anti-aircraft fire of convoy and escort. The second, much more aggressively conducted, was largely blunted by some excellent shooting from the US destroyer *Wainwright* who had just joined the convoy to refuel from a tanker. Three ships were hit by torpedoes. Two were lost but the third, the Russian tanker *Azerbaijan*, was, in Broome's words, 'holed but happy'. In the midst of the hubbub, Broome flashed to *Wainwright*: 'Was original 4th July as noisy as this?' 'I wasn't there,' was the reply, 'but I guess negative.' It seemed that, provided the ammunition lasted out, PQ17 could look after itself, although the U-boats, whose homing signals could now be detected by every D/F received in the convoy and on almost every bearing, had yet to take part.

Hamilton's cruisers were still in company for most of 4 July. At 1230 the Admiralty had given Hamilton discretion to continue east of longitude 25° 00 E, as long as Tovey had not given him contrary orders. That afternoon Tovey had signalled Hamilton, referring to the Admiralty signal of 1230, telling Hamilton, 'Once the convoy is to the eastward of 025 degrees East or earlier at your discretion you are to leave the Barents Sea unless assured by Admiralty that TIRPITZ cannot be met'. Hamilton replied: 'Intend withdrawing to westward about 2200/4 on completion of destroyer oiling.' But now the Admiralty signalled Hamilton, repeating to Tovey: 'Further information may be available shortly. Remain with convoy pending further instructions.'

The 'further information' was of course the intercept revealing that *Tirpiz* was about to enter Alta. Until now discretion to take decisions as necessary had been left to the men on the spot. But now Pound had made up his mind and intervened from afar. At 2111 on 4 July he signalled Hamilton, repeating to Tovey: 'Cruiser force withdraw to westward at high speed.' Twelve minutes later he signalled to Broome, repeating to Hamilton and Tovey: 'Owing to threat from surface ships convoy is to disperse and proceed to Russian ports.' And finally, thirteen minutes later, to the same addressees: 'My 2123/4th. Convoy is to scatter.'

It was not just what the signals actually said, although that was quite disturbing enough, it was the way they arrived in such quick succession which created a crescendo of alarm. 'This one was lethal,' Broome said of the final signal; 'it exploded in my hand.' Both Hamilton and Broome naturally thought that *Tirpitz* must be about to fall upon the convoy. Everybody searched the horizon, fully expecting to see the fighting top of a capital ship and the ominous flashes of her broadsides.

To his 'dying regret', as he called it, Broome obeyed the signal. Destroyer escort and cruiser covering force withdrew to the west, expecting to encounter *Tirpitz* herself at any moment. But, as time passed, apprehension turned to uncertainty and then to foreboding, until the first pitiable cries for help came out of the ether, from merchantmen being attacked by aircraft and U-boats. PQ17 lost another twenty ships, ten to bombing and ten sunk by U-boats. Stalin, with the ignorant impertinence of the landsman, asked if the Royal Navy had any sense of glory.

Not everybody at the OIC agreed with Pound that *Tirpitz* had sailed. In particular, Commander Norman Denning, the Intelligence Officer with special responsibility for appreciations about the German surface fleet, had wanted to add to the ULTRA signal sent to Tovey at 1918 on 4 July (that *Tirpitz* had arrived at Alta fjord at 0900 that morning and her destroyers and torpedo-boats had been ordered to refuel) the comment that the evidence was that *Tirpitz* was still in Altenfjord, but this was deleted after some discussion. Pound asked Denning why he thought *Tirpitz* had not sailed.

There was, of course, no direct positive proof. But there was a good deal of negative evidence. Denning was convinced that, after what the Germans thought was *Tirpitz'* lucky escape against PQ12, they would not risk her until they could be sure she was in no danger from the Home Fleet's battleships and aircraft carriers. The sighting reports available to the Germans had no such reassurance: if anything, the opposite – the Enigma had revealed that early that day a German aircraft had sighted Hamilton's cruisers and reported that his force included a battleship. A later report from a U-boat showed that it had also sighted Hamilton's ships and reported them as 'heavy enemy forces', and this U-boat had been ordered to shadow 'the battleship formation'. But a later decrypt showed that a German aircraft had correctly reported Hamilton's force as consisting of four heavy cruisers with destroyer escort.

Furthermore, the U-boats had not been ordered to keep clear of the convoy, to leave the way clear for *Tirpitz*, and their transmissions suggested they were still in contact with it; there was none of the W/T activity normal when German heavy units were at sea; and there had been no sightings by British or Russian submarines. Pound was not satisfied and asked if Denning could assure him that *Tirpitz* was still in Altenfjord – an assurance which Denning could not give.

The Naval Section at Bletchley Park agreed with Denning's appreciation. There had been no *Offizier* signals nor indecypherable transmissions since *Tirpitz'* arrival. The weight of negative evidence suggested that *Tirpitz* was still in harbour. But the Deputy Director of OIC was not able to convince Pound. He returned later to try again to persuade Pound that not only had *Tirpitz* not sailed but she would not do so until the Germans had accurately located the British heavy ships. But Pound had already made up his mind that *Tirpitz* and the other heavy ships could reach PQ17 by 0200 on 5 July and the convoy should be scattered. Exhibiting the classical psychological behaviour pattern of a man who does not wish to be diverted from his pre-chosen path, Pound ordered PQ17 to scatter.

The first ULTRA signal to Tovey of 5 July, timed at 0238, informed him: '1. It is not repeat not known if German heavy forces have sailed from Altenfjord, but they are unlikely to have done so before 1200B/4th. 2. It appears that Germans may be in some confusion whether a battleship is in company with CS1. Germans do not repeat not appear to be aware of position of C-in-C Home Fleet.'

In fact the enemy now had a much better picture of the Home Fleet's whereabouts. At 0700 on 5 July a German aircraft sighted and reported the Home Fleet some 500 miles away from the convoy (which had already been scattered). This confirmed the accurate aircraft report of Hamilton's force of the previous afternoon, that there were no British heavy units anywhere near the convoy. Raeder was, at last, able to obtain Hitler's permission.

Tirpitz, Scheer, Hipper, seven destroyers and two torpedo-boats – the largest and most powerful force the German Navy had sent to sea since the Channel Dash – began to sail from Altenfjord between 1100 and 1130 on 5 July, intending to attack PQ17 on the morning of 6 July. An Enigma decrypt had revealed *Tirpitz* signalling her intentions, and an ULTRA of 1517 that afternoon told Tovey: 'At 1145/5th TIRPITZ stated that she would be ready in Rolvoysund [the western exit from Altenfjord] at 1430'. The German ships were sighted on their way at 1700 on the 5th by the Russian submarine *K.21*, by an aircraft at 1816, and at 2029, when they were steering east off North Cape, 300 miles from where PQ17 had scattered, by the submarine HMS/M *P.54.*

But the German heavy ships were recalled late in the evening of 5 July, much to the disgust of their officers and ship's companies. The German High Command, always nervous about the safety of the big ships, and, as in this venture, for ever encompassing their admirals about with cautions and restrictions and admonitions to take no risks, decided that, because of the success the U-boats and the Luftwaffe were already enjoying against the scattered remnants of PQ17, Operation KNIGHT'S MOVE was not worth the risk to the big ships.

The Enigma for the period from noon on 5 July to noon on 6 July was not broken until the morning of the 6th, so it was not until an ULTRA of 1317 on 6 July that Tovey received the news: 'At 2219/5th *Gruppe Nord* directed that operation KNIGHT'S MOVE was to be broken off.' The same ULTRA revealed instructions to U-boats to search for the convoy which was widely scattered as far as 70 degrees north, to the minesweepers and anti-submarine patrols in the Altenfjord area, and orders to the tanker *Dithmarschen*, believed to be at Altenfjord, to be at one hour's notice from 1200 on 6 July.

The obvious implications were in the Comment appended to the signal: 'This is assumed to mean that attack on the convoy by surface forces is abandoned and that TIRPITZ and ships in company are returning to Altenfjord'. The German ships were, in fact, sighted by a PR Spitfire at Altenfjord at 1045 on 7 July and they reached Narvik at 0200 on 8 July. *Tirpitz* had never been nearer than 300 miles to PQ17, but the threat of her presence had been enough to win a major victory.

Ironically, in the case of PQ17, the Enigma had for once given Pound a little too much information too early. Merely keeping together would not have ensured the convoy's safety. PQ17 might well have had to scatter at some time late on 5 or early on 6 July. But in the meantime, whatever the threat, real or imagined, PQ17 should have been allowed to preserve its formation and identity as a convoy until the last possible moment, and the final decision to scatter should have been left to Broome or Hamilton. All the lessons of naval history since the Middle Ages have showed again and again that the safest way of passing merchant ships across the seas is by convoy and escort, and the entity of ships in convoy should only be broken as a very last resort.

After PQ17, no more convoys were sailed until PQ18, of forty ships, sailed from Loch Ewe on 2 September, 1942. The strong escort included the aircraft carrier HMS *Avenger*, a fighting escort of sixteen destroyers commanded by Rear Admiral Burnett flying his flag in the anti-aircraft cruiser HMS *Scylla*, two anti-aircraft ships, four corvettes, three minesweepers, four trawlers and two submarines.

It was not to be expected that PQ18 could escape detection. In fact the close escort was sighted by Focke Wulf Fw.200s on 6 September, the convoy itself on the 8th. But by then the Admiralty had already circulated their estimate, obtained from the Enigma, of the locations of the twenty U-boats expected to be in position to attack, and an estimate of German strength in bombers and torpedo-bombers.

On 9 September, as a result of the aircraft sightings, the Germans redisposed their U-boats, but these new arrangements were signalled to ULTRA recipients the next day. On the night of 10 September it was learned from the Enigma that 'two enemy battleships [*Scheer* and *Hipper*], one cruiser [*Koln*], five destroyers and three escorts' had sailed from Narvik steering north. Earlier that day, at 1420, this force had reported being attacked by four torpedoes (actually fired by the submarine HMS/M *Tigris*) which exploded some 3,000 metres astern. *Tigris* and other submarines had been placed in their positions on patrol

71

as the result of a large amount of information gained from the Enigma during the previous weeks on the precise routes steered by the German heavy ships in their sortie against PQ17. The German plans to repeat that sortie against further convoys had also been promulgated to ULTRA recipients.

The German ships arrived in Altenfjord early on 11 September, whence it was intended they were to sail against PQ18. Their presence at Altenfjord was revealed by the Enigma and promulgated by ULTRA signal later that morning of the 11th, and confirmed by PR flights on 14, 15 and 16 September. Intelligence also hinted that *Tirpitz* was suffering from engine defects and would not take part unless her presence was essential. In the event, largely as a result of typically cautionary orders from Hitler, the German ships did not sail against either PQ18 or the homeward convoy QP14 and both operations were cancelled.

In spite of so much information from ULTRA, PQ18 came under heavy air attack and eventually lost ten ships to aircraft and another three to U-boats, although the escorts' anti-aircraft fire and *Avenger's* aircraft inflicted what the Germans themselves called 'painful losses' on the Luftwaffe, and sank *U–589*. But if the Germans had also used their heavy ships, which were conveniently placed at Altenfjord, PQ18 might well have suffered a disaster equivalent to PQ17.

After PQ18 Arctic convoys were again suspended for a time. Experiments, largely unsuccessful, were made in sailing ships individually. Of thirteen ships sailed by the middle of November, 1942, only five arrived in Russia; four were sunk, three turned back and one was wrecked. Meanwhile, the Enigma continued to reveal U-boat patrol positions, general movements, and their strength in the Arctic, which had risen to twenty-five by mid-November. Supported by the Naval Attaché in Stockholm's sources, the Enigma also continued to reveal the movements of the major German warships, although not precisely or early enough for any attempt to intercept them. By the end of October *Tirpitz*, reported to be in need of refit, had gone down to Trondheim and *Scheer* had withdrawn to the Baltic, leaving only *Hipper* and the light cruiser *Koln* in the far north.

Through the Enigma it was learned that Luftwaffe strength in the north, especially in torpedo bombers, had been much reduced. QP15 with twenty-eight ships, destroyer and cruiser cover, therefore sailed from Archangel on 17 November. The Enigma also warned that the Germans were aware of QP15's sailing and that *Hipper* and *Koln* were being prepared to attack. Four submarines were stationed off Altenfjord to intercept the two ships. Thus, had the German ships actually sailed, the Enigma might well have been the saviour of this convoy. However, by 20 November (as the Enigma also showed) the operation had been cancelled because of bad weather. QP15's ships arrived at Loch Ewe between 30 November and 3 December, after being scattered by gales and losing two ships to U-boats.

From the beginning of November, 1942, onwards, the Enigma began to give an ominous picture of the build-up of German naval strength. The cruiser *Nurnberg* arrived at Trondheim on the 17th, after an abortive attempt by the RAF to attack her on passage from Bergen on the 15th, and reached northern Norway on 5 December. By then it had been deduced from references to them in the Enigma that *Lutzow* and *Prinz Eugen* might leave the Baltic early in December and could possibly be followed by *Scharnhorst*. All three had been taking part in exercise attacks on convoys. From the Enigma and photo-reconnaissance, it seemed possible that *Tirpitz, Hipper, Lutzow, Prinz Eugen, Scheer* and four 6″ gun cruisers, possibly also *Scharnhorst*, might all be operational by mid-December.

If all these ships had indeed gone north, they would have formed the most powerful surface fleet the German Navy had ever had and perhaps the strongest in the world at that time. However, *Tirpitz* remained under repair at Trondheim, *Scheer* was refitting in Germany, *Prinz Eugen* stayed in the Baltic and *Scharnhorst*'s hour was yet to come. But *Lutzow* did sail and joined *Hipper* and *Koln* at Narvik, where the Enigma reported she had arrived on 12 December.

The Germans certainly planned to send *Lutzow* into the Atlantic, but only after she had attacked the next Arctic convoy. But this intention was not revealed by the Enigma, and Admiral Tovey, the C-in-C Home Fleet, took the precautions of reestablishing the cruiser patrol in the Denmark Strait and of sending the battleship *Anson* up to Hvalfjord in Iceland.

Convoy JW51A of sixteen ships, sailed from Loch Ewe on 15 December and arrived at Kola on Christmas Day, unsighted and unscathed (although five of the ships were subsequently lost to aircraft or mines after arrival). The second half, JW51B, of fourteen ships, sailed on 22 December, escorted by three *Hunt* Class destroyers, three corvettes, two trawlers and a minesweeper. The convoy was joined on Christmas Day by the 17th Destroyer Flotilla, under Captain R. St. V. Sherbrooke, in *Onslow*, with *Obedient, Obdurate, Orwell* and *Achates*. The three *Hunts* and one corvette departed, leaving Sherbrooke's destroyers to take the convoy onwards to Russia. Also at sea was Force R under Rear Admiral R. L. Burnett with the cruisers *Sheffield* and *Jamaica* which had escorted JW51A through to Kola and now returned to cover JW51B. In the deep field were the battleship *Anson*, wearing the flag of Admiral Fraser, Flag Officer Second-in-

Command of the Home Fleet, the cruiser *Cumberland* and three destroyers.

The convoy was blown south of its track by gales and was sighted and reported by *U–354* south of Bear Island at about midday on 30 December. The Enigma had already revealed the arrival of *Lutzow* and *Hipper* at Altenfjord on 19 December. Burnett, an ULTRA recipient, was informed of this and warned that the German ships could be expected to sail. He was also informed by ULTRA that two U-boats were in the area and two more were in the neighbourhood of the ice-edge. ULTRA signals on the 28th and 29th gave Burnett details of the position of the ice-edge, as reported by the U-boats, and the news that the Germans knew of his departure from Kola and were expecting shipping through the Bear Island channel. Burnett was told in a further ULTRA, on 30 December, that up to 0045 that day the indications were that the German Admiral Commanding Cruisers (Kummetz) was still at Altenfjord,

In fact, *Hipper* (wearing Kummetz' flag), *Lutzow* and six destroyers had sailed on the 30th, after receiving *U–354*'s report. But this most important information of all was not conveyed to Burnett because, unluckily, no Enigma was decrypted on 31 December. And so, at 0830 that day, when JW51B was by then under the imminent threat of attack, Burnett still did not know of *U–354*'s sighting nor that the German squadron had sailed.

The Battle of the Barents Sea, as it was called, was a confused action, divided into several separate engagements and lasting several hours, in which both sides were hampered by poor visibility and uncertainty about the identity of radar contacts.

At 8.30 on the 31st the main convoy of twelve ships was steering east, with eight escorts. The trawler *Vizalma*, with one merchantman, was about 45 miles to the north. The minesweeper *Bramble* was some 15 miles to the north-east. *Sheffield* and *Jamaica* were 30 miles north of the convoy. Also, at that time, *Hipper* and three destroyers were 20 miles astern of the convoy and just crossing its wake, while *Lutzow* and her destroyers were some 50 miles to the south of the convoy, and closing.

At about 8.20 the corvette *Hyderabad* in the close escort sighted two strange destroyers but thought they were the expected Russian destroyer reinforcements and made no report. Ten minutes later *Obdurate* also sighted the same ships and closed them. At 9.30 the strangers (actually the three destroyers escorting *Hipper*) identified themselves by firing on *Obdurate*. Sherbrooke saw the gunflashes and turned towards, telling the other three destroyers to join him.

Sherbrooke had prepared a plan in the event of attack by surface ships. His five destroyers would concentrate on the threatened side, while the convoy turned stern-on and retired, under cover of smoke and the close escort. Meanwhile Sherbrooke's destroyers would dart out towards the enemy, threatening torpedo attack.

The plan worked. Four times *Hipper* attacked the convoy and each time the destroyers drove her off, while *Achates* laid a smoke screen in front of the convoy. Just after 10.30 *Hipper* came across the unfortunate minesweeper *Bramble*, who had been detached to search for a straggler, and sank her. But *Hipper* had no other success until the fourth attack on the convoy, when her hitherto erratic gunnery suddenly improved and she hit *Onslow* with an 8" shell, which badly damaged her and wounded Sherbrooke.

Sherbrooke continued to direct the flotilla for another half an hour, until turning over command to the captain of *Obedient*, who led the remaining four destroyers out for another attack in which *Achates* was hit and her captain killed. *Achates* afterwards sank, but meanwhile *Hipper*, fearing torpedoes, turned away for the last time and suffered a most unpleasant surprise when she herself came under fire from *Sheffield* and *Jamaica*, closing from the north.

Kummetz had also had a plan. He had split his force into two so that Hipper and her destroyers could attack from the north and drive the convoy towards *Lutzow* approaching from the south. This plan also worked perfectly. *Lutzow* encountered the convoy at a range of only two miles and at a time when the escorts were engaged in beating off *Hipper*. *Lutzow* had in fact been sighted earlier with her destroyers by *Hyderabad* who, however, maintained the same Trappist silence and made no report. But *Lutzow*'s Captain hesitated, fumbled his approach, was disconcerted by a snow-storm, waited for the weather to clear, then made no attack, and so let slip the sort of golden chance which comes to a naval officer once in a lifetime. Pursued by *Sheffield* and *Jamaica*, the damaged *Hipper* retired at reduced speed to the west, without attacking any of the merchantmen.

The convoy therefore lost only *Achates* and *Bramble* from the escort. On the enemy side, *Hipper* had been hit three times by Burnett's ships and was only saved from more serious damage by a snowstorm which hid her at a critical time. Whilst retiring, the German destroyer *Friedrich Eckholdt* suddenly appeared from a snow squall within 4,000 yards of *Sheffield* (having possibly mistaken her for *Hipper*) and was quickly sunk.

The Enigma for 31 December was broken at about midnight and ULTRA signals early on 1 January, 1943, confirmed that the German force had included *Lutzow*, *Hipper* and six destroyers and that one destroyer had been sunk. Early in January the Enigma revealed that

Lutzow was undamaged, but signals concerning *Hipper* were in the 'officer only' key. Not until 24 January was it confirmed *Hipper* had been hit and her No. 3 boiler room flooded.

Kummetz' failure was a catastrophe for the German Navy. A furious Hitler, who had been promised a great success against a convoy to Russia, ordered the big ships to be scrapped. Admiral Raeder resigned and was replaced by Dönitz. By contrast, on the British side, Captain Sherbrooke won the Victoria Cross, while Burnett, the captains of *Sheffield* and *Jamaica*, the captains of the other destroyers and the senior surviving officer of *Achates*, were awarded DSOs or Bars to their DSOs, with forty-six other awards and fifty-four Mentions in Despatches.

Dönitz, who had a better way with Hitler than his predecessor, managed to persuade the Führer at least to reprieve what Dönitz claimed were the more effective of the big ships. He promised a sceptical Hitler success before too long.

The full effect of the Barents Sea débâcle upon the German Navy's reputation was not known to OIC for a long time, but throughout 1943, as in 1942, the Enigma continued to yield information of the movements of the German heavy ships and the OIC now had a great deal of experience in interpreting the tell-tale signs and hints the Enigma decrypts provided that something was afoot: increased numbers of Luftwaffe reconnaissance flights, movements of fighter squadrons from Germany to Norway, sailing signals and route orders of escorts and minesweepers, the transfer of operational control over ships from one flag or regional authority to another, unusual instructions to U-boats to report on British air and sea patrols and radar surveillance, or an increase in traffic in the 'Officer only' key.

Lutzow's Atlantic venture was cancelled. *Hipper* and *Koln* returned to the Baltic in February, 1943. After one false start with *Prinz Eugen* in January, *Scharnhorst* arrived in the north, without *Prinz Eugen*, in March. As two more Arctic convoys sailed, JW52 in January, JW53 in February, with return convoys RA52 and 53 from Kola Inlet, the OIC expected a more belligerent reaction from Dönitz, if only to safeguard his own reputation with Hitler. Late in March, *Tirpitz*, *Scharnhorst* and *Lutzow* all moved up from Narvik to Altenfjord. The Enigma revealed that the enemy believed a convoy had sailed for Russia and was flying reconnaissance patrols to search for it. The Arctic convoys were suspended again, after RA53 had arrived on 14 March.

Dönitz, who had been such a brilliant commander of the U-boat arm, was to prove only a mediocre Commander-in-Chief. In May there was a brief flurry of alarm when the Enigma revealed that all the ships in Altenfjord – *Tirpitz*, *Scharnhorst*, *Lutzow*, the 5th and 6th Destroyer Flotillas, and the 5th Torpedo Boat Flotilla – had come to three hours' notice for steam after a report of another convoy. But two weeks later the Enigma showed that in fact the enemy squadron would only sail on firm evidence from air reconnaissance. In June it seemed that the enemy ships might be about to break out into the Atlantic. But, once again, nothing happened.

On 6 September, 1943, *Tirpitz*, *Scharnhorst* and ten destroyers sailed from Altenfjord to carry out a bombardment of the shore installations occupied by an Allied meteorological party on the island of Spitzbergen. The Enigma had given details of greatly increased Luftwaffe reconnaissance flights in the area beforehand but PR evidence from Russia that the German ships had sailed on 7 September did not reach the Admiralty until the next day. Thus the German sortie caught the Home Fleet by surprise. Admiral Fraser sailed from Scapa Flow at 1930 on the 8th, with *Duke of York*, *Anson* and five destroyers, but turned back when he realized he was too late. In fact, Operation ZITRONELLA, as it was called, was not much more than a propaganda exercise. It proved to be the only occasion on which *Tirpitz* ever fired her main armament in anger, and then only against an inoffensive shore target.

Later that month *Tirpitz*, *Scharnhorst* and *Lutzow* were themselves the targets of a supremely daring sortie by five 'X' Class midget submarines. The Enigma, with PR and visual reports of sightings by a Secret Service agent at Altenfjord, gave up-to-date information of the German ships' movements and berthing arrangements until the time the X-craft, and the orthodox submarines which towed them to the target area, left to carry out the operation (codenamed SOURCE). Further information from the Enigma after the force had left showed that *Scharnhorst* would be away from her anchorage, carrying out gunnery trials, on 22 September, the day of the attack. But, for fear of compromising the source, it was not possible to transmit this information to the submarines on passage and *X.10*, the X-craft allocated to attack *Scharnhorst*, therefore made a fruitless entry into the fjords. *X.8*, allocated to attack *Lutzow*, was lost on passage.

But *Tirpitz*, the main target, was badly damaged by charges placed underneath her or very close to her by *X.6* and *X.7* (whose captains were both awarded the Victoria Cross). The Enigma did not reveal the exact extent of the damage but clearly it was severe and later Enigma decrypts in the following months showed that *Tirpitz*'s ship's company were being sent on leave and repairs would not be completed until March, 1944.

Keeping track of the movements of German heavy ships, even with the aid of Enigma, was made more difficult because the German dispositions often seemed to defy logic. With *Tirpitz* temporarily but seriously disabled, and with winter drawing on, when Allied Arctic convoys would probably be resumed, the Germans might have been expected to keep as many heavy ships in the north as possible. But, in the days before, during and after the X-craft attacks on *Tirpitz*, the Enigma began to reveal some of the customary signs – increased Luftwaffe reconnaissance, transfer of fighters to Norway, requests for markboats and radio beacons – which usually accompanied the passage of a major unit.

It could have been *Tirpitz* going back for repairs. In fact it was *Lutzow*, who was undamaged and, though some time out of refit, might have been retained, with *Scharnhorst*, for another sortie against the convoys. *Lutzow* left Altenfjord on 23 September, reached Narvik on the 24th, and sailed again on the 26th. An aircraft sighted her with five destroyers early on the 27th, off Kristiansand. A striking force of torpedo-bombers of 832 Squadron Fleet Air Arm (ironically, the same squadron which had failed in its attack on *Tirpitz* at sea in March, 1942), with Coastal Command Beaufighter escort, flew from Sumburgh in the Shetlands to look for *Lutzow* off the Norwegian coast. Unfortunately, when they reached the coastline they searched to the north when *Lutzow* was actually only some forty miles to the south.

Lutzow avoided aerial mines laid on her expected route and eventually reached Gdynia on 1 October. The Enigma and other intelligence had provided an excellent chance to intercept her. Her escape was therefore a great disappointment – and the subject of a subsequent enquiry. But for *Lutzow* herself ocean warfare was over. In 1944 she supported the seaward flank of the German army in the Baltic. She was finally wrecked and stranded by air attacks on Swinemunde in April, 1945.

Scharnhorst and the damaged *Tirpitz* were now the only German heavy ships left in the Arctic. Admiral Fraser, who was now C-in-C Home Fleet, took advantage of the new situation, and of some very accurate Enigma intelligence about enemy shipping movements along the Norwegian coast, to sail from Scapa Flow on 2 October with *Duke of York*, *Anson* and the US carrier *Ranger*. Their object was to carry out an air strike on the Norwegian port of Bodo. This would be the first time an Allied aircraft carrier had operated in this way so near the Norwegian coast since 1940.

The attack, codenamed Operation LEADER, was a copy-book use of ULTRA and a complete success. *Ranger* reached her flying-off position, about 140 miles off Bodo, before dawn on the 4th. The Enigma had revealed a promising collection of enemy shipping gathered in the harbour. One group of twenty of *Ranger*'s Dauntless dive-bombers and a second of ten Avenger torpedo-bombers flew with their fighter escorts very low up the fjord and caught the enemy completely by surprise. Five ships of 20,753 tons were sunk, including a loaded trooper transport. Another seven ships were damaged, among them a large tanker which was known (also through the Enigma) to be taking fuel up to Altenfjord. Three of *Ranger's* aircraft were lost to flak.

Scharnhorst – 'lucky Scharnhorst' as the German sailors called her – had escaped the attack by midget submarines. But she could not escape the constant attention of the OIC, especially as the Enigma began to reveal, from September, 1943, onwards, that she was exercising frequently, was to remain at Altenfjord for the winter and, by mid-October, was at full operational fitness and readiness for war. Her progress was carefully watched, for she was still a major threat on the flank of convoys to and from Russia which restarted with RA54A, leaving Archangel on 1 November, 1943, and JW54A, which sailed from Loch Ewe on 15 November and reached Kola unobserved on the 24th. Convoy JW54B, which sailed on 22 November, was also unobserved. So too was the next westbound convoy, RA54B, which left Archangel on 26 November, although the Luftwaffe searched for both of them.

Meanwhile, at Scapa Flow, Admiral Fraser spent some time every afternoon sitting in the armchair of his day cabin in *Duke of York*, thinking about *Scharnhorst* and planning how he would dispose of her. It seemed certain to him, as it was to the OIC, that *Scharnhorst* would attack a convoy to Russia sooner or later, and the danger would grow as the weeks passed. For JW55A Fraser took *Duke of York* through to Kola to give battleship cover the whole way. The convoy arrived safely, but Fraser suspected that, with every convoy that passed, the chance of a sortie by *Scharnhorst* increased. The Enigma reinforced his suspicions, revealing on 18 December that the enemy had anticipated that a convoy was at sea, had allocated patrol areas to U-boats, ordered air reconnaissance, and most ominously, had brought *Scharnhorst's* Battle Group in Altenfjord to three hours' notice for sea.

A stream of ULTRA signals continued to supply Fraser with information on U-boat traffic, positions of the attacking areas assigned to them, warnings of intended Luftwaffe reconnaissance and flights, reports of hydrophone contacts and a mass of detail on U-boats' fuel and torpedoes remaining, and weather conditions. This continuing supply of rapid and accurate intelligence enabled Fraser to handle his forces in an imaginative and confident manner which had a decisive effect upon events to come.

The Enigma showed that the Battle Group at Altenfjord reverted to six hours' notice on 21 December. But the respite was only temporary.

Unknown to Fraser or the Admiralty, Dönitz had at last obtained Hitler's permission for *Scharnhorst* to be used against the next convoy to be sighted, if the chances of success appeared reasonable.

Convoy JW55B, of nineteen ships, sailed from Loch Ewe on 20 December, and the westbound RA55A, left Kola on 23 December. Both had strong destroyer escorts, and RA55A had a further close escort in Force 1, of the cruisers *Belfast*, *Sheffield* and *Norfolk*, under Vice Admiral R. L. Burnett, which also sailed from Kola on 22 December.

JW55B was sighted by a German meteorological aircraft at 1045 on 22 December. Fraser, who was by then at Akureyri in Iceland, was informed of this sighting by ULTRA signal of 0146 on 23 December. JW55B's covering force, Force 2, of *Duke of York*, flying Fraser's flag, with the cruiser *Jamaica* and four destroyers, sailed from Akureyri at 10 p.m. on 23 December and carried out a 'night encounter with *Scharnhorst* exercise' on passage.

In the next twenty-four hours a succession of ULTRA signals told Fraser that the German Battle Group at Altenfjord had been brought once again to three hours' notice at 1300 on 22 December, that the enemy aircraft had reported forty transports in the convoy, that the Germans had at first suspected the convoy was a landing force heading for Norway, and that eight U-boats had been ordered to form a patrol line south-west of Bear Island. A further ULTRA signal, of 0550 on 24 December, informed Fraser that the enemy appreciated that the convoy was making for the Bear Island area and that it was covered by 'a strong battle group'. This signal also gave Luftwaffe intentions for 24 December and, finally, the news that, at 2324 the previous evening, 23 December, *Scharnhorst* had been informed that 'no German U-boat was in contact with convoy bound for North Russia'.

None of these later ULTRA signals bore directly upon *Scharnhorst*'s intentions, but the mention of *Scharnhorst* in the signal of 0550 was an indication that she might sail at last. An ULTRA signal of 1025 on 24 December revealed that, at 1342 on the 22nd, Admiral Northern Waters had requested Admiral Polar Coast to make preparations for the departure of the Battle Group. However, this ULTRA signal also included Admiralty comment that, up to 0700 on 24 December, there had been no signs that the Battle Group had left Altenfjord.

Nevertheless, on the morning of 24 December, Fraser decided that JW55B was dangerously exposed. Although German surface forces had never before made a sortie to the west, the convoy was entirely unsupported and Fraser was uneasy that a surface attack might be imminent. At noon on the 24th JW55B was only 400 miles from Altenfjord and the shadowers had caught up again. One aircraft reported the convoy's course and speed at 1220 on the 24th (a signal which was decrypted and repeated to Fraser in an ULTRA signal of 0210 the next day). Fraser also decided that radio silence was, in the circumstances, not as important as keeping the widely scattered elements of the scene in touch.

At 1201 Fraser therefore broke radio silence with a signal to the Admiralty, to Burnett, and the escort commanders of JW55B and RA55A, asking RA55A's escort commander to consider diverting his convoy to the north after passing Bear Island and the transfer of four of his destroyers to JW55B. Fraser also gave his own position, course and speed. He broke silence again at 1325, to JW55B's escort commander, ordering the convoy to reverse course until 1700. (Because of very bad weather and equally bad station-keeping by the convoy, this order could not actually be carried out: JW55B therefore complied with the spirit if not the letter of Fraser's signal, and decreased speed for a time.) At the same time Fraser increased Force 2's speed to 19 knots.

By the afternoon of 24 December the enemy knew JW55B's position and could estimate its future course and speed. They knew nothing of RA55A. They suspected, but had not confirmed, that heavy British ships were at sea. No U-boats were in touch with either of the convoys or the covering forces.

By midnight on 24 December the time taken to break the Enigma messages was only about twelve hours. For instance, an ULTRA of 0215 on 25 December gave the revised patrol areas for eight U-boats south-west of Bear Island – positions which they had only been ordered to take up at 1423 the previous afternoon. But the speed of decryption improved. One U-boat reported at 1901 on 25 December that the convoy (JW55B) had passed over it in the position given in the signal, steering 060 degrees. News of this U-boat report was passed to Fraser by ULTRA at 1350 – only $4\frac{1}{2}$ hours later. At 1045 the other seven U-boats were ordered to operate on the basis of this U-boat's sighting report. This, too, was passed on by ULTRA at 1557 – only five hours later.

On Christmas Day there were at last stirrings of activity in Altenfjord. At 1056 Scharnhorst and the 4th Destroyer Flotilla were ordered to be at one hour's notice for sea by 1300. At 1158 the minesweeper R.121 was ordered by an 'Emergency' message to proceed forthwith to Scharnhorst in Langfjord, and to receive further orders there. At 1516 the Battle Group reported 'readiness for sea at 1630'. At 1527 Admiral Northern Waters at Narvik signalled to the Battle Group 'Most Immediate, OSTFRONT [the codename for the Battle Group's sortie] 1700/25/12'. At 1715 the patrol vessel V.5903 was informed by Scharnhorst that she would pass outward bound at 1800. In fact Scharnhorst had cleared the inner boom of Langfjord by 1955 and was joined in the outer fjord by an escort of five Z-Class destroyers.

The Enigma key had changed at midday on 25 December and the first decrypts of the afternoon signals reached the OIC during the middle watch of the 26th. An ULTRA of the 'OSTFRONT' signal of 1527 (with the British codeword EPILEPSY substituted for OSTFRONT) was despatched at 0130. Then, making a deduction from the signal activity from Altenfjord, the Admiralty transmitted at 0217 on 26 December the dramatic 'Emergency' ULTRA signal '*Scharnhorst* probably sailed 1800A/25 December', addressed to a wide range of ULTRA recipients including, of course, Fraser and Burnett. As the base of the Secret Service agent at Altenfjord was opposite Kaafjord and a long way from Langfjord, where *Scharnhorst* was berthed, the agent did not report *Scharnhorst*'s departure and this ULTRA signal, early on 26 December, was therefore the only indication from any source that *Scharnhorst* had sailed. For the benefit of JW55B's escort, and others who were not ULTRA recipients, the Admiralty also broadcast another general message at 0339: 'Admiralty appreciates *Scharnhorst* at sea.'

An ULTRA signal of 0230 on 26 December told Fraser that 'Force 2 (his own) does not repeat not yet appear to have been sighted' and he knew that Forces 1 and 2 were now both steering courses which, barring something unforeseen, should intercept *Scharnhorst*. But he now decided that 'the safety of the convoy must be the primary object' and, to ensure that, accurate knowledge of everybody's whereabouts outweighed the importance of radio silence. At 0401 on 26 December he ordered Force 1 and the convoy to signal their positions, and gave his own. At 0628 he broke silence yet again, to order the convoy to alter to the north and Burnett to close the convoy in support.

On the morning of 26 December, as the adversaries closed each other, ULTRA provided more information: that the Battle Group had told the German Admiralty on leaving the fjords the previous night that anticipated weather conditions in the operational zone 'greatly impaired offensive action', and that an aircraft which had shadowed JW55B on 25 December had reported no support group within 50 miles.

There were to be other ULTRA signals that day, but ULTRA's main work was now accomplished. *Scharnhorst* was at sea. Fraser had been given all the latest intelligence. It now only remained for him, the man on the spot, to carry out the execution. By the time Fraser received two later ULTRA signals – that U-boats had been told that *Scharnhorst* and five destroyers had passed through the northern exit of Altenfjord at 2300 the night before, with the intention of attacking the convoy at 0900 on 26th, and that U-boats had been ordered to operate against the convoy themselves – Burnett's Force had already been in action.

The German intelligence had been only a shadow of the British. The B-Dienst service and the Luftwaffe had provided much valuable information which had been either ignored or edited in transmission so that crucial words were missing. The German staff's plotting and assessment of the changing situation had been weak. The much-maligned Luftwaffe had reported the convoy accurately several times. U-boats had been in contact and one at least had shadowed for some hours. Vital information was withheld from *Scharnhorst* which could have saved her.

Errors in staff work and weaknesses in intelligence were compounded by a combination of rough weather and poor seamanship, so that *Scharnhorst* lost contact with her destroyer screen and was therefore totally alone as well as utterly caught by surprise when, at 0926 on 26 December, starshell from the cruiser *Belfast* burst directly above her.

Belfast's radar had detected *Scharnhorst* closing from the east at 0840 at a range of 25,000 yards. *Sheffield* reported 'Enemy in sight, range 13,000 yards' at 0921. After a brief gun action in which *Norfolk* was the only British ship to fire but scored one and possibly two hits, *Scharnhorst* steered first to the south and then hauled right round to the north-east at over 30 knots.

Burnett could not follow at that speed, so gave up the chase. Rightly reasoning that the enemy would try again, Burnett steered north-west so as to keep his ships between the convoy and the enemy. Fraser had ordered four of JW55B's destroyers to join Burnett. By 1050 Burnett's cruisers, with their new destroyer screen, were perfectly placed, 10 miles ahead of the convoy.

Once again, it was *Sheffield* who, at 1221, reported 'Enemy in sight'. Another gun action followed, in which all three British cruisers took part and scored hits, but *Norfolk* was hit and damaged. *Scharnhorst*, who for the second time had been caught by surprise, turned away and fled to the south-east. Burnett followed, knowing that this course would lead their quarry directly towards Fraser in *Duke of York*. Soon *Norfolk* dropped out of the chase because of a fire, and *Sheffield* because of an engine defect. *Belfast* continued to trail at a distance, with the destroyers, making regular reports on *Scharnhorst*'s position, course and speed which were eagerly read and plotted all over the world.

Fraser's staff in *Duke of York* now calculated that the first radar contact of the enemy would be a minute either side of 1615. The first contact, range 45,500 yards, or nearly 23 miles, was at 1617. Force 2 closed their target steadily until, at 1647, for the third and the last time that day, *Scharnhorst* was caught utterly unawares, with turrets still trained fore and aft, by starshell from *Duke of York*, followed by broadsides from the flagship's 14″ guns at a range of 12,000 yards.

Once again *Scharnhorst* turned and fled to the east and, while returning fire with her main 11″ armament, appeared to be gaining on her pursuers and making good her escape. At 1840 a bitterly disappointed Fraser signalled to Burnett that he saw little hope of catching *Scharnhorst* and was proceeding to support the convoy. But almost at once the range steadied and then began to come down. A crucial shot from *Duke of York* had slowed *Scharnhorst* sufficiently to allow the destroyers to close and fire torpedoes. *Scharnhorst* finally sank at about 1945, after sustaining at least thirteen 14″ shell hits, possibly a dozen hits from the cruisers, and eleven torpedo hits. There were thirty-six survivors, from a ship's company of about 2,000.

Tirpitz was now alone in the Arctic.

8 | THE END OF TIRPITZ

While the Germans worked through the winter of 1943/44 to repair the damage done to *Tirpitz*, their progress was monitored by the SIS agent at Altenfjord, by PR Spitfires and by Enigma decrypts. By the end of the year the precise extent of the damage was still not clear but in the months following the attack *Tirpitz* requested additional electrical power, gunnery materials, special welding equipment and cranes. An Enigma of 2 January, 1944, gave 15 March as the completion date for hull, main engine and electrical repairs. On 27 January, 1944, OIC assessed *Tirpitz*'s prospects and concluded that hull, engineering and electrical repairs would be completed as expected by 15 March, but gunnery repairs would take longer and, until they were completed, *Tirpitz* would not be operationally fit for sea. Even when all these repairs had been completed, *Tirpitz* would still not be operationally effective for long periods at sea, as she had not docked for two and a half years.

In February and March, 1944, evidence accumulated that *Tirpitz* would very probably be ready for sea in mid-March. In February the SIS reported that continuous work was in progress on her. The SIS agent at Altenfjord reported on 3 March that she had fired her guns, on the 11th that she was ready to sail and on the 15th that she had sailed. By 14 March the SIS and a PR flight from Russia had confirmed that she was in her berth. But she had indeed sailed, because on 18 March the Enigma disclosed her report on her sea trials. There was a possibility, but no firm evidence, that she was likely to sail south.

The Arctic convoys began again in 1944 when JW57 sailed from Loch Ewe on 20 February. The size of the convoy (forty-two ships and a tanker) and its safe passage showed how the increasing strength of convoy escorts and the use of ULTRA were shifting the balance of power in the Arctic. JW57's escort included no less than seventeen destroyers, the cruiser *Black Prince*, the carrier *Chaser*, a covering force of three more cruisers, and shore-based aircraft of Coastal Command. The U-boats mounted what their headquarters called 'a grand slam' attack, using all fourteen available U-boats deployed in two patrol lines. But the positions of these lines were revealed by the Enigma and signalled by ULTRA on 14 and 22 February. Not only was the convoy able to divert to a safe route but the U-boats themselves came under attack. One U-boat was sunk by the destroyer *Keppel*, a second by a Catalina of 210 Squadron Coastal Command, and several others were harried and attacked by *Chaser's* Swordfish. Not one ship from the convoy was lost, but the destroyer *Mahratta* was torpedoed and sunk by a U-boat.

The westbound convoy RA57 which sailed on 2 March did even better. The Enigma showed where fifteen U-boats were deployed and the convoy made a wide detour to the east on leaving Kola to avoid them. The move was not wholly successful, the convoy being located by the U-boats two days later and one ship was torpedoed and sunk. But *Chaser's* Swordfish retaliated by sinking two U-boats, sharing a third with the destroyer *Onslaught* and damaging two others.

The enemy were very much discouraged by the losses they had incurred around these two convoys. Five U-boats had been sunk and several more damaged, for the loss of a single merchantman and a destroyer. The U-boats blamed the weather, which certainly had been bad, 'depth charge and hydrophone pursuits' by the escorts, and, above all, attacks by aircraft, especially carrier-borne aircraft which the enemy realized had caused them the most casualties. The enemy did not, however, suspect the Enigma. The U-boats were forced to change their tactics, to stay dived by day and attack by night. This in itself amounted to a tactical defeat for the U-boats, to which ULTRA had made a large contribution.

On 21 March, a few days before the next convoy, JW58, was due to sail, an ULTRA to Admiral Fraser summed up the *Tirpitz* situation: '*Tirpitz* is unlikely to proceed to sea for operations against a well-escorted convoy but might do so if sure she had no heavy ships or aircraft carriers to contend with. It is known that the enemy attach great importance to intercepting supplies to Russia and this may influence them to take more than normal risk with *Tirpitz* in her present condition. It should therefore be assumed that *Tirpitz* may be operationally effective and battleship cover for convoy JW58 should be given.' However, the same ULTRA signal informed Fraser that *Tirpitz* was sending a cruising turbine by air to Mannheim on 2 April, which suggested she would still be in Altenfjord at least until then.

JW58, which sailed on 27 March, was enormous, the largest Arctic convoy of the war, with forty-nine ships and the US cruiser *Milwaukee* (being transferred to the Russians) and a huge escort of twenty destroyers, five sloops of Captain F. J. ('Johnny') Walker's famous 2nd Escort Group from the Western Approaches, four corvettes, the light cruiser *Diadem* and two escort carriers, *Activity* and *Tracker*.

The Enigma on 20 March showed that the U-boats had been informed that another eastbound convoy was due which would be 'decisive for the war in the east'. U-boats were ordered to stay dived by day and to concentrate their attack on the first night. By 26 March the Enigma had revealed U-boat strength in the Arctic to be sixteen at sea and another thirteen in harbour. After the Luftwaffe sighted the convoy on 30 March, the U-boats were dispatched at top speed to form a patrol line east of Bear Island, to prepare to attack on the night 31 March–1 April. But these moves were also revealed by Enigma and in the battle that followed Walker's sloop *Starling* sank one U-boat, the destroyer *Beagle* and *Tracker*'s aircraft a second, *Keppel* a third (and her second of the year) and aircraft from both *Tracker* and *Activity* a fourth. Carrier aircraft also shot down six enemy shadowers. This was another tremendous convoy victory. One merchantman from JW58 was damaged by ice and had to return to Iceland. No other ship was lost or damaged. RA58 westbound scored yet another victory – one merchant ship lost, three U-boats sunk.

Admiral Fraser, in *Duke of York*, his second-in-command Vice Admiral Sir Henry Moore in *Anson*, with *Belfast*, the aircraft carrier *Victorious* and five destroyers, sailed from Scapa Flow on 30 March, 1944, to cover JW58 and also to carry out an attack by carrier aircraft on *Tirpitz* (Operation TUNGSTEN). Fraser's force (Force 1) was joined at sea by Force 2, of the cruiser *Royalist* wearing the flag of Rear Admiral Bisset (Rear Admiral Escort Carriers), with the aircraft carrier *Furious*, the escort carriers *Searcher*, *Emperor*, *Pursuer*, and *Fencer*, the cruisers *Sheffield* and *Jamaica*, five destroyers and two oilers.

The Fleet Air Arm had trained long and hard and carefully for TUNGSTEN. The latest information on anti-aircraft gun sites had been incorporated in a scale model of Kaafjord, where *Tirpitz* was lying. A special bombing range was built at Loch Eriboll, on the west coast of Scotland, where the local topography resembled Kaafjord. The attack was to be made in two strikes by Nos 8 and 52 Wings, each Wing providing twenty-one Fairey Barracuda torpedo bombers, armed with bombs, from *Victorious* and *Furious*. Each strike would be escorted by ten Corsairs from *Victorious*. Twenty Wildcats from *Searcher* and *Pursuer* and ten Hellcats from *Emperor* would provide flak-suppression. Meanwhile, Seafires from *Furious* and Wildcats from *Fencer* would fly CAPs (Combat Air Patrols) over the force.

When Admiral Fraser received reports of the success of JW58's escorts, he decided that he need no longer continue to cover the convoy and could concentrate instead upon TUNGSTEN. ULTRA, with more information about *Tirpitz*, reassured Fraser that JW58 no longer needed carrier protection from the danger of surface attack, and also gave him a chance to bring forward TUNGSTEN by twenty-four hours.

Such was the speed of decryption that, on 31 March, the Enigma revealed that *Tirpitz* had reported, earlier that same day, that she was at anchor in Altenfjord and was intending to return to her net enclosure in Kaafjord. Good weather was essential for the operation; the SIS agent had been told to send two-hourly reports from the area of *Tirpitz'* anchorage. His first, reporting fine weather, was not received until 1700 on 2 April and would not, by itself, have been early or decisive enough to influence Fraser. Much more important was an Enigma decrypt of 1 April revealing that *Tirpitz* had postponed the remainder of her programme of full power trials for two days (almost certainly because of the turbine sent to Mannheim) and would now very probably sail to complete the trials on 3 April. Fraser decided that this news gave his forces a better chance of finding *Tirpitz* in her berth. He ordered the time of the attack to be advanced to 0530 on 3 April.

Emperor, *Searcher* and *Pursuer* were then some distance away from the main force and had to steam at full speed for more than twenty-four hours to keep their rendezvous in the afternoon of 2 April with Admiral Moore, who was in charge of the strike force. An ULTRA of 0435 on 3 April disclosed that *Tirpitz* was to sail at 0530 that day. But this did not affect the timing of the strike. By the time the signal was received, the operation was already underway.

Flying off began exactly on time at 0415. The first wave of the strike, twenty-one Barracudas, with fighters for escort and flak-suppression, formed up and took departure at 0437 for the target, which was about 120 miles away. The second striking force, of another twenty-one Barracudas and forty fighters, followed at 0525.

The first strike took *Tirpitz* utterly by surprise, arriving without warning overhead within minutes of her sailing time. The Barracudas actually caught *Tirpitz* as she was in the very act of shortening in her anchor cable and was just about to put to sea. There was no fighter opposition, and, to begin with, no anti-aircraft fire. While the fighters strafed *Tirpitz*'s gun positions and upper deck and the flak sites ashore, the bombers closed to begin their dives and the first bombs were away at 0529.

Ten Barracudas carried a single 1,600 lb armour-piercing bomb, twenty-two carried three 500 lb semi-armour-piercing bombs, and ten

ALUMINIUM ON ACTIVE SERVICE

From a painting by NORMAN WILKINSON, O.B.E., R.I.

The Catch of the Season

A RIPPLING wake of water in the Gulf of Aden revealed a prying periscope to the alert watch on H.M. Trawler "Moonstone." Depth charges thundered below. Soon, and in apparent haste, one of the largest Italian submarines broke surface and at once engaged the Trawler with torpedoes, two 3-inch guns and smaller arms. The "Moonstone" replied with her solitary gun, scoring a number of direct hits. Calculated on her smaller fire-power, she stood little chance of survival. But it is in engagements against great odds that the Royal Navy is seen at its fighting best. The "Moonstone" lived up to this fine tradition and

had the further glory, heightened by comedy, of towing her adversary back to port after its prudent surrender. The catch of the season, indeed!

Exploits like these, and there have been many in this war, indicate the confidence we can place in our armed forces. On land, sea and in the air they grow stronger every day in equipment and machines of war in which aluminium alloys are used to maximum advantage. This versatile metal is providing high strength for heavy duty and lightness to reduce that great obstacle to

efficiency and economical operation—deadweight.

When hostilities cease aluminium will be available for an increasing range of applications. Our Research and Development Department is ready now with constructive proposals for every industry. Please write.

IMPORTANT NOTICE. *Owing to the shortage of paper supplies, it will not be possible to continue our offer of fine art prints. We greatly regret, therefore, that applications cannot be accepted for reproductions of the above illustration.*

NORTHERN ALUMINIUM COMPANY LTD.

Head Office : Banbury, Oxfordshire.   Telephone : Banbury 2244

Publicity triumph but possible security lapse: Story and pictures of *Moonstone's* capture of *Galileo Galilei* appeared at once in the British press, and in magazine advertisements, complete with painting by Norman Wilkinson, only weeks after the event.

The German commerce raider *Atlantis*, betrayed by ULTRA, and sunk by HMS *Devonshire*, 22 November, 1941. Seen (top) from *Devonshire's* Walrus aircraft, and (below) making smoke and trying to escape.

The secret capture: *Bulldog* taking *U110* in tow, 9 May, 1941.

Four-rotor 'Enigma' coding machine, used by the German Navy, of
the type captured from *U110* in May, 1941.
Grand Admiral Karl Donitz, *Befehlshaber der Uboote* (BdU), who
refused to accept that the German Enigma codes had been broken.

The German trawler/weather-reporting ship *Muenchen*, whose
capture north-east of Iceland on 7 May, 1941, provided priceless
Enigma cypher keys. (Picture from a German PoW).

A great chance lost, after ULTRA had revealed *Tirpitz'* passage
south. Tracks of torpedoes from *Victorious'* Albacores, missing
astern, seen from *Tirpitz*, 9 March, 1942.

The seemingly innocuous Enigma intercept which caused Admiral
Sir Dudley Pound to order convoy PQ17 to scatter, 4 July, 1942.

T O O   0740

FROM: C IN C FLEET

TO: ADMIRAL COMMANDING CRUISERS

IMMEDIATE

ARRIVING ALTA 0900. YOU ARE TO ALLOT ANCHORAGES TIRPITZ
OUTER VAGFJORD (AS RECEIVED). NEWLY ARRIVING DESTROYERS
AND TORPEDO BOATS TO COMPLETE WITH FUEL AT ONCE.

Scharnhorst at sea: Painting by the German artist Bock, showing her power and grace, presented to a former Captain as a farewell gift. Two ULTRA signals betrayed her sailing and led to her destruction, 26 December, 1943.

U118, mine-laying U-boat, attacked and sunk by Avengers of USS *Bogue* on the return journey after mining Halifax on 12 June, 1943. 17 survivors rescued by USS *Osmond-Ingram*. 30°48′N.33°49′W.

Reassuring picture of Admiral Cunningham saluting on an
apparently unharmed flagship *Queen Elizabeth* in Alexandria which
appeared in the British press. *Queen Elizabeth* had in fact been
badly damaged by an Italian 'charioteer' attack on 19 December,
1941.

U175 on surface during attack by USCG cutter *Spencer*, 17 April, 1943.

'A target of the utmost priority'. Two supply U-boats *U461* and *U462* with *U504*, betrayed by ULTRA and circling desperately on the surface, Bay of Biscay 30 July, 1943. All three U-boats were sunk.

carried high-explosive or anti-submarine bombs. The first strike hit *Tirpitz* with five armour-piercing (two and possibly three of them 1,600 pounders) and four high-explosive bombs, with another very near miss, probably with an anti-submarine bomb, which caused hull damage.

Tirpitz' guns' crews and control position were thoroughly disrupted by the strafing, but she had begun to move back into her net defences, smoke floats had been ignited and partly obscured her, and there was some anti-aircraft fire from ship and shore, when the second strike arrived overhead at about 0630. *Tirpitz* received at least four and probably five more bomb hits, although the only 1600 pounder to hit did not explode. While the Barracudas bombed *Tirpitz*, the fighters flew down the fjord attacking smaller vessels and set a large tanker on fire.

The strike aircraft returned safely to their carriers, with one Barracuda from the first strike lost to flak. Another had crashed into the sea, killing the crew, on take-off. Admiral Moore intended to carry out a second strike on the following day but changed his mind because he believed that *Tirpitz* was badly damaged, and also because of the fatigue and strain already suffered by the aircrews in carrying out what had been a very dangerous operation. The weather worsened overnight, so the operation would very probably have been cancelled in any case.

Tirpitz' upper decks and superstructure were quite extensively damaged, with 122 men killed and another 316, including her Captain, wounded. But the ship's vitals were not nearly as seriously damaged as had been hoped and expected. In fact, none of the bombs had penetrated the main armour belt. The attackers had been too eager and, in their anxiety to obtain the maximum number of hits, had dropped their bombs from too low an altitude. *Tirpitz* was put out of action for only three months.

It was as well for the Allies that the Germans remained absolutely confident that the Enigma was inviolate. Even the least suspicious of intelligence officers might just have wondered why, after *Tirpitz* had been so many months under repair, a powerful and clearly well-briefed and trained force of enemy aircraft should just happen to arrive overhead, not only on the day but at the hour, even at the very minute, when *Tirpitz* was putting to sea. In fact the Germans later claimed they had anticipated the attack and had expected another.

There was a dearth of information about the damage done to *Tirpitz* in TUNGSTEN. An Enigma on the day of the actual attack showed that *Tirpitz* had been hit several times. But there was no more information (because *Tirpitz* was communicating by land-lines from her berth) until June, when the Enigma gave some details about the numerous casualties. But it seems that the worst damage was done to the morale of *Tirpitz'* Captain and ship's company. After all their hard work and training, all the hopes they had cherished of being at last able to get their ship to sea and achieve something to retrieve the good name of the German Navy had been wrecked in the space of a few minutes. It does, with hindsight, seem astonishing that the German naval staff never noticed or questioned the glaring coincidence that enemy aircraft should appear at precisely the right moment – for them. The Germans continued to place absolute faith in the Enigma.

Admiral Fraser had decided against another attack. *Tirpitz* would not be caught by surprise again. The nights were shortening. There would be no convoy at sea to distract the enemy's attention a second time. But under the strongest urging from Admiral Cunningham, the First Sea Lord, who felt that another attack should be made as soon as possible, before the enemy had had a chance to recover, a strike by aircraft from *Victorious* and *Furious* (Operation PLANET) was planned for 23 April. The ships sailed to carry out the attack, but it was cancelled because of bad weather, and the aircraft attacked shipping in Bodo harbour instead.

On 15 May *Victorious* and *Furious* flew off a powerful striking force of twenty-seven Barracudas, escorted by thirty-six fighters, (Operation BRAWN), but they were frustrated by thick cloud over the whole target area. Yet another attempt on 28 May (TIGER CLAW) was also abandoned because of bad weather. These failures were not regarded as serious. There were to be no more Enigma decrypts until June but meanwhile the Naval Attaché in Stockholm had reported that it would take eight weeks from the time of the TUNGSTEN attack to repair the underwater damage caused by the near miss. By mid-May opinion in the Admiralty was that *Tirpitz* would be out of action for at least another three months and not fully operational for another five.

However, these estimates were optimistic. The SIS agent had already reported that *Tirpitz'* main engines were untouched and early in July it was very probably this agent who reported that *Tirpitz* was exercising in Altenfjord. At the same time ULTRA, which had so much to do with *Tirpitz'* life and death, always hovering over her like some malignant familiar perched on a witch's shoulder, was once more suggesting that *Tirpitz* might be getting ready for sea. Enigma decrypts showed on 9 July that the Luftwaffe were transferring bombers to Norway and also (on the 11th) Messerschmitt Me.110 fighters. The Battle Group was also instructed to 'report the date for the start eight days in advance'. It was concluded that *Tirpitz* was probably about to try and move south, some time after 16 July. Clearly it was time for another attack.

On 17 July, in Operation MASCOT, the Fleet Air Arm mounted another massive attack, of forty-four Barracudas, escorted by eighteen Corsairs, eighteen Hellcats and twelve Fireflies. But the Germans were ready, having had about fifteen minutes' warning. They had established an observation post on a nearby hilltop with a direct telephone line linking the observers to *Tirpitz'* gun control, including the directors for her main 15″ armament. The anti-aircraft gun defences had been strengthened and more efficient and quicker-acting smoke-generating equipment provided. Further, the Germans had warning from their own B-Dienst Service. There had been the suspicion that the Germans were alerted by intercepts of Admiral Moore's special flag officers' W/T during Operation PLANET, and there was definite evidence from the Enigma that they had been alerted by intercepts of British carrier R/T while the ships were on passage for BRAWN.

When the strike arrived overhead, *Tirpitz* was already almost completely hidden by smoke. All her guns were manned and the anti-aircraft fire was very heavy. The Barracudas had to bomb 'blind' through the smoke and flak, which included rounds from *Tirpitz's* main 15″ armament. They scored one near-miss. One Barracuda and one Corsair were lost to flak. A second strike that day was thwarted by fog.

The Enigma showed that *Tirpitz* had suffered no serious damage from MASCOT, and by the end of July there were SIS reports that she was under way again. In fact she put to sea for exercises (for the last time) with the 4th Destroyer flotilla on 31 July and 1 August. Another series of attacks (Operations GOODWOOD I, II, II and IV) was mounted on 22, 24 and 29 August. Five carriers, *Indefatigable, Formidable, Furious, Nabob* and *Trumpeter*, took part in one or more of the attacks, some of which involved between sixty and eighty aircraft. One direct hit with a 1600 lb bomb was achieved on 24 August. The bomb pierced *Tirpitz'* main armour and penetrated as far as her keel but did not explode (and when examined by the Germans was found to be only half-full of explosive). Eleven aircraft were lost during the GOODWOOD attacks and, while the ships were retiring after GOODWOOD I on 22 August, a U-boat sank the frigate *Bickerton* and badly damaged the carrier *Nabob*. Enigma decrypts showed that the damage done to *Tirpitz* was insignificant but one, from *Tirpitz* on 24 August, was an urgent request for the assistance of a Luftwaffe bomb disposal squad to render a bomb safe (obviously the 1600 pounder).

A big ship needed a big weapon, bigger than the Fleet Air Arm could deliver. It was clearly a task for Bomber Command's 12000 lb

91

'Tallboy' bombs. At Kaafjord *Tirpitz* was out of range for a round flight by Lancaster bombers loaded with 'Tallboys'. But the Russians gave permission for the bombers to land and refuel in Russia. On 15 September, 1944, in Operation PARAVANE, twenty-seven Lancasters of Nos 9 and 617 Squadrons took off to attack *Tirpitz*; twenty-one carried Tallboys, the other six each carried twelve 400 lb JW Mk II mines.

The bombers attacked through flak from ship and shore, but there were no fighters. *Tirpitz'* shape rapidly disappeared under a smoke screen, and only sixteen 'Tallboys' were dropped, but one scored a direct hit on *Tirpitz's* fo'c'sle, went through the deck, penetrated the ship's side and exploded below the waterline on the starboard side. But the damage done could not be confirmed for some time. An Enigma decrypt of 16 September referred to the hit having 'serious consequences'. On 25 September a signal to all naval attachés stated that *Tirpitz* had been hit by a heavy bomb but that, because the attacking aircraft could not have seen the results, only slight damage was being admitted publicly, but photo-reconnaissance and SIS agents' reports in the next fortnight confirmed that *Tirpitz* had been seriously damaged.

Although the Allies did not know it until after the war, this was the end of *Tirpitz'* operational career. Examination showed that repairs would take nine months. At a conference on 23 September, attended by Dönitz and the German naval staff, it was decided it was no longer possible to make *Tirpitz* ready for sea and action again. On 29 September an Enigma decrypt was received of a general message from Dönitz to all U-boats: 'After successfully defending herself against many heavy air attacks the *Tirpitz* has now sustained a bomb hit, but by holding out in the operational area the ship will continue to tie down enemy forces and by her presence confound the enemy's intentions.' This last was in fact an admirable description of *Tirpitz's* main role, as a 'fleet in being', ever since her arrival in Norway.

But *Tirpitz'* war history was not over. An Enigma decrypt of 16 October caused some alarm in the Home Fleet when it disclosed that *Tirpitz* had moved the day before, under her own steam but also with the assistance of tugs, to a new berth off Haakoy Island, near Tromso. The Germans were still sure that an Allied attack on northern Norway was likely. Here, at Tromso, complete with her nets and booms and anti-aircraft batteries, *Tirpitz* was intended to act as a floating heavy battery for the defence of northern Norway and here, on 18 October, she was sighted by aircraft from the carrier *Implacable*.

Tromso was just within return range of Lancasters, if they were stripped of armour and mid-upper and rear gun turrets, and fitted with overload fuel tanks. On 29 October thirty-two Lancasters tried again in Operation OBVIATE. Harassed by flak and hindered by cloud, they scored one near miss on *Tirpitz'* port quarter (revealed by an Enigma decrypt which also referred to 800 tons of water being admitted to the hull).

Finally, in Operation CATECHISM, on 12 November, 1944, thirty-two Lancasters took off to administer the coup de grâce. There was no cloud, no smoke-screen, and no fighters. Twenty-nine 'Tallboys' were dropped from between 12,500 and 16,000 feet, in a total time of eight minutes. Two direct hits were scored, both on the port side, one level with the bridge, the other alongside X turret, and there were other near-misses along the port side and on the starboard quarter. *Tirpitz* listed 20 degrees to port, then heeled over to 70 degrees. One of the hits started an internal fire and, just after the last bomb had fallen, there was a huge explosion which blew X turret out of the ship. *Tirpitz* rolled further over to port and capsized. Many of her men were trapped inside her and eighty-seven were eventually rescued by cutting holes in the ship's bottom. But over 1,000 of her complement of about 1,700 were lost.

Tirpitz' final demise was confirmed by the Enigma next day, and there was one last sad postscript: the Enigma also revealed that *Tirpitz* had asked for air cover before this final attack, but none appeared.

9 | THE WAR AGAINST THE U-BOATS
1941–42

'The only thing that ever really frightened me during the war,' wrote Winston Churchill, 'was the U-boat peril.' For a time, in 1941, it seemed that Churchill's worst fears might come to pass. In the spring of that year the U-boat arm was poised to launch a new offensive against the convoys, using 'wolf-pack' tactics, attacking on the surface and at night. But the breakthrough in the Enigma in May and June was to transform the situation, although not at once. From May, 1941 onwards, British intercept stations received every signal transmitted to or by the U-boats. From the beginning of June, 1941, and for the next two months, the U-boats' '*Heimisch*' home waters Enigma traffic was read currently, i.e. within an hour of its transmission, although there continued to be days and times when delays were longer.

The benefits of the break-through were enormous and eventually affected every aspect of the battle against the Atlantic U-boats. Until then the pattern of U-boat operations, and hence the best ways of rerouting convoys, had had to be deduced from Coastal Command aircraft reports of U-boat sightings and D/Fs of U-boat transmissions. But from the Enigma there came at once a flood of new information. The U-boats themselves normally only transmitted their short signals, but the Head of the U-boat Arm, *Befehlshaber der U-boote* (BdU), exercised a close central control over the dispositions of U-boats and their attacks. BdU regularly transmitted lengthy situation reports and detailed instructions to U-boats on patrol. Decoded, these signals gave the OIC enough data to be able, not just to reroute convoys with confidence, but to study U-boat behaviour in general and in detail, their patrol areas and transit routes, their offensive capacities and their weaknesses (such as torpedo misfires, common in the Norwegian campaign, but hitherto unknown to Allied intelligence), and the tactics and methods used in their attacks. From the Enigma decrypts the Submarine Tracking Room in the Admiralty was able to produce daily a virtually complete Atlantic chart with the current position of every U-boat accurately marked on it. As the OIC gained experience, in time they even came to know the names, personalities and idiosyncrasies of individual U-boat commanders.

But in mid-May, 1941, there were still stutters in decrypting. BdU issued redisposition orders to the 'West' Group of U-boats on 14 May. The delay in decryption was then about seven days and the OIC therefore did not receive the Enigma until 21 May. This was too late to save the convoy HX126, homeward bound from Halifax and unescorted when, on 19 May, it was sighted and attacked by the first of the 'West' Group, U–94, which sank two ships before losing contact. The convoy was then in 41° West, the furthest west any convoy had been attacked thus far in the war. The next day, 20 May, U–557 made two attacks and sank three ships. Between that evening and the following morning, by which time the convoy had become scattered, U–111, U–98, U–94 (again) and U–93 all made contact and each sank one ship.

The mauling of HX126 led to radical improvements in convoy escort. Until then eastbound convoys were escorted only for the first part of their voyage, when their escort left to join a westbound convoy, leaving the original convoy to proceed alone until it met another escort from Iceland or from the United Kingdom. This left a gap in mid-ocean escort, and it was in this gap that HX126 had been attacked. From the experience of HX126 it was clear that convoys had to be escorted the whole way across the Atlantic. This was achieved by the formation of a Newfoundland Escort Force, based on St John's. Ships of the Royal Canadian Navy supplied the local escort in Newfoundland waters and the ocean escort for the first stage of the Atlantic passage, as far as a Mid-Ocean Meeting Point (MOMP) in about 35° West. There a British escort from Iceland would take over and escort the convoy as far as the Eastern Ocean Meeting Point (EastOMP), in 18° W, where a Western Approaches escort group would take the convoy into Scottish waters. After HX126, long-range Catalina flying boats were transferred to the RCAF, to extend air cover over the convoys. There was still a 'black gap' in mid-Atlantic, where air cover could not reach, but at least it was reduced to about 300 miles.

When the 'Heimisch' Enigma began to be read currently, the rerouting of convoys which this made possible was soon noticed by the enemy. Suddenly the U-boats were having such difficulty in finding convoys that BdU, suspecting an internal breach of security, changed the method by which positions at sea were given in Enigma signals. Until then, signals gave positions by referring to a secret grid (the whole grid for the North Atlantic had been recovered from U–110).

But from 16 June the Enigma traffic began to refer to fixed points with names such as Franz, Oscar, Herbert and Siegfried and gave positions in terms of bearings and distances from those fixed points.

This complication caused only a short delay. By July GC & CS had largely solved the problem. In August, BdU introduced another method, of addressing U-boats by the names of their commanders instead of their numbers. Because U-boat commanders moved from U-boat to U-boat this did make it more difficult for OIC to be sure of the whereabouts of particular U-boats, but BdU found this system cumbersome and liable to lead to misunderstandings and miscalculations. On 11 September the system was changed again, to one where the coordinates of grid references were encoded separately before the message text was encyphered in the Enigma. But, after some delay, GC & CS solved this problem also. Finally, in November, 1941, when BdU was still clearly uneasy about security, an even more complicated process was introduced: the Christian name, surname and address of one of a number of imaginary persons indicated the particular table that was to be used at any given time for encoding the details of the grid coordinates. By changing the names and addresses in use at frequent and irregular intervals, the BdU could disguise the positions given in signals. The system was successful and resisted analysis until June, 1944, when a copy of the 'address book' was captured from U–505.

The first convoy to benefit directly from ULTRA was the homeward-bound HX133, of forty-nine ships, which sailed from Halifax on 16 June. By then the evasive routing made possible by the Enigma was being so successful that the U-boats had made no sightings since 1 June, and in fact made none until 1335 on 23 June, when U–203 sighted and reported HX133. BdU had reformed the 'West' Group with four U-boats on 1 June and added more boats as they arrived. However, it seemed to BdU beyond coincidence that U-boats were no longer sighting convoys. Not for the first (or the last) time BdU was suspicious of security and in particular suspected that the 'West' Group had been compromised and was being avoided. BdU broke up the Group and by 20 June had spread no less than twenty U-boats over a great arc of the central and northern Atlantic.

U–203 closed HX133 on the night of 23 June and sank one straggler before losing contact. On 24 June U–203 chanced across another convoy, the outward bound OB336, and sank two ships from it. Meanwhile U–203's sighting and BdU's orders to other U-boats to converge on HX133, had been revealed by the Enigma. OB336 was ordered to divert out of danger, but human failing frustrated the achievement of ULTRA and the best-laid plans of the Admiralty. The signal to alter course was received in the Commodore's ship, not by the Petty Officer Telegraphist, who was sick, but by a junior and inexperienced telegraphist, who did not know how to decode it, was afraid to ask, put the signal in his pocket and said nothing about it for 27 hours.

On 24 June *U–79* sighted the westbound convoy OB336 and called up *U–71*, which was driven off, and *U–371* and *U–651*, which each sank one ship. Although five U-boats continued to shadow OB336, they had no more success. The Admiralty rightly decided from the Enigma intercepts that HX133 was the more seriously threatened convoy and ordered most of OB336's escort to join HX133, bringing its escort up to thirteen ships, actually outnumbering the U-boats. In the battle which lasted over five days, HX133 was attacked at 7 p.m. on 24 June, and again at about 11 p.m., and at midnight on the 26th, and there was a fourth attack at 0030 on 29 June. Some eight or nine U-boats were in contact, but happily every U-boat which made an attack subsequently lost contact and dropped astern. In all, from HX133, and from OB336 with its depleted escort, eleven ships of about 57,000 tons were sunk. Two ships were damaged but managed to keep up.

The battle was by no means one-sided. At 7.35 a.m. on 27 June, one of HX133's escort, the corvette *Nasturtium* got a clear asdic contact, but unfortunately she had no depth-charges left. A second corvette, *Celandine*, was summoned to the scene. She had depth-charges but could get no asdic contact. In a prolonged attack which was joined by a third corvette, *Gladiolus*, *Nasturtium* guided *Celandine* over the target as she dropped four patterns of depth-charges, while constantly reassuring *Celandine* (who still had no target contact) that her charges were not being wasted.

Finally, at 12.17 p.m. after nearly five hours of depth-charging, during which *Celandine* never had a single asdic contact, there was a strong smell of oil and a widely-spreading slick, in the midst of which a U-boat suddenly came to the surface. The Captain and all but four of the crew of *U–556* abandoned ship, before their U-boat dived again for the last time, and were picked up by the corvettes.

The last attack on HX133 at 0030 on the 29th had been made by *U–651* who later collided with a merchantman in the darkness and was forced to stay on the surface. At 5.30 that morning a small black cloud of smoke was sighted from the bridge of the destroyer *Malcolm* who closed at full speed. The small cloud (actually of diesel smoke) was seen to contain a U-boat conning tower. The U-boat dived, but *Malcolm* had too good an attacking datum to miss, ran in and made one accurate attack with a full pattern of charges which blew *U–651* to the surface. The Captain and crew abandoned ship, to be picked up by *Malcolm* and a second destroyer, *Scimitar*.

July and August, 1941, were comparatively light months for sinkings by U-boats. In August there were twenty U-boats waiting for targets south-west of Iceland, but the U-boats made no pack attacks during the month. Convoys were sighted and reported but, through the Enigma, were evasively routed. BdU moved the U-boats eastwards, nearer Ireland, but this brought them well within range of Coastal Command, whose aircraft made eighteen attacks on U-boats during August. *U–452* was sunk by a Catalina and the trawler *Vascama* on 25 August, and two days later a Hudson of 269 Squadron, piloted by Squadron-Leader J. H. Thompson, pulled off a tremendous coup by attacking and forcing *U–570* to surrender. It was later commissioned as HMS *Graph*.

The lull suggested to some optimists that the worst of the Battle of the Atlantic might be over. There were even suggestions, which the Admiralty had strenuously to resist, that aircraft should be removed from Coastal Command and put back to bombing shore targets in Europe. The figures for September, 1941, fifty-three ships of 202,820 tons sunk by U-boats, showed that the 'lull' was over. Most of these losses were inflicted upon a few unfortunate convoys. The fate of SC42 showed what could still happen if there were any delay in breaking the Enigma.

The convoy, a large one of sixty-four ships, sailed from Sydney, Nova Scotia, on 30 August, escorted by the Canadian 24th Escort Group, of the destroyer *Skeena* and three corvettes. The '*Markgraf*' group, of fourteen U-boats, twenty miles apart, was disposed in a line south-west of Iceland. Their presence was known, but not their position, due to a delay in decrypting the Enigma – one of the temporary delays, this time caused by 'the U-boat Captain's name' change in encoding positions. Even so, SC42 was diverted far to the north, rounding Cape Farewell, the southern tip of Greenland.

The convoy might have escaped, had it not been making so much smoke (the convoy's Commodore had already complained that their smoke was visible for 30 miles) which, on 9 September, was sighted by *U–85*, the northernmost boat in the pack. *U–85*'s attack failed but its report brought three more U-boats to the scene. At 7 p.m. that evening SC42 made another diversionary turn, to the north-east, so that it was actually steering towards Greenland. But it was of no avail. When the sun went down a brilliant hunter's moon arose, and the U-boats, all four of them actually inside the columns of the convoy, went to work. *U–432* sank four ships, *U–82* sank one ship (*Empire Hudson*, one of the first catapult armed merchantman, equipped with a Hurricane fighter for the defence of the convoy), and *U–652* torpedoed a tanker. For a time there was bedlam inside the convoy, with merchantmen firing in all directions at surfaced U-boats and *Skeena* chasing one particularly bold U-boat up and down the ranks of ships. *Skeena* obtained an asdic contact but broke off her attack to rescue survivors. At one point three of the four escorts were astern of the convoy picking up survivors. By dawn eight ships had been sunk.

U–432 shadowed the convoy all day, during which one corvette left to tow the torpedoed tanker to Reykjavik, and thus when the U-boats closed in again at nightfall they outnumbered the depleted escort by two to one and sank another seven ships.

But once again the battle was not entirely one-sided in the end. The Canadian corvettes *Chambly* and *Moosejaw* out on a training exercise, were ordered to reinforce SC42's escort. On their way to join, they surprised *U–501* astern of the convoy and carried out one sharp attack which blew the U-boat to the surface. *Moosejaw*, attempted to ram and, after she had run alongside the U-boat for some time, her sailors were surprised to find a German-speaking stranger on their upper deck. It was the U-boat Captain, who had abandoned his ship.

During the night the escort was further strengthened by three more corvettes and a trawler, and the 2nd Escort Group of five destroyers arrived from Iceland at noon the next day. This, with air cover from Iceland, redressed the odds and that evening the destroyers *Veteran* and *Leamington* sank *U–207*, which had sunk three ships of SC42 the previous night. U-boats did mop up two cripples astern of SC42 but the main convoy steamed into a providential fog bank and lost no more ships.

The convoy escorts improved, under the pressure of hard operational experience, and they also had the overt assistance of the United States Navy, although America was still officially neutral. Meanwhile, the U-boat arm was suffering from some dilution of its most experienced commanding officers. The 'aces' who had begun the war were beginning to drop out, either killed or captured. However, the number of operational U-boats was continuing to rise ominously, from sixty-five in July, 1941, to eighty in October. On 1 September the OIC assessed the current U-boat strength as 184, with losses to date of forty-four (the actual figures were 198 and forty-seven). Apart from the treatment of SC42, other events in September showed once again what could happen if the U-boats gathered in strength or if there were any hitch in the Enigma.

With or without the Enigma, the quality of the escort captains could make the life-saving difference to a convoy's fate. HG72 left Gibraltar on 10 September, 1941, and was attacked by four Italian U-boats, *Da*

Vinci, Morosini, Torelli and *Malaspina*. But the escort, of the destroyers *Faulknor* (Captain de Salis), *Avondale, Encounter,* and *Nestor,* and the sloop *Deptford,* joined later by two more destroyers, *Boreas* and *Wild Swan,* from Plymouth, held the ring so successfully and drove off their attackers so comprehensively that HG72 lost not a single ship. The reports of that convoy were passed around the various Admiralty departments, as a perfect example of how a convoy should be escorted.

On the other hand, nothing, not even the Enigma, could have saved SL87, homeward-bound from Sierra Leone. An inexpert and ill-organized escort, of the ex-US Coastguard cutter *Gorleston,* the sloops *Bideford* and the Free French *Commandant Duboc,* with the corvette *Gardenia,* encountered four highly experienced U-boat commanders, including Dönitz's son-in-law Gunther Hessler (*U–107*). After four days of attacks, the convoy split into two groups. During many of the attacks only one escort was with the convoy, the others being dispersed to transmit signals, or to pick up survivors, or to carry out what they called 'dusk sweeps', or, in *Gorleston's* case, to tow a damaged ship, or, in *Gardenia's* case, to leave early because of shortage of fuel, having not topped up before sailing.

Of eleven ships in SL87, seven (of 33,000 tons) were sunk. A board of enquiry concluded that the convoy 'was not afforded maximum protection' due to 'lack of leadership and balance and to the fact that the escort group were untrained and mixed'. The C-in-C Western Approaches, Admiral Noble, sombrely minuted on the papers that 'arrangements have been made that the CO of *Gorleston* shall not in future act as the Senior Officer of an Escort Group'.

However, the Enigma did provide one chance of avenging SL87. It revealed a U-boat rendezvous, planned for 27–28 September, at Tarafal Bay, on St Antoa, the most northerly of the Cape Verde Islands. There *U–111* was to meet and transfer torpedoes to *U–68* and *U–67,* which had both taken part in the attacks on SL87. When the U-boats approached, the submarine *Clyde* was waiting. In a series of sightings and rapid attacks at close range, *Clyde* fired torpedoes at *U–111* and *U–68,* but missed and the torpedoes, probably exploding on the shore, alerted the targets. *Clyde* collided with *U–67* during another attack, and was herself damaged. All three U-boats escaped, but on 4 October *U–111* had a chance encounter off Madeira with the anti-submarine trawler *Lady Shirley* and was sunk after a brief but fierce depth-charge and gun battle.

If all three U-boats had been sunk, the ambush might have been worthwhile. But coming as it did so soon after the offensive against *Bismarck's* supply ships, this operation risked jeopardizing the secret of ULTRA for no great tangible reward. BdU was certainly made suspicious by the appearance of an Allied submarine so apparently fortuitously at a very remote rendezvous. In November, 1941, BdU reviewed the intelligence situation. It was once again assumed that the Enigma was inviolate. Internal security was as safe as it could be made. BdU accepted the assurances but nevertheless remained convinced that British intelligence had more regular and more accurate information about U-boat dispositions than could be justified by British sightings, D/F fixes and Traffic Analyses – all the usual 'cover stories' for ULTRA. There was something amiss, but BdU did not know what it was and was baffled by it.

For the rest of September events around the convoys showed once again that, despite improvements in escort, losses mounted whenever there was a delay in breaking the Enigma, and wherever the enemy could get enough U-boats to the scene. On the 11th the enemy introduced the more complex method of disguising grid coordinates by coding them separately. For weeks afterwards the instructions to U-boats could only be guessed at, or deduced from past experience.

With this temporary advantage, the U-boats attacked two convoys on the Gibraltar route. They sank six ships of 9,500 tons (including the rescue ship *Walmer Castle*) from the outward OG74, although this convoy was the first ever to be accompanied by an escort carrier, *Audacity*, and nine ships of 25,000 tons (including the catapult ship *Springbank*) from the homeward HG73 and only broke off on 28 September, after a four-day battle, because they had expended all their torpedoes.

Nevertheless, the total tonnage sunk during September was less than the monthly averages earlier in the year, although the enemy now had nearly twice as many U-boats at sea. October was even better. In that month the delay in reading the Enigma was reduced to an average of twenty-six hours, compared with delays of fifty hours in August and forty-one in September. Also, the OIC and GC & CS jointly managed to reduce the uncertainties caused by the new system of encoding grid positions. As a result, for the last three weeks of October, no U-boat patrol lines sighted any convoy, and fifteen convoys were diverted safely. Three Atlantic convoys were sighted by U-boats on passage to join their patrol lines. Of these three, only SC48 was heavily attacked.

In fact SC48 was one of only two October convoys to suffer serious losses, but its experience showed again what the U-boats could do if given the opportunity. The slow eastbound convoy sailed with fifty ships but was scattered by bad weather and had only thirty-nine ships when it was sighted on the night of 14–15 October, some 400 miles south of Iceland, by *U–553*, which was on its way to join a newly formed patrol line southeast of Cape Farewell. *U–553* sank two ships

101

at once and its report brought up another eight U-boats, of whom *U–568* sank a third ship the next day.

On 16 October SC48's original escort of four corvettes was reinforced by a US Navy escort group of four destroyers from ON24, and by the destroyer *Broadwater* and the Free French corvette *Lobelia* from Reykjavik. Nevertheless, five U-boats gained contact during the afternoon. That night six ships were sunk and the corvette *Gladiolus* was lost, without trace and with all hands, torpedoed probably by *U–553*. The US destroyer *Kearny* was also torpedoed (the US Navy's first casualty of the war) and was escorted to Hvalfjord. Finally, *U–101* torpedoed *Broadwater* who was later abandoned and sunk.

The other October convoy to suffer was HG75, homeward bound from Gibraltar, sighted by *U–71* shortly after midnight on 23 October. U-boats were in contact almost continuously for the next five days and sank five ships including the catapult ship *Ariguani*. The escort also suffered: the destroyer *Cossack* was torpedoed, with heavy loss of life, on 23 October, and foundered on the 26th. Two Italian U-boats were lost: *Ferraris* sunk in a gun action with the destroyer *Lamerton*, and *Marconi* through unknown causes.

Sinkings by U-boats in October, 1941, were thirty-two ships of 156,554 tons, a large decrease on September's total of fifty-three ships of 202,820 tons. On analysis, there was an even more encouraging lesson in the October figures: of those thirty-two ships fourteen were sunk more than 600 miles from Coastal Command bases, where there was no air cover; twelve were sunk between 600 and 400 miles from air bases, where air cover was intermittent; and no ships at all were lost within 400 miles of bases, where air cover was plentiful. Clearly the U-boats had become reluctant to operate within range of air cover.

The figures continued to decline in November, to thirteen ships of 62,196 tons, the best month of the year. In that month evasive routeing as a result of the Enigma had become so successful that BdU abandoned the practice of extending all the U-boats in one patrol line, and formed them instead into four smaller lines which were constantly on the move around the Atlantic in the search for targets. Furthermore, on 22 November the U-boats were ordered to concentrate off Gibraltar and the offensive against shipping in the Atlantic was virtually abandoned for the time being. From September, 1941, onwards U-boats began to move through the Straits of Gibraltar into what Dönitz rightly termed 'the trap' of the Mediterranean. Hitler also insisted on a strong U-boat presence in Norwegian waters, to guard against an Allied invasion of Norway (a favourite obsession of his).

As a result U-boats sank only nine ships of 45,931 tons in the Atlantic in December, but sinkings in other areas took the monthly total of losses to U-boats up to twenty-six ships of 124,070 tons. The withdrawal of the U-boats, coupled with the mastery which GC & CS had achieved over the Enigma, had resulted by December, 1941, in a very small, and only temporary, Allied victory in the Atlantic. But any advantage which might be gained from this was more than outweighed by the effect of the Japanese entry into the war the same month. The total sinkings of British, Allied and neutral ships in December, 1941, soared to nearly 600,000 tons, 431,000 tons in the Pacific.

By December, 1941, the cryptographic battle, that ceaseless struggle of both sides to break the other's codes, was taking a clear swing in favour of the enemy. From September, 1941, after a difficult period since August, 1940, the German B-Dienst Service began to read the Royal Navy's main cypher, Naval Cypher No. 2, with less and less delay. By December the B-Dienst Service was also starting to read a special cypher, Naval Cypher No. 3, which the Admiralty had introduced in the summer for Anglo-American-Canadian communications in the Atlantic, and especially the control of the Atlantic convoys.

The increasing confidence of the B-Dienst Service began to show in the dispositions of the Atlantic U-boats from late October, 1941, although alert evasive routeing using the Enigma saved every convoy except SC52. Through the B-Service, the 'Raubritter' group of eleven U-boats was formed and directed against SC52 on 31 October. The convoy was sighted by U–374 on 1 November and five U-boats closed to attack. On 3 November U–202 sank three ships in two attacks, U–203 sank two ships and U–569 one, for a total of six ships of 22,300 tons, before the U-boats lost contact in poor visibility. This was much the heaviest loss from a single convoy in that month.

From 7 November another group, 'Stortebecker', of eight U-boats, was directed west of Spain by the B-service against SL91 but because of evasive routeing neither the U-boats nor air reconnaissance had found the convoy by the 11th and the operation was unsuccessful. Similarly, on the 12th, after their attacks on SC52, the 'Raubritter' line was deployed against ONS33 but failed to find it. 'Stortebecker's' next objective, directed by the B-Service, was OS11 but neither the U-boats nor the aircraft provided from 16 November could locate the convoy. BdU now abandoned the long single search line and deployed the U-boats instead in three loose lines, 'Stortebecker', 'Godecke', and 'Benecke', to intercept an OG convoy which had been forecast by the B-Service. But they had no success and from 22 November the U-boats began to pass through the Straits of Gibraltar into the Mediterranean.

By the end of November only three U-boats, all with little fuel remaining, were still in the North Atlantic. They formed the 'Letzte Ritter' group and were deployed on information from the B-Dienst

103

Service against OG77, which sailed for Gibraltar on 26 November. This convoy was actually sighted by aircraft on the 28th, but it then vanished and searches on 29 and 30 November and 1 December failed to find it.

During the month of December BdU carried out a major redeployment of U-boat strength. By the 8th all twelve U-boats on patrol in the Atlantic were concentrated in the area off Gibraltar. By the 15th twenty U-boats had passed through the Straits of Gibraltar into the Mediterranean. Hitler still insisted that U-boats be kept in the north and, by March, 1942, the number of U-boats in Norwegian waters had risen to twenty-four. By contrast, on 1 January, 1942, there were only six U-boats in the Atlantic, all on patrol near the Azores.

BdU was once again made suspicious by the comparatively high failure rate in the latter half of 1941, against convoys which had been accurately located by the B-Dienst Service. It was indeed mathematically unlikely that so many U-boats should sight nothing, no matter how accurately they were directed, and so many convoys should randomly change course at what was always the most opportune moment for them.

In fact there *was* a correlation between the evasive routeing of the convoys and the contents of the Enigma signals. There was bound to be. No matter how carefully the Admiralty guarded the ULTRA secret, how cautiously they used the information from the Enigma, and how ingenuously and skilfully they fabricated appropriate 'cover' stories, there had to be a connection if the Enigma information were used over a long enough period. But the Germans failed to detect it, because it was concealed by their own comparative lack of success in breaking British codes between August, 1940, and September, 1941, and because there were other excuses: air cover had driven the U-boats into mid-Atlantic where they were deprived of reconnaissance information from the long-range Focke Wulf Kondors. The closely packed search lines, used until almost the end of 1941, had enabled the U-boats to concentrate quickly and in strength upon a sighted convoy; but by their nature they also reduced the U-boats' own reconnaissance range. There might also have been a psychological block which discouraged any German suspicion of the Enigma. They believed it was absolutely secure, because they wanted to believe it was secure. Once again, assurances were given from the highest level that the Enigma was invulnerable.

BdU's continuing anxiety about security led to the most serious cryptographic setback of the war for the Allies. From the spring of 1941 naval Enigma decrypts and captured material had referred to the possibility that a fourth wheel might be added to the Enigma machine.

The series of changes in encoding grid coordinates in signals to U-boats, introduced in the last six months of 1941, also suggested that the first use of the fourth wheel would be in a new key for the Atlantic U-boats. It was known by the end of 1941 that fourth wheels were being issued to U-boats, and it was hoped that it would not be long before someone 'jumped the gun' and used the fourth wheel in error. In fact, in December, 1941, when one such signal was transmitted on the U-boat frequency, the telegraphist responsible then compounded his error by repeating the signal using only three wheels. From this, GC & CS were able to work out the wiring of the fourth wheel.

The blow fell on 1 February, 1942, when the Germans introduced the fourth wheel for a new key, used by all U-boats except those in the Arctic (who continued to use 'Heimisch'). The new key was named 'Triton' by the Germans, 'Shark' by GC & CS. The flow of priceless Enigma material on the U-boats in the Atlantic was cut off, literally overnight.

This was bad enough. Worse, the enemy achieved a major crypto-graphic success in February, 1942. The German B-Dienst Service had begun its cryptographic attack on British Naval codes well before the war and, by April, 1940, was reading between 30 and 50 per cent of the traffic in the British Naval Cypher No. 1 without much delay. But on 20 August, 1940, Naval Cypher No. 1 was replaced by Cypher No. 2, which gave the B-Dienst much more difficulty, until an inex-plicable change of encoding procedure in September, 1941, made their task much easier. The B-Dienst once again began to read much of the traffic, until 1 January, 1942, when Naval Cypher No. 2 was replaced by No. 4, against which they never achieved anything like their earlier success.

The B-Dienst's most important success was against Naval Cypher No. 3, a reserve US Navy Cypher, introduced in June, 1941, for use by the British, US and Canadian Navies. The B-Dienst soon realized that this cypher was carrying much of the Atlantic convoy traffic and concentrated their efforts on it. By February, 1942, they had broken it and were able to read most (sometimes as much as 80 per cent) of the signals.

Thus, at the very time when the Allies suffered a serious crypto-graphic reverse, the enemy made a major advance. The effect of this was not felt immediately in the Atlantic because the U-boats concentrated their attacks in the first months of 1942 on shipping off the east coast of the United States. In spite of the lessons of all past naval history, and the experience of the war so far, the United States Navy declined at first to escort merchant shipping in convoy. For a few months, while the US Navy tried every expedient except convoy and escort, the U-boats enjoyed a happy time, executing what one distinguished American naval historian called 'a merry massacre' on unescorted merchant ships along the eastern American seaboard.

As the weeks passed and became months without the Enigma, the charts in the Submarine Tracking Room became less accurate and more conjectural. The Tracking Room had much experience of U-boat ways and could make intelligent guesses at their whereabouts, but there was no substitute for the hard crisp authentic Enigma information.

Meanwhile, the German cryptographic success was accompanied by a dramatic increase in the number of U-boats at sea, which climbed from twenty-two in January, 1942, to sixty-one in May, to eighty-six in August and soared to over 100 in October. With the belated introduction of convoy off the east coast of America in the summer of 1942 the U-boats began to return to the Atlantic. The main onslaught on the convoys opened in August and September, when the U-boats located twenty-one out of sixty-three convoys that sailed, attacked seven of them and sank forty-three of their ships.

From August, 1942, onwards there were some fierce battles in and around the convoys, with the U-boats resuming determined attacks in daylight, in a way they had not done during the previous ten months. On 1 August twelve U-boats of the 'Pirat' patrol line lay in wait for ON115, whose Canadian escort group, C3, had already driven off repeated U-boat attacks on 30 and 31 July, and had sunk U–588. The convoy was sighted by U–552 on 3 August and its report brought up five more U-boats, which sank three ships before the Canadians drove them away again.

Most of the U-boats which had attacked ON115 formed a new 'Steinbrinck' Group, of eight boats, east of the Newfoundland Bank where, on 5 August, U–593 sighted SC94, of thirty-six ships escorted by another Canadian group, C1, of one destroyer and two corvettes, with three British corvettes. Another hectic battle took place, from 5 to 10 August, in which eleven ships were lost, but the destroyer Assiniboine rammed, depth-charged, shelled and finally sank U–210 on 6 August. The corvette Dianthus rammed, depth-charged, machine-gunned and finally sank U–379 on the 7th.

SL118, of thirty-four ships homeward bound from Sierra Leone, was attacked by four of the eight U-boats in the 'Blucher' Group on 17 and 18 August. Four ships were lost and the armed merchant cruiser Cheshire was torpedoed. But the convoy was vigorously defended: the air and surface escort made twenty counter-attacks, including eight depth-charge attacks by escorts and three by Liberators. U–333 was damaged and the rest were driven off. Four days later, in a long battle

106

which began on 22 August, the thirty-six ships of ON122 were attacked by seven U-boats of the '*Lohs*' Group. Again, the escort group, B6, (the destroyer *Viscount* and four Norwegian-manned corvettes) counter-attacked with tremendous vigour: the convoy lost four ships but the escorts made thirty attacks with depth-charges and two with the new 'Hedgehog' ahead-throwing mortars, damaging *U–605* and *U–256*.

The key to many convoy battles was radar. Where it was lacking or defective, the convoys were once again very vulnerable. In September, directed by the B-Dienst, thirteen U-boats in the '*Vorwarts*' Group waited to ambush ON127. The convoy had thirty-two ships, escorted by the Canadian Group C4, of two destroyers and three corvettes, with one British corvette. The convoy was first sighted on 5 September but was then lost until the 10th, by which time it was outside air cover. In a fierce three-day battle, in which for the only time in 1942 and 1943 every U-boat taking part (thirteen in this case) fired torpedoes, the destroyer *Ottawa* and seven merchantmen, of more than 50,000 tons, were sunk, and four ships were damaged. The escorts' radar was unserviceable at crucial times in the battle. No U-boat was sunk, although *U–659* was damaged on 11 September.

Those last four months of 1942, when there were over 100 U-boats at sea, were some of the most successful of the war for the U-boat arm, from the point of view of professional achievement. Forming and reforming into fresh searching groups, very appropriately named after carnivores such as Leopard, Puma and Panther, with a flow of accurate and timely intelligence from the B-Dienst Service, and some quick and thorough sighting and reporting amongst themselves, as well as to and from BdU, the U-boats seemed able to go from convoy to convoy almost at will.

In October SC104 was found by several U-boats and attacked over a period of nearly a week, losing seven ships. In a seven-day battle ten U-boats attacked SL125 off Madeira and sank thirteen ships. In November SC107 was attacked by seven U-boats and lost fifteen ships. ON144 fought a four-day battle with a pack of six U-boats and lost six ships and the corvette *Montbretia*, who was hit twice while going at full speed and sank without stopping, taking with her the Captain and forty-six of her people. HX212 lost twelve ships and ONS154 thirteen in fierce battles at the end of the year.

The escorts were by no means swamped. Most encouraging for the Allies were the successes scored by aircraft. From 5 October, when *U–582* was sunk by aircraft of 269 Squadron, aircraft went on to sink another fifteen U-boats by the end of the year. Nevertheless, by the beginning of November the U-boat arm had about 200 operational boats, and another 170 doing trials or training. The Germans had by then lost 135 boats, the Italians fifty-three. The figures showed that the Allies were not sinking more than a third of the monthly output of new U-boats.

Happily for the outcome of the battle, the decision was taken in November, 1942, to provide more long-range aircraft for the Atlantic. It was a crucial, indeed a war-winning decision, and it was not taken a moment too soon. By the end of 1942 the U-boats had sunk 1160 ships of more than six million tons and another crisis in the battle was looming. But, even more happily for the Allies in the Atlantic, in December, 1942, GC & CS finally broke back into the U-boat 'Shark' Enigma.

10 | THE U-BOAT WAR, CONVOYS TM1 AND SC118, *January–March, 1943*

On 22 November, 1942, GC & CS was urged by the OIC to pay 'a little more attention' to the 'Shark' Enigma. The U-boat war was 'the one campaign which Bletchley Park are not at present influencing to any marked extent – and it is the only one in which the war can be lost unless BP *do* help.' The note of urgency was matched by the rising figures of merchant tonnage sunk by U-boats in the last months of 1924: 485,413 tons in September, 619,417 in October, and 729,160 – the highest monthly tonnage sunk during the whole war – in November.

It was therefore with great satisfaction, and even greater relief, that Pound was able to signal to Admiral King, the US Chief of Naval Operations, on 13 December: 'As the result of months of the most strenuous endeavour a few days' U-boat traffic will be readable in the immediate future and this may lead to better results in the near future.' However, Pound emphasized the need for caution, so as not to lose this most precious of secrets. 'You will, I am sure,' he went on, 'appreciate the care necessary in making use of this information to prevent suspicion being aroused as to its source. We have found this especially difficult when action by routeing authorities outside the Admiralty is required. It would be a tragedy,' Pound concluded, 'if we had to start all over again on what would undoubtedly be a still more difficult problem.'

Ironically, the loss of the U-boat Enigma from February to December, 1942, very probably helped to conceal that the Enigma had been broken earlier. The Enigma 'black-out' happened to coincide with the U-boat offensive along the east coast of America. Had the U-boats continued to concentrate as before on the North Atlantic routes, the enemy would surely have noticed the improvement in their performance against the convoys and could hardly have failed to link it with the change from the three- to the four-wheel Enigma.

For the Admiralty, one of the first and most important results of the break into the 'Shark' Enigma code was that it soon revealed what the 'blackout' had hitherto concealed — that the enemy had broken into Naval Cypher No 3, the 'convoy code'. The enemy had naturally tried as hard as the Admiralty had to conceal their cryptographic success, but a correlation was bound to appear over a long enough period and the Admiralty, being perhaps more sceptical and less confident of their codes than the German naval staff, deduced the enemy's success from evidence in the German signals during the early months of 1943.

But the break into the 'Shark' key did not have a noticeable effect for some time. Meanwhile, the B-Dienst Service's mastery over Naval Cypher No. 3, coupled with a lack of air cover, could still prove fatal, as was brutally demonstrated by the fate of the slow westbound convoy ONS154 late in December, 1942.

The convoy, of forty-five ships, escorted by the Canadian escort group C1, had been diverted to the south and was out of range of air cover from Iceland when it was first sighted on 26 December by *U–664*, one of ten U-boats of the '*Spitz*' line, which had been lying in wait for ONS154 since the 24th. A three-day battle began that night, in which the escorts sank *U–356*, but the '*Spitz*' U-boats attacked again and again and were joined by another nine U-boats of the '*Ungestum*' group, waiting some distance to the west. In one of the worst convoy maulings of the war, fourteen ships of more than 73,000 tons were sunk, including the convoy commodore's ship *Empire Shackleton*, and a tanker was torpedoed. Also lost, with all hands, was the special service ship HMS *Fidelity*, on 30 December.

In spite of this disaster, monthly figures for U-boat sinkings were actually down in December, to 330,816 tons. This was principally because, after the Allied TORCH landings in November, BdU had diverted a large number of U-boats to the south to search for convoys en route to North Africa. But because of the excellent security, both cryptographic and physical, given to the TORCH convoys, the U-boats had no success against them in 1942. Yet, ironically, it was to be a TORCH convoy which suffered the first disaster of 1943.

Convoy TM1, of nine valuable tankers intended for the North African campaign, sailed from Trinidad for Gibraltar on 28 December, 1942. BdU knew nothing of its sailing or its route, but certainly learned from agents in Trinidad that tankers were loading for Gibraltar. The escort group was B5, under Commander Boyle, in the destroyer *Havelock*, with the corvettes *Pimpernel*, *Saxifrage* and *Godetia*.

There were defects in the corvettes' radar sets, and *Havelock*'s High Frequency Direction Finding (H/F D/F) equipment was also not working properly. However, the voyage was without incident until about 4.30 p.m. on 3 January, 1943, when, quite by chance, the convoy was sighted by *U–514*, which happened to be on passage to the West Indies, and reported as 'about ten ships with destroyers, course 070, speed 9 knots'.

U–514 was ordered to 'stick at it without fail', to report at two- to four-hour intervals and to attack. *U–514* closed the convoy after dark, and sank one tanker at about 9.45 p.m. *U–514* was not detected or attacked by the escort but was sighted on the surface, passing through the columns of the convoy from ahead, and was fired on by several of the tankers.

At that time information from the Enigma was patchy. It was known that the *'Delfin'* Group, of six U-boats, had been patrolling between Madeira and the Azores since 29 December, hoping to inter-cept TORCH convoys, and had been ordered on 3 January to sweep to the south. But there was no information from the Enigma from noon on 3 January until the morning of 9 January, and a critical period for TM1, from noon on 3 January to noon on the 5th, remained blank. Acting on the last appreciation of the *'Delfin'* Group's movements, OIC ordered TM1 at 2.05 p.m. on the 3rd to alter course after dark and to steer well to the southward of the original route. This would, with hindsight, have been a safe course. But Commander Boyle decided to stay to the north, where he expected to find better weather for refuelling the escort. This proved to be a most unfortunate decision.

Meanwhile, BdU had lost touch. *U–514*'s W/T was defective and *U–125*, which was about 250 miles to the east, never gained contact with TM1. It seemed that the convoy had escaped. BdU expressed displeasure and warned all U-boats to avoid a repetition. *'Delfin's'* sweep to the south was cancelled and the U-boats were ordered instead to proceed at full speed south-east to search for TM1. But at 8.35 p.m. on 3 January *U–182*, outward bound for the South Atlantic, happened to sight the nearest ships of GUF3, a convoy from Gibraltar to New York, then about 400 miles west of Madeira. *U–182* was detected and depth-charged, and lost contact. BdU still thought GUF3 more promising, but the convoy proved to be too fast and escaped to the west before the U-boats could be deployed in its path.

This diversion might have saved TM1, but, after further reports from *U–514* and *U–125*, BdU decided to turn back to the original quarry. At 6 p.m. on 5 January, apparently acting almost on intuition, BdU ordered the *'Delfin'* boats to form a new line for 7 January, 180 miles long, about 650 miles south-west of the Canary Islands and about the same distance north-east of TM1's last reported position.

The more southerly route ordered by OIC on 3 January would have taken TM1 some 120 miles clear of the U-boat line. But on the northerly course chosen by the escort commander TM1 was sighted by *U–381*, the third boat from the northern end of the line, at 3 p.m. on 8 January. BdU at once ordered four more boats, *U–511* and *U–522*, outward bound for the South Atlantic, and *U–128* and *U–134*, homeward bound from patrols in the St Paul's Rocks area, to join the line.

The main battle therefore took place that night of 8/9 January. *U–571* was attacked and driven off by *Pimpernel*, but *U–436* sank two tankers, was depth-charged by *Havelock* and retired for repairs. *U–536* sighted flares from the convoy, attacked three times, claimed three hits at about 11 p.m., another hit at 5.30 the next morning, followed almost at once by three hits on 'overlapping tankers'. *U–571* attacked three tankers at 7 a.m. but was depth-charged, damaged and driven off by *Havelock*. During that day four more U-boats attacked and were all driven off.

On the following day, 10 January, one crippled tanker was finished off and a ship sailing independently north of the convoy was sunk. The U-boats were back in force by the evening and sank one final tanker. BdU was still demanding 'the last tankers must also fall', but a Sunderland flying-boat arrived on the morning of the 11th and at once forced U-boats to dive. The U-boats were called off that evening. The last two remaining tankers of TM1 reached Gibraltar on 14 January without further mishap, but seven tankers had been lost.

Had the Enigma been available in time, it would still have been possible to redirect TM1 so as to avoid the U-boats, even after Boyle had made his decision not to make the original diversion. Thus TM1's experience was the sum result of that unfortunate routeing decision, defects in radar and H/F D/F, a decrypting 'black-out' at a crucial time, and a lack of air cover, which all combined to give the U-boats the chances they needed. BdU had wiped the Admiralty Tracking Room's eye in a most painful way. As one officer who worked in the OIC, Lieutenant-Commander Beesly, wrote many years later: 'TM1 was but one example of the unending battle of wits between BdU and the Tracking Room. We lost some and we won some. This was one we definitely lost.'

But the Tracking Room had its many successes to set against TM1. Ironically, the U-boats themselves were largely responsible for the Tracking Room's seemingly uncanny knack of not only tracking but anticipating U-boats' movements. For the U-boats were the most talkative opponents in the whole history of naval warfare. 'Have sunk one steamship for certain and one tanker (probable) in Square 8852,' signalled Korvetten-Kapitan Herbert Schultze, of *U–432*, to BdU in

October, 1942. 'Set one tanker on fire on 15 October. My present position is Square 8967. Have 69 cubic metres of fuel oil left. Have two [air] and one [electric] torpedoes left. Wind south-west, force 3 to 4. Pressure 996 millibars. Temperature 21 degrees [above freezing].'

This lengthy signal was only one of dozens which BdU received and sent every day. Every U-boat outward-bound from the French ports had to report by signal when it had cleared the Bay of Biscay. U-boats from Norway or the Baltic had to signal as soon as they crossed 60° N. Unless a U-boat had sailed for a specific task, or for a particularly remote area, its patrol destination and operational orders, decided by BdU in the light of the latest tactical situation, were signalled to it at sea. U-boats were not allowed to deviate from their orders without signalling first to ask, and then receiving, permission from BdU.

In every signal a U-boat had to include its present position. If it failed to do so, or if it made no signals at all for several days, BdU would order it to report. BdU signalled the fuelling rendezvous when U-boats were to replenish from a 'milch cow' U-boat, indicated which U-boats were to refuel, in what order and at what times, and how much fuel each U-boat was to receive. After replenishment, the 'milch cow' was required to signal whether or not the U-boats nominated had been refuelled and how much fuel and stores now remained.

BdU ordered the forming and reforming, even the naming, of the U-boat patrol lines. Every U-boat commander was addressed by name and told which line to join and which place in the line to occupy. BdU signalled the latest information on expected convoys. When a convoy was actually sighted, BdU then decided which U-boats would attack, and in what order, and from which direction, and even at what time. A U-boat sighting and shadowing a convoy was required to transmit medium-frequency homing signals for the benefit of other U-boats in the vicinity, and to send detailed descriptions to BdU on high-frequency. When reception was bad, BdU nominated U-boats to relay signals to those in contact and to relay back their signals to BdU.

Neither BdU nor the U-boats ever seemed to realize the great dangers to themselves, and the enormous benefits to the Allies, of all this signalling. These long and frequent messages were not only invaluable to intelligence but also to H/F D/F operators in ships at sea, providing accurate bearings and often, by their strength, a good estimate of range. Time after time the escorts ran down a H/F D/F bearing and found the U-boat at the end of it. Two or more simultaneous H/F D/F bearings from different escorts would give an accurate position fix. A few U-boat commanders returning from patrol commented on the curious coincidence that a W/T transmission was so often followed quickly by an attack, and suggested there might be some connection. But BdU and the staff could conceive of no such thing. Any U-boat commander who persisted in this crankish notion was accused of having a bee in his bonnet or, worse, lacking sufficient aggressive spirit.

The immense volume of U-boat signal traffic, continuing ceaselessly day and night, provided Allied intelligence with priceless raw material which, when decoded and examined over a length of time, eventually gave the Admiralty Tracking Room staff their almost eerie knowledge of their opponents. In time they came to know BdU's foibles, the characters and likely reactions of BdU's staff, and the personalities and professional standings, in BdU's eyes, of individual U-boat captains.

However, this psychological mastery was still a long way short of being achieved at the beginning of 1943. January brought almost incessantly appalling weather in the Atlantic. Gale followed gale, hampering the U-boats, who sank thirty-seven ships of 203,128 tons, a comparatively light monthly loss. But the figures began to rise steeply and ominously in February to sixty-three ships of 359,328 tons, in a series of large-scale attacks on convoys. It soon became clear to OIC that in December, 1942, BdU had embarked upon what was nothing less than a second major U-boat assault on the convoys, using many more U-boats than at any previous time in the war, and only the very bad weather of January had delayed the campaign from reaching its full climactic intensity.

The battle around SC118 showed, once again, how fatally easy it was for a convoy to suffer heavy losses if there was a break in the Enigma, if the escort were not properly trained together as a group, and if the escort commander made a mistake such as placing most of his ships to leeward of the convoy, on a night when the U-boats were attacking, as they often did, from downwind.

Yet, ironically, for most of the time, SC118 was very ably handled and defended. The first shadowing U-boat was firmly sunk. Air cover duly arrived, on time, and the surface escort was reinforced, in time. Counter-attacks were properly and satisfactorily carried out. H/F D/F on the rescue ship *Toward* gave consistently accurate bearings. Had not the escort group been what the Admiralty called ' a scratch team', then, in the Admiralty's opinion, SC118 'might have been one of the highlights of the U-boat war'. Nevertheless, the hard truth emerged that, at a time when the escort had been increased to twelve ships, the U-boats still managed to regain the initiative.

SC118, of sixty-four ships, sailed from New York on 24 January, 1943. The escort group was B2, the 'scratch team', of the destroyers *Vanessa* (Lieutenant-Commander Proudfoot), *Vimy* (Lieutenant Stannard VC) and *Beverley*, with four corvettes including the Free French *Lobelia*, the US Coastguard cutter *Bibb* and the rescue ship *Toward*.

It seems that SC118 was first betrayed by a survivor from the tanker *Cordelia*, a straggler from HX224, which had lost three ships. The man was picked up by *U–632*, which had sunk his ship on 3 February, and he told his rescuers that another large convoy was following his own along the same route. There were then some sixty U-boats north of latitude 50° N, but most of them were not well placed to intercept SC118. There were twenty-one U-boats in the '*Haudegan*' Group, off Cape Farewell, who were still somewhat scattered after chasing a convoy south of Greenland. A smaller '*Jaguar*' Group was off Newfoundland. Another group of nineteen U-boats who had been patrolling west of Iceland in about longitude 25° W had just dispersed. Seven of these boats, with another two outward bound U-boats, formed the '*Pfeil*' Group which was positioned across the route of HX224, hoping for the promised second convoy to follow.

Unfortunately for OIC, and for SC118, information from the Enigma for 19 January to 1–2 February had not been received and vital details about the '*Pfeil*' Group of U-boats, who were best placed to attack SC118, was not received until 7th, by which time the convoy was fighting for its life. Meanwhile the only possible evasion was to alter the convoy's course to the southward, to avoid the '*Haudegan*' Group.

The first sighting was by *U–187*, of the '*Pfeil*' Group, on the forenoon of 4 February. The rest of that Group, with three of the '*Jaguars*' and five '*Haudegans*', who were also to take part, were all exhorted by BdU: 'Convoy is probably destined for Murmansk – at them! Operate ruthlessly, to relieve the Eastern Front!' But *U–187*'s sighting report was detected by H/F D/F in *Toward* and in *Bibb*, and shortly afterwards *Beverley* sighted the U-boat itself, carelessly loitering on the surface about seven miles ahead of the convoy.

Beverley and *Vimy* closed the spot at full speed as the U-boat dived and dropped smoke floats to establish the datum position. They then carried out four careful, measured depth-charge and Hedgehog attacks, the last of which stove in part of the U-boat's hull so that it had to blow main ballast tanks to reach the surface, where the crew abandoned ship. Most of them were picked up before *U–187* sank. 'Got him!' signalled Stannard (who was now to get a DSO to add to his VC) to *Vanessa*.

While *Vimy* and *Beverley* were dispatching *U–187*, the convoy was sighted by *U–402* which was joined that afternoon by four more U-boats. They all attacked and were all driven off. One of them, *U–609* (Korvetten-Kapitan Rudloff), regained contact during the night and

115

was to stay in touch with SC118, with only short breaks, for the next three days.

BdU had not yet been able to assess the situation properly and was further confused that evening when the convoy made a large emergency turn to starboard. The three porthand columns misunderstood or misheard the Commodore's sound signal to turn and stood on to the north on their original course. The convoy thus became divided and the two sections gave the U-boats the impression that there were two convoys, a fast and a slow.

On 5 February U–609 was still in contact and brought up five U-boats which all tried to attack. A sixth U-boat claimed one hit but no ship was lost until 1 p.m. that afternoon when U–413, the first of the 'Jaguar' Group to take part, sank a straggler. Several U-boats were driven off, or reported defects during the day, and eventually BdU became restive, urged the U-boats to give their enemy no respite, warned them not to lose the convoy again, and once more exhorted them, 'Remember the Eastern Front'.

By the morning of 6 February the missing 'rump' had rejoined, the convoy had formed up again in good order, and for a time it seemed that the U-boats had fumbled their chance. SC118 was now about 720 miles south-west of Iceland and 820 miles west of Londonderry, and the eagerly awaited Very-Long-Range Liberators arrived on cue. Eleven U-boats reported sighting aircraft and four were actually attacked with bombs and cannon fire. By that evening of the 6th the U-boats were in some disarray. Several had been forced down or driven off. U–465 was badly damaged and withdrew. Even U–609 had lost contact.

The convoy lost another straggler that day, sunk by U–266, who reported that it had taken the Master and Chief Engineer prisoner, and obtained from them information on the convoy's formation and progress. But, apart from that, BdU had had no fresh reports and was signalling displeasure that more U-boats had not made better use of U–609's shadowing reports. By contrast, the escort could feel quietly confident, especially when they were joined during the day by the US destroyers Babbitt and Schenk and the US Coast Guard cutter Ingham from Iceland.

Four U-boats, U–438, U–262, U–456 and the persistent U–609, regained contact during the evening. All four were driven off, together with U–267, damaged by depth-charges, and U–624, hunted and depth-charged for four hours. But, during the night, in spite of these setbacks, the U-boats wrested back the initiative.

Proudfoot, the escort commander, was afterwards bitterly criticized by Captain Gilbert Roberts, head of the Western Approaches Tactical

School, for placing most of his escorts on the convoy's bow, when the wind was astern and the U-boats were known to prefer attacking downwind. During the night of 6–7 February, at least three U-boats slipped into the convoy's ranks from astern and eight ships including *Toward* were lost. As so often in the Atlantic, a few U-boats did most of the damage. One particularly able and bold U-boat captain could turn a battle. Six of those eight ships were lost in two attacks before dawn by *U–402* (Korvetten-Kapitan Freiherr Siegfried von Forstner).

U–262 and *U–614* also sank a ship each during the night. But Rudloff's long trail in *U–609* was over. At about 4.30 a.m. on the 7th *U–609* was detected by the Free French *Lobelia*, commanded by the very able Lieutenant-Commander de V. De Morsier, and was sunk with all hands in one sharp deadly attack.

Nevertheless BdU sensed that the U-boats had done well during the night and at 7.45 ordered repeated attacks, despite the air cover. BdU advised the U-boats to get ahead of the convoy: 'The broad formation is the most favourable for submerged as well as surface attack.' The U-boats did their best. Eleven of them were still in positions where they were able to attack, although some were now short of torpedoes. *U–456* and von Forstner in *U–402*, joined later by U–438, all made contact with the convoy at some time during the day. Von Forstner pursued his quarry all day and was forced down or driven off no less than seven times.

Another U-boat in contact was *U–624*, which transmitted a very long signal just after 5 p.m., recounting the experiences of the night before. But the garrulous *U–624* tarried too long and was sighted on the surface shortly after 6 p.m. by Liberator 'J' of 220 Squadron, who dropped three depth-charges close to the U-boat's port bow. After the explosions had died away, there was tremendous underwater activity and bubblings, followed by wreckage and miscellaneous débris bobbing to the surface.

BdU sent a special signal of commendation to von Forstner and urged him to stay in touch. This he did and, while the other U-boats lost contact one by one and fell by the wayside (three of them, *U–135*, *U–89* and *U–614*, all reported being forced to dive by aircraft), von Forstner closed SC118 again during the night of 7–8 February and sank one final ship just after 1 a.m. In the evening of 8 February, when SC118 was 450 miles north-west of Londonderry, even von Forstner abandoned the chase and headed south-west to rendezvous with the supply U-boat. As late as 9.30 p.m. on 9 February BdU was still urging all U-boats to search at high speed on zigzagging courses until dawn. But nobody complied.

Of nineteen U-boats which made contact with SC118, three were sunk and four badly damaged. The U-boats had sunk ten ships and *Toward*. One of the ships lost, the American troopship *Henry R. Mallory*, went down with great loss of life due to confusion and poor lifeboat drill. In the end BdU seemed displeased with the U-boats' final performance, although they had not been favourably placed to attack when SC118 was first sighted, and some of the U-boats had already been on patrol for some weeks. BdU sent congratulatory signals to von Forstner, to *U–609* (being unaware that Rudloff and his crew were dead) and to *U–262*, but to nobody else.

The bad weather continued in February, 1943. There was an almost unbroken succession of fierce westerly and north-westerly gales in the Atlantic from November, 1942, throughout that winter until April, 1943. Convoys and U-boats had to battle, not only against each other, but against some of the worst weather of the whole war.

Meanwhile, ashore, the cryptographic contest continued, with the B-Dienst struggling to provide BdU with the information needed to deploy U-boats ahead of a convoy in good time, while the GC & CS and OIC battled as hard to give the Tracking Room enough warning to be able to divert a convoy out of danger. This contest was evenly balanced for much of February 1943. Of the homeward bound convoys, HX223 lost only one ship, HX224 two and a straggler. HX225 was not sighted at all by the U-boats, nor was HX226. SC119 and SC120 were unscathed.

Of the outward convoys, ONS165 was attacked by the '*Typhoon*' Group of U-boats and lost one ship and one straggler, but the destroyers *Fame* and *Viscount* sank a U-boat each. ONS167, only sighted by chance, lost two ships. But the fate of the convoy between these two, ONS166, showed how much more effective the U-boats were when they were previously disposed in a patrol line in front of a convoy than when they had to try and gain an attacking position after a convoy had been sighted, and what timely advice from the B-Dienst Service, coupled with lack of air cover in the infamous mid-Atlantic 'gap', could do to a convoy, however ably defended.

ONS166, of sixty-three ships, was escorted by A3 Group, of mixed nationalities, commanded by Captain P.R. Heineman USN, with two US Coastguard Cutters, *Spencer* and *Campbell*, the RN corvette *Dianthus*, and four Canadian corvettes, with the Polish destroyer *Burza* joining later. The weather was so bad, with constant north-westerly gales, that ONS166 averaged only four knots for the first four days, and by 20 February, when *U–604* sighted the convoy, there were as many as nine stragglers. Nevertheless, the convoy was immensely cheered on the following evening when *Spencer*, on her way with *Dianthus* to assist a Liberator attacking a U-boat on the convoy's port beam, sighted another U-boat on the surface. *Spencer* attacked with gunfire and then with depth-charges before she had to leave – too early in Heineman's opinion. However, she had indeed sunk *U–225*.

U–604 was one of sixteen U-boats, in two groups, which B-Dienst reports had enabled BdU to deploy ahead of ONS166. That night of 21–22 February ONS166 passed out of range of air cover and a five-day battle began, which stretched over 1,000 miles of sea. No less than seventeen U-boats in all were in contact with the convoy at one time or another. Although Heineman's ships determinedly fought them off, the U-boats eventually sank fourteen ships, of more than 85,000 tons, including the rescue ship *Stockport*, torpedoed like *Toward* when she was rejoining the convoy from astern (and therefore behaving very much like a straggler).

On the escort's side, *Campbell* and *Burza* attacked *U–606* on 22 February. *Campbell* finally sank the U-boat by gunfire and ramming, after which *Campbell* herself was left helpless and had to be taken in tow by *Burza*. Heineman's multi-national group was thereafter nicknamed 'Heineman's Harriers'.

On 1 March, 1943, there were nearly seventy U-boats – more than ever before – at sea in the north Atlantic, and the number was increasing with every day. There was also a cryptographic setback for GC & CS during that month. One of the main ways of breaking into the 'Shark' Enigma had been through a code book the U-boats used for their short weather reports. A copy taken from *U–559*, sunk north of Port Said on 30 October, 1942, had greatly helped GC & CS to break the 'Shark' key in December. On 10 March, 1943, the U-boats began to use a new book and OIC and the Admiralty Tracking Room faced another Enigma blackout. However, despite the most pessimistic forecasts, GC & CS broke back in nine days. Marvellous achievement though this was, it was unfortunately not enough to forestall another convoy disaster.

March 1943, was a good month for the B-Dienst Service, who enjoyed a consistently successful period. On 3 March, B-Dienst decrypted part of the routeing instructions for the fifty-nine-ship SC121. Forewarned, BdU deployed two groups, the '*Westmark*' of seventeen U-boats and the '*Ostmark*' of nine in the convoy's path. It was *U–405*, one of the '*Westmark*' boats, which duly sighted SC121 on 6 March; in such bad weather and heavy seas, several ships were straggling.

The escort was Heineman's Harriers, of *Spencer* and the US destroyer *Greer*, with the corvette *Dianthus* and two Canadian corvettes *Rosthern* and *Trillium* who had been with ONS 166. Heineman was an aggressive and very able commander but he and his ships had had only the barest minimum time in harbour for rest and recovery after their experience with ONS 166. Heineman's Harriers sailed again with tired crews and numerous defects in their Asdics, radar, W/T and H/F D/F, caused by the very bad weather and lack of time for repairs.

The battle began on the night of 6–7 March and lasted for five days during which the seventeen U-boats involved pursued the convoy eastwards night and day, in bitter cold and unusually bad weather even for March, 1943, with Force 10 gales, frequent storms of hail and rain, mixed with blinding snow blizzards. The escort was reinforced by the arrivals of *Bibb, Ingham* and *Babbitt* and RAF Liberators, all from Iceland on 9 March, and by the corvettes *Mallow* and *Campion* on the 10th. Many U-boats were driven off in counter-attacks, but they still sank thirteen ships, of nearly 60,000 tons, before they finally broke off on 11 March. No U-boats were sunk.

As the battle around SC121 was ending, far to the south-east another battle around the next eastbound convoy, HX228, was just beginning. 'Shark' decrypts for 5–7 March had revealed that the '*Raubgraf*' Group of U-boats was waiting in HX228's track, and it was therefore diverted in plenty of time to a more southerly course. But this diversion was itself decrypted by the B-Dienst Service, who thus obtained HX228's new course, and its estimated position for 8 March. Thirteen U-boats of the '*Neuland*' Group were deployed to search for it.

The diversion to the south nearly saved HX228. But the sixty-ship convoy was sighted at midday on 10 March by the most southerly '*Neuland*' boat, U–336, which was detected by H/F D/F and driven off. The convoy was defended by a very experienced escort group, B3, under Commander A. A. Tait, in the destroyer *Harvester*, with another destroyer *Escapade*, the Polish destroyers *Garland* and *Burza*, the corvettes *Narcissus* and *Orchis*, and the Free French corvettes *Aconit*, *Roselys* and *Renoncule*. The escort was also reinforced from 5 to 14 March by the 6th Support Group, of the American escort carrier USS *Bogue* and the destroyers USS *Belknap* and *Osmond-Ingram*.

The main battle took place during the night of 10–11 March. The shadower was U–444, who summoned up five more U-boats, including U–221, commanded by an up-and-coming ace, Kapitan Leutnant Trojer. U–221 sank two ships and hit a third. Trojer said later that he 'fired two torpedoes at two large overlapping merchant ships. First torpedo hit. Ship disintegrated completely in flames and a vast cloud of smoke. Hundreds of steel plates flew like sheets of paper through the air. A great deal of ammunition exploded. Shortly afterwards scored another hit on a freighter, which also exploded. From bows to bridge the ship was underwater. Heavy débris crashed against my periscope which now became difficult to turn. The whole boat re-echoed with bangs and crashes.'

120

Trojer was so near his next target he had to go astern to avoid it. The detonation of his own torpedo was so close it caused his periscope 'to go completely black' and heavy fragments of the stricken ship rained down as though the U-boat itself was under gunfire. In the same attack U–757 hit a Norwegian ammunition ship, *Brant County*, which blew up with an explosion so violent that U–757 itself was damaged.

That night three U-boats fired the new FAT (*Flachen Absuchender* or *Feder Apparat Torpedo*) 'pattern-running' torpedoes. These could be fired from a target's beam and, when they had run the estimated range, turned onto the target's estimated course and 'weaved' either side of it for some distance. This was the first time they had been used in action, and none of them hit.

U–444 sank one ship but was sighted on the surface by *Harvester* whilst withdrawing and was forced to dive. *Harvester* made a quick accurate attack with depth-charges which blew U–444 to the surface. After some violent manoeuvres, *Harvester* rammed the U-boat and was locked together with it for some time with her port propeller entangled in the U-boat's hydroplanes. U–444 broke away and made off, badly damaged, but was found an hour later, still on the surface, by *Aconit* (Lieutenant-Commander Lavasseur) and was sunk by ramming.

Harvester meanwhile made the best way she could on one shaft to rejoin her convoy. But the starboard engine also broke down on the following morning. *Harvester* lay immobile until shortly before noon when U–432 hit her with two torpedoes. *Harvester* broke in two and sank, taking Tait and most of his ship's company with her. But, once again, *Aconit* was there to take revenge. She located U–432, attacked and damaged it with depth-charges, and finally finished it off on the surface with gunfire and ramming – her second U-boat kill of the day.

Attacks by four or more U-boats were repulsed later that day, 11 March, and the last shadower, U–590, was driven off on the 12th. The convoy had lost four ships and an escort, but two U-boats had been sunk. The escort carrier *Bogue* had much less effect upon the battle than had been hoped and expected. The weather prevented flying for much of the time and *Bogue* had mostly remained within the body of the convoy, because of the great danger of U-boat attacks, and her freedom of movement, to fly off and land her aircraft, seems to have been seriously restricted.

Those same 'Shark' decrypts of 5–7 March also affected the courses of the next two eastbound convoys, SC122 and HX229, both of which were routed to the south instead of taking their intended north-easterly course along the coast of Newfoundland. But, as it happened, these diversions were not enough to prevent SC122 and HX229 experiencing the biggest single convoy disaster of the war. BdU was about to demonstrate what the U-boats could do if there was adequate advance intelligence warning and enough U-boats favourably placed to take full advantage of it.

11 | THE U-BOAT WAR,
CONVOYS HX229 AND SC122
March, 1943

'*Die grosste Geleitzugschlacht aller Zeiten* – the greatest convoy battle of all time', proclaimed German radio, with some justifiable hyperbole, on 20 March, 1943. Signals from U-boats who took part in this 'greatest convoy battle' claimed to have sunk thirty-two merchant ships, of 186,000 tons, and one destroyer. A jubilant broadcast from BdU confirmed the number of sinkings, but increased the tonnage to 204,000. BdU's claim was exaggerated, but that was no consolation for the Admiralty. The truth was quite bad enough.

SC122 sailed from New York on 5 March, 1943. Several ships had joined and left by 12 March, when the convoy came under the care of its ocean escort, but the final order was fifty ships (with one, *Clarissa Radcliffe*, already a straggler) disposed in thirteen columns. The ocean escort was a strong and experienced one, B5 Escort Group, under Commander R. C. Boyle DSO in the destroyer *Havelock*, with the frigate *Swale*, the corvettes *Buttercup*, *Godetia*, *Lavender*, *Pimpernel* and *Saxifrage*, the US destroyer *Upshur*, and the trawler *Campobello*. The rescue ship was *Zamalek*.

The faster convoy HX229, of forty ships in eleven columns, sailed from New York on 8 March and was met by its ocean escort, B4 Escort Group, on the 14th. B4 was also an experienced Group but its leader, Commander E. C. L. Day, had had to remain in St John's, Newfoundland, while repairs were completed to the asdic dome of his destroyer *Highlander*. Temporary command devolved on Lieutenant-Commander G. J. Luther, in the destroyer *Volunteer*, who actually belonged to B5 and was therefore a stranger to the ships in B4. Luther was an anti-submarine warfare specialist, who believed in taking the offensive against the U-boats. But he had made only one previous Atlantic convoy crossing, during which no U-boat had been detected,

123

and had never commanded an escort group. With *Volunteer* were the destroyers *Beverley*, *Witherington* and *Mansfield*, who were joined on the 15th by the corvettes *Anemone* and *Pennywort*. There was no rescue ship.

At that stage of the war there were so many ships in New York waiting to sail and the pressure to clear them was so great that a third convoy HX229A, of thirty-nine ships, sailed on 9 March, escorted by 40th Escort Group, of four sloops and two frigates. This convoy was routed to the north of its two predecessors and although it was in no sense intended as a decoy, was to become a source of confusion to BdU.

SC122 and HX229 were to have been routed to the north so as to pass through 60° N 35° W (about 300 miles east of Cape Farewell, the southernmost point of Greenland). But the 'Shark' decrypts of 5–7 March revealed a group of sixteen U-boats disposed in a patrol line across the convoy path. Both convoys were therefore rerouted to the south. But there was then a Shark 'blackout' until p.m. on 17 March, an interval which proved to be critical for both convoys.

Meanwhile, on 12 March, the B–Dienst Service learned the original route of HX229 from a decrypt of a signal of 4 March. Another decrypt, of a signal of 12 March, obtained in the forenoon of 14 March or the afternoon of the 15th, gave the B–Dienst Service a position for HX229 on the new route. A third decrypt obtained at about the same time, from a signal of 13 March, revealed that HX229 was to proceed on a course of 089°, and not its original 028°, and that SC122 was to proceed on a course of 073° or 067° (B–Dienst was not sure which).

With the benefit of these decrypts, BdU was able to throw his U-boat packs across the likeliest convoy paths. At that time a reorganized 'Raubgraf' Group of nine U-boats, which had just been searching unsuccessfully for ONS169, was spread out in a patrol line to the north-east, in advance of SC122's original course. But when the decrypts provided fresh information on SC122's new more easterly courses, BdU decided that SC122 was steering 067° and ordered the 'Raubgraf' Group to move first to the south and then, later on 15 March, after a period in which no ships had been sighted, some 45 miles to the east. A much larger 'Stuermer' Group, of eighteen U-boats, formed from U-boats which had operated against SC121 and some new arrivals, was drawn up further to the east but also in SC122's anticipated path. A third 'Draenger' Group, of another eleven U-boats, which had operated against HX228, lay even further to the east and south, to lie in wait for HX229. By 15 March, therefore, BdU had disposed no less than thirty-eight U-boats in positions where they were likely to intercept SC122 or HX229.

BdU knew the convoys' routes, but not how far along them the convoys had advanced. SC122, with a westerly gale behind it, made

124

better progress than BdU had expected. By the time the '*Raubgraf*' Group had taken up its more easterly position, SC122 was already through the line and some 75 miles to the east of it. The '*Raubgraf*' boats continued to search for SC122 until midday on 15 March when, no contact having been made, BdU decided that the correct course should have been decrypted as 073° (and not 967°). He ordered the '*Raubgraf*' boats to move 15 miles to the south and to sweep along a course of 073°.

BdU knew that HX229 was somewhere to the south and astern of SC122, but did not know its exact position. In fact, HX229 had also made such good progress that it was ahead of BdU's estimate, and was the first of the two convoys to be sighted.

It was one of the '*Raubgraf*' boats, U–91, which sighted and reported a destroyer (in the outer screen of HX229) steering north-east on the evening of 15 March, and assumed it was the convoy. Three more '*Raubgraf*' boats were ordered to take action on U–91's report, while the rest were to carry on steering east at 7 knots. BdU's instructions were that if the four '*Raubgraf*' boats operating on the report had not gained contact during the night, all nine boats were to regroup in a new patrol line ahead of the convoy's path by 1900 on 16 March. Long before that, just after midnight on the 16th, U–91 had obtained a hydrophone contact and steered to investigate. Even so, the convoy might still have managed to steam clear, but by ill luck it was sighted at 0725 that morning by U–653, which was not from any of the three Groups but had withdrawn for repairs after sinking a straggler from ON170 on 12 March, and just happened to be in the vicinity.

BdU thought U–653's sighting was the SC convoy. In fact, it was HX229. BdU's mistake was understandable: not only was HX229 some distance ahead of where BdU expected it, but BdU had been further misled by another garbled decrypt which suggested, erroneously, that the HX convoy had been diverted again to a course of 350° and was therefore some way away to the north-west.

But, whatever the convoy's number, at 0800 on 16 March BdU ordered the whole '*Raubgraf*' Group to 'get up and at 'em!' He also summoned up more U-boats: U–228 and U–616, which had been refuelling, and eleven boats of the '*Stuermer*' Group, which had been patrolling to the north-east ahead of both convoys since 1900 on 14 March and which were now closing on a course of 260°. BdU reassured the U-boats that the escort was a weak one and there was no air cover.

On that day, 16 March, the U-boats began to stream towards the convoy's reported position. Six '*Raubgraf*' boats, U–758, U–664, U–84, U–615, U–91, and U–600, and the singleton U–653, all made contact with the convoy or stragglers at some time during the afternoon. At 1516 *U–653* reported that it had been forced to dive by the escort and at one stage the convoy had passed right overhead. BdU signalled general instructions to all U-boats that afternoon: 'Good position is of the greatest importance in this area on account of the very irregular currents where the Gulf Stream and the Labrador Stream meet. After sinking vessels proceeding independently, operate at once at maximum speed against the convoy.'

More U-boats were approaching by the hour. *U–89*, which had been on its way to refuel, and *U–603*, both made contact that evening. Even this was not enough: at 2053 on 16 March BdU ordered the '*Draenger*' Group, on patrol to the eastward, to operate against the convoy, adjusting their speed so as to arrive during the afternoon of 17 March.

The first boat to attack, at 2200 that evening, was *U–653* which sank the Norwegian *Elin K*. Next was *U–758*, which sank the Dutch *Zaanland* and torpedoed the American Liberty ship *James Oglethorpe*; the ship turned back towards St John's but was later finished off, with great loss of life amongst her crew, by *U–91* (Kapitan-Leutnant Walkerling). The '*Raubgraf*' boat *U–435*, though having a defective starboard main motor, torpedoed and damaged another Liberty ship, *William Eustis*, in the early hours of the 17th. This ship was abandoned by her crew, shelled as a wreck by the escort, and finally finished off by *U–91*. At about 5 a.m. on the 17th *U–600* (Kapitan-Leutnant Zurmuhlen) hit three ships with one FAT salvo which sank the 12,000 ton tanker *Southern Princess* and crippled the Royal Mail steamer *Nariva* and the American *Irenee Dupont*. Both these were dispatched by the scavenging *U–91*, which had also sunk *Henry Luckenbach*, with the loss of almost her entire company, an hour earlier. *U–91* also claimed two more ships damaged in its attacks and BdU ordered other U-boats in the area to sink them and to take at least one prisoner, preferably the Master or the Chief Engineer, from each ship. Though several U-boats searched, only *U–603* saw any ships but had no torpedoes left.

Thus, when dawn came, HX229 had lost eight ships. The U-boats' task had been made easier because Luther, having no rescue ship, had allowed two of the escorts to drop astern to pick up survivors; it was always difficult for an escort commander to decide the balance of importance between present survivors and future attacks, and whatever decision he made was bound to be controversial.

U–600 and *U–435* both continued to shadow after their attacks until they lost contact, *U–600* at about 10 a.m. on 17th, and *U–435*, because of its engine defects, in the afternoon. But meanwhile the first two '*Stuermer*' boats, *U–228* and *U–190*, had closed the convoy during the night. Walkerling in *U–91* had previously signalled that the escort was weak, but this was not the experience of other U-boats who found Luther's group only too ready to counter-attack. *U–89* had been driven off shortly after 5 a.m. that morning and had to retire to a supply U-boat to refuel. At 0850 on the 17th *U–228* attempted an attack with one torpedo on *Volunteer*, Luther's own ship, but missed and was heavily attacked, driven down and damaged by depth-charges from *Volunteer* and *Beverley*.

Meanwhile, away to the north-east, Kapitan-Leutnant Manfred Kinzel in one of the 'Stuermer' boats, *U–338*, had sighted SC122, in bright moonlight, at about 2 a.m. on 17 March. Once again, it was a case of most damage being done by a few U-boats. Kinzel reported the sighting and closed at once to attack, sliding between two escorts and firing a salvo – one of the most successful in the whole battle of the Atlantic – of five torpedoes, of which four hit and sank *Kingsbury*, *King Gruffydd* and *Fort Cedar Lake* and the Dutch *Alderamin*. Not content, Kinzel surfaced, pursued the convoy, and sank his fifth ship, the American *Granville*, that afternoon.

Two more 'Stuermer' boats, *U–665* and *U–631*, arrived ahead of HX229 at daylight on the 17th but, also at daylight, the situation changed dramatically, for convoys and U-boats, with the arrival of air cover, at the unprecedented ranges of 1,000 miles, for HX229, and 900 miles for SC122. By noon two U-boats had been attacked and forced down.

Kinzel had signalled details of his success, but his transmission was not picked up, either by BdU or the Allies. But his first sighting signal, at 0202 on the 17th, had caused BdU some puzzlement. BdU still believed, from the misleadingly garbled decrypt of 15 March, that HX229 was away to the north-west and that the convoy presently under attack was SC122. But Kinzel's signal showed that SC122, if it was SC122, was much further to the north and east than had been supposed. Furthermore, another U-boat, *U–439*, signalled at 0818 on the 17th, just before it was forced down by an aircraft, that it had sighted smoke clouds even further to the north and east. BdU ordered Kinzel to confirm his sighting position and, as a precaution (still knowing nothing of Kinzel's successes), ordered six of the 'Stuermer' Group to close *U–338*'s sighting position, having assumed that these ships were a faster group of the main convoy. But while BdU was still trying to tease some meaning out of a jumble of contact reports and attacks, there was even more confusion. When Kinzel eventually transmitted another position report later, the coordinates given in his signal must have been encyphered wrongly, because they seemed to show that *U–338* really was in contact with HX229 and not SC122. The error was not realized for another 24 hours. BdU therefore cancelled the order to the 'Stuermer' boats. However, almost at once U–527 reported more smoke clouds from the same area up to the north. BdU then ordered U–439 to confirm his earlier 'smoke clouds' report and once more ordered the 'Stuermer' boats to close the position, which was, in fact, SC122.

The general position now was that HX229 was catching up SC122, and pulling the U-boats after it, until HX229, SC122 and several U-boats were all very close together and thus a comparatively small area of the Atlantic Ocean was densely populated by a great mass of merchant shipping in two convoys, with their escorts, all wallowing about in very heavy seas and a following westerly wind, who were surrounded by U-boats: the 'Raubgraf' boats following up from the west, the 'Stuermer' boats closing from the north-east and east, while the 'Draenger' boats still lay in wait to the south-east.

Meanwhile, the U-boats were still trailing HX229 during the forenoon of 17 March, with two 'Stuermer' boats, U–631 and U–384, in contact. They penetrated the convoy screen just after 1 p.m. and sank two ships: U–384 sank the British Coracero and possibly the Dutch East Indiaman Terkolei (also possibly shared by U–631). Both U-boats were counter-attacked, while the convoy drew away out of range. There were no more attacks on HX229 that day. U–600 and U–134 were still shadowing, but were put down by aircraft. The convoy ran over both boats at about teatime and both lost contact. U–221, the nearest and most dangerous of the 'Draenger' boats, was bombed by aircraft before Trojer had had a chance to sight the convoy, and thus he did not find HX229 until the following day.

However, 17 March continued to be a busy day for SC122. Five 'Stuermer' boats apparently passed astern of the convoy while approaching HX229 but another six U-boats were still searching. One 'Stuermer', U–305, sighted SC122 at 1.45 p.m. but was at once driven down and depth-charged by an aircraft (the first of four aircraft attacks on this U-boat on 17 and 18 March). A second 'Stuermer', U–439, also found the convoy but was attacked and kept down for four hours. Both convoys had suffered grievously, but there is no doubt that the presence of the aircraft prevented a massacre.

After Kinzel had sunk Granville, his fifth victim from SC122, on the afternoon of 17 March, he was counter-attacked by Godetia and Upshur. The weather had worsened, with the wind rising to a full gale, bringing heavy snow blizzards, but the two escorts stayed with their target and depth-charged U–338 for four hours. Kinzel, on his first patrol, was a determined and persistent opponent. Although U–338 was damaged in these attacks, Kinzel tried again on 18th, was depth-charged and damaged by Lavender, but attacked again and was damaged a third time by a Sunderland on 19 March before he finally gave up. But late in the evening of 17 March, another determined U-boat captain, Kapitan Leutnant Bahr, also on his first patrol in *U–305*, closed SC122 (although he had already been attacked by aircraft three times that day) and sank *Port Auckland* and *Zouave*.

That evening BdU decided that, after all, there must be two convoys, in close proximity to each other, and ordered six 'Stuermer' boats and the northern half of the 'Draenger' line to operate against HX229. These dispositions were still unknown to the OIC because the Shark 'blackout', which had begun on 11 March, had still not ended. However, it was still possible for the OIC to draw general conclusions from the actual appearance of an undecrypted signal – the type of Enigma code being used, the number of letter groups, even the length of the signal – and decide whether it was a U-boat position report, or a sighting report, or orders from BdU for U-boats to take up new dispositions.

It was also still possible to strengthen the escort. By the morning of 18 March HX229 had five escorts: *Volunteer*, *Beverley*, *Anemone*, *Pennywort* and *Witherington*, who had to detach later in the day. (*Mansfield* had already had to leave, because of shortage of fuel.) Five escorts did not seem much but it was more than the convoy had had for much of the time when, for one reason or another, the escorts had dropped to three or even two and for a period to none at all. But Commander Day in *Highlander* joined during 18 March, and more reinforcements were on the way.

The most dangerous, indeed the only really effective, opponent on 18 March was Trojer in *U–221* who found HX229 and attacked at about 3.30 p.m. He sank the Blue Star Line refrigerated ship *Canadian Star* and the Liberty ship *Walter Q. Gresham*, but was himself then attacked by aircraft, broke off his patrol and started for home.

No other U-boat captain could match Trojer that day. *U–134* attacked just before 7 p.m., and shadowed until he was driven off. *U–610* and *U–439* both reported counter-attacks and both gave up. *U–441* made several attempts to attack between 3.30 and 5 a.m. on the morning of the 19th but achieved nothing. At least seven more U-boats stayed in touch with the convoy until the forenoon of 19th, but none of them made an attack.

Late on 18 March the Master of the American *Matthew Luckenbach* decided that, as he had a 15-knot ship and this was only a 9-knot convoy, he would do better alone at his full speed and, against strict convoy orders, forged ahead. This behaviour, known as 'romping', was much rarer than straggling but just as dangerous and *Matthew Luckenbach* was duly sunk by *U–527* and *U–523* the next day, though happily with no loss of life. The last casualty actually in convoy was the Greek *Caras*, torpedoed early on 19 March by *U–666* and finished off later by *U–333*. Lastly, there was *Clarissa Radcliffe*, who had been a straggler for days and was never seen or heard from again. Possibly she was the independent ship which *U–663* claimed to have sunk at about 2 p.m. on 18 March.

The action began to slacken late on 19 March and ended on the 20th when BdU decided that air cover was too heavy. At 9.34 a.m. on the 19th, *U–384* was attacked and sunk by a Sunderland of 201 Squadron about 40 miles astern of HX229. This was the only U-boat to be sunk during the battles around HX229 and SC122. However, HX229's surface escorts expended 229 depth-charges, in making eleven attacks, and damaged five U-boats. SC122's escort used sixty-nine depth-charges in seven attacks and damaged two U-boats. Aircraft flew thirty-two sorties in support of the convoys, made twenty-five sightings of U-boats, dropped eighty depth-charges in twenty-one attacks, damaged six U-boats and sank one. Forty-one U-boats had taken part, of which thirty-three U-boats in all made contact with the convoys at one time or another and there were seventeen torpedo attacks. They sank thirteen ships from HX229 and another nine from SC122, for a total tonnage of 146,596. The trawler *Campobello* was also lost through bad weather.

The number of U-boats operating in the North Atlantic, already seventy on 1 March, had grown steadily throughout the month, so that on 22 March, when the battles around HX229 and SC122 had just ended, Pound informed the Anti-U-boat Warfare Committee that 'we could no longer rely on evading the U-boat packs, and, hence, we shall have to fight the convoys through them'. On the 30th, after the losses from HX229 and SC122 had been studied, he told the committee that although very bad weather, defects in the escorts and patchy air cover could all be held partly responsible for the losses, a state had nevertheless been reached where 'the Atlantic is now becoming so saturated by U-boats that the practice of evasion is rapidly becoming impossible'.

When the first successful U-boats from HX229 and SC122 began to return from their patrols, German propaganda quite justifiably proclaimed a great victory and gleefully crowed over the episode in a way it had not been able to do since those first happy halcyon days of October, 1940. If nothing else, the celebrations over the feats of this new generation of U-boat aces did help to take the German people's minds off the recent catastrophe suffered by the Sixth Army at Stalingrad.

For the Allies, it did indeed seem to be one of the darkest times in the whole battle of the Atlantic. Forty-one ships had been lost in the first ten days of March. In the next ten days, another fifty-four were lost, for a total loss of more than half a million tons. Nor was there the consolation of knowing that equivalent losses were being inflicted upon the U-boats; only seven U-boats had been sunk around the convoys in the same period. The total sunk by U-boats in March, 1943, was 108 ships, of 627,377 tons. From all causes, 120 ships of 693,000 tons were lost that month – the worst figures since November, 1942.

The Admiralty's own appreciation of the situation was that 'the Germans never came so near to disrupting communications between the New World and the Old as in the first twenty days of March, 1943'. But much more ominous than the sheer scale of the losses was the fact that nearly two-thirds of those ships had been sunk *whilst in convoy*. The loss of twenty-two ships from HX229 and SC122, following the terrible experiences of SC121 and ON166, and further losses from convoys such as HX228, sent shock waves of alarm around the Admiralty. Such losses did make it appear that if the enemy had as much accurate intelligence as he appeared to have, and enough U-boats favourably placed, as he clearly did have, then evasive routeing certainly would become impossible and putting ships in convoy and sending them out to meet the U-boat packs would be like herding dumb animals together and driving them into an abattoir.

In some quarters, the principle of convoy itself began to be questioned and there was talk of a return to independent routeing, which had proved so bloodily insufficient from 1914 to 1917. 'It appeared possible,' wrote the Naval Staff, 'that we should not be able to continue convoy as an effective system of defence.' This was an admission of a possibility which had the most appalling implications. Convoy was the very rock and foundation stone of Allied strategy in the war at sea. Convoy had been the Navy's very present help in trouble since medieval times. It was unthinkable that convoy could fail. Yet, that very possibility was apparently being considered.

In fact, the gloom over HX229 and SC122 was tending to obscure some real successes which had been happening at the same time. HX229A, besides temporarily confusing BdU, had passed by far to the north with only one loss, a tanker wrecked on an iceberg. The next eastbound convoy, HC230, had also lost only one ship, a straggler. SC123, which had the services of the carrier USS *Bogue* and her group, and ONS1 were both completely unscathed.

It was at this stage in the war at sea, when matters appeared at their blackest, that ULTRA performed one of its most valuable services to the Allied cause, by giving a vital sense of confidence to those who

131

knew its secret. For, significantly, the general mood of alarm and despondency about convoy was certainly not shared by the staff of OIC who, through the Enigma decrypts, rubbed their minds daily against those of BdU and his staff. Every day, in the decrypts, OIC could read the U-boat captains' constant complaints about the ever-increasing threat from the air, and they could sense in BdU's signals to his U-boats his underlying uneasiness, his reluctance to reprove and his eagerness to encourage. It was quite clear in the OIC that BdU was not behaving at all like a commander who was just about to accomplish a great victory. On the contrary, he was looking much more like a man who was slowly losing his power to control events, and knowing it.

In truth, the principle of convoy was as sound as it had ever been. Nothing of real importance had changed. Of the twenty-two merchant ships lost from HX229 and SC122, fifteen were sunk during a period of 24 hours when the convoys were without air cover. Most of the sinkings were the handiwork of no more than four U-boats; for instance, four of SC122's nine losses occurred during one determined moonlight attack by Kinzel in *U–338*. HX229 had had a weak escort, with an inexperienced escort commander, and no rescue ship. Even so, several of the attacks might have been successful; given a little more luck, a little more time, and one or two more ships in the right places, and probably two of those near-misses by Luther's ships would have been kills.

The horrific shipping losses of March, 1943, prompted President Roosevelt to enquire where the Very-Long-Range Liberators were being employed. It had been agreed at the Casablanca conference in January that more VLR aircraft were to be allocated to the Atlantic. It transpired that, at a time when the US Navy had seventy VLR Liberators in the Pacific, not one VLR Liberator was employed between Newfoundland and Iceland. A total of 225 VLR Liberators was allocated to the Atlantic and the first twenty were operational by the end of March, 1943.

The effect of the arrival of these VLR aircraft over and around the convoys was immediate and almost magical. It was as though the skies were literally clearing and even the weather had begun to improve. At last the infamous mid-Atlantic 'gap' was closed and from that moment the battle began to swing away from the U-boats.

The improvement took place over a matter of weeks. No longer was there this nightmare feeling of helplessness, of being surrounded by shoals of predatory U-boats waiting in lines to intercept the convoys which had no escape, no means of routeing available. In convoy after convoy, the feeling now was that the escorts were improving with

132

every trip, while the U-boats' confidence was beginning to falter, especially under the ever-increasing fear of air attack.

On 4 April *U–530*, which was returning from patrol, sighted HX231, just west of the '*Lowenherz*' Group patrol line. *U–530*'s report brought up another five boats and two more in the night. BdU urged them to attack at once, stressing the importance of attacking on the first night (in strong contrast to his earlier advice against SC118 in February, that the 'main blow' should come later) but the sixty-one ship convoy was very ably defended by the Escort Group B7, of the frigate *Tay*, the destroyer *Vidette* and four corvettes. The U-boats sank six ships, of which three were stragglers, but Liberators of No. 86 Sq RAF sank *U–635* on 5 April and during the following night *U–632* attacked and missed the corvette *Alisma* but was then sunk by *Tay*. The 4th Support Group, of four destroyers, joined the convoy in the morning, and with the air escort, drove off the six U-boats still in contact. BdU was dissatisfied by the performance of so many U-boats (actually thirteen '*Lowenherz*' boats, with the sighter *U–530* and two more boats in the area) sinking only six ships, and reprimanded them for excessive use of radio!

Convoys continued to be attacked by U-boats placed in their path by information from the B-Dienst Service, but none of them suffered losses on the scale of HX229 and SC122. On 10 April ON176 was sighted by *U–404* of the '*Adler*' Group of ten U-boats deployed south of Greenland and lost two ships and the destroyer *Beverley*. On 11 April the '*Lerche*' Group of ten boats was deployed to intercept HX232. BdU's orders for this deployment and his exhortations to the U-boats to show 'healthy hunter and warrior instincts' were decrypted and the Submarine Tracking Room could see HX232 heading straight for the line. HX232 was ordered to make a drastic alteration of course away. But the convoy was nearer the '*Lerche*' boats than estimated and the alteration was not enough. *U–584* sighted the convoy where it had expected to sight it and three ships from HX232 were lost in that first night. But five U-boats had to break off action with ON176 and HX232 because of damage. All they received for their pains was a reproof from BdU who suspected them of not pressing home their attacks.

On 14 April the '*Meise*' Group was ordered to operate against SC126, but through the 'Shark' Enigma SC126 was diverted safely away. Four days later, an augmented '*Meise*' Group of twenty-one U-boats was placed ahead of HX234. The convoy was sighted by *U–306* on the 21st. But only one ship was lost. While closing HX234, some of the '*Meise*' boats came across ONS3 and ON178. They sank three ships, but three U-boats were sunk and there were no more U-boat

133

successes in attacks on convoys for the rest of April. SC127 was successfully diverted, and ONS4 and ON179 were evasively routed away from attacks. Thus, April, 1943, was a much better month: U-boats sank fifty-six ships of 327,943 tons – bad enough, but only just over half the figures for March.

The figures were at least encouraging. Even more heartening, for the OIC if for nobody else, was the reaction of BdU to the figures, and to the increasingly vehement complaints from U-boats at sea about the severity of air attack and the efficiency of the escorts in following up aircraft sightings. At last it began to be impressed upon the U-boats that silence was golden. From mid-April they were ordered to maintain strict W/T silence whilst in a patrol line.

May, 1943, was the crucial month in the Atlantic. From the beginning of that month the total number of U-boats at sea began to climb to its peak. On 10 May the OIC estimated that the number of operational U-boats at sea was 128, 'the highest ever known'. Worse, most of them were fresh into battle: ninety-eight had sailed in April and most of those during the second half of the month. On 3 May the number of U-boats positively identified by the OIC at sea in the North Atlantic was over sixty and that would surely be an underestimate. Their positions and deployments were not known precisely because there had been an interruption in the flow of 'Shark' Enigma decrypts. The settings had not been broken since 26 April.

But enough was known or could be deduced to show that BdU was now summoning the U-boat Arm for a supreme effort. The U-boats would be disposed so as to eliminate any chance of missing the eastbound convoys. There would be so many U-boats that even with the help of the 'Shark' Enigma decrypts there would be no chance of evasive routeing. BdU was confident. 'On the basis of the available information,' said the German summary, 'and an appreciation of the new pattern [of patrol lines] it was estimated on 1 May that by 3 May all routes would be blocked from 53° N, 48° W around to 46° N, 38° W.' On the morning of 28 April, 1943, one of the 'Star' Group of U-boats on patrol south of Iceland sighted ships in the most easterly column of convoy ONS5 and began to shadow. A climactic battle in the Atlantic struggle was about to begin.

12 | THE U-BOAT WAR, CONVOY ONS5
May, 1943

Convoy ONS5 took departure from the United Kingdom, bound for Halifax, on 21 April, 1943. There were forty-three ships, of nine nationalities: British, American, Greek, Panamanian, Dutch, Danish, Norwegian, Yugoslavian and Polish (although the Pole had to turn back after a few hours because of engine trouble). The ocean escort, which joined off Oversay on the 22nd, was the battle-hardened and very experienced B7 Escort Group, led by Commander P. L. Gretton in the destroyer *Duncan*, with the frigate *Tay* and the corvettes *Sunflower*, *Snowflake*, *Pink* and *Loosestrife*. There were two trawlers, *Northern Gem* and *Northern Spray*, as rescue ships, and two escort oilers, *British Lady* and *Argon*.

ONS5 was routed unusually far north, in the hope of avoiding U-boats. Unfortunately the weather was very bad. Many of the ships, being westbound, were in ballast or lightly loaded and rolled prodigiously. Station-keeping became even more difficult than usual and ONS5's speed, officially $7\frac{1}{2}$ knots, dropped to only one or two knots for long periods when the convoy was virtually hove to. In the event this very slow progress gave the U-boats more time to get into position.

The Shark Enigma intercepts were available from 20 to 26 April, when there was a break of several days, until 5 May. It was known that the '*Amsel*', '*Specht*' and '*Star*' Groups of U-boats were in the general area of Newfoundland, but, because of the break, no details were known and therefore it was not possible to choose a safe evasive route for ONS5.

By 26 April BdU had already made his dispositions with the aid of the B-Dienst Service which had first reported SC127. The '*Amsel*' ('Blackbird') Group, of ten U-boats, had been formed east of Newfoundland to attack SC127 but, through the 'Shark' Enigma inteccepts, the convoy was successfully diverted. After another fruitless search, for ONS4, the '*Specht*' ('Woodpecker') Group of twenty U-boats was formed to the north-east of the '*Amsel*' to lie in wait for HX235. But this convoy, too, was safely diverted so as to pass between the '*Amsel*' and '*Specht*' Groups. It also had the benefit of the 6th Support Group, including USS *Bogue*, whose aircraft drove off the five '*Amsel*' boats which did approach the convoy on 28 April. On the same day BdU formed a '*Star*' ('Starling') Group, of sixteen U-boats, in a patrol line south of Iceland, to wait for ONS5.

ONS5 meanwhile had encountered a moderate gale on the 26th, blowing from the west-north-west, dead in the convoy's teeth. Two ships collided and one had to divert, alone, to Iceland. However, the escort was strengthened by the destroyer *Vidette* who joined on the 26th with three merchant ships from Iceland. But W/T transmissions, classified as coming from a U-boat, were detected early on 28 April, and in fact *U–650*, one of the '*Star*' Group, sighted the convoy later that morning. *U–650* began to shadow and, although forced to dive several times by US Navy Catalina flying boats of VP.84 Squadron, succeeded in bringing up two more '*Star*' boats, *U–386* and *U–378*.

At noon on 28 April *Duncan* detected a U-boat transmitting from dead ahead of the convoy and apparently quite close. The escorts were soon in action. That night *U–386* was depth-charged and damaged by *Sunflower*. *U–650* and a third '*Star*' boat, *U–532*, first attacked *Duncan* and *Snowflake* and were then themselves counter-attacked. When daylight came on 29 April *U–532* was attacked again, by *Tay*, and *U–528* was damaged by a VP.84 Catalina. So far the honours had gone to the air and sea escort. But at 5.35 a.m. on the 29th the American *McKeesport* was torpedoed by a fourth '*Star*' boat, *U–258*, and sank some hours later.

The C-in-C Western Approaches had ordered the 3rd Support Group, of the destroyers *Offa*, *Oribi*, *Penn* and *Panther*, to reinforce ONS5's escort and the first of these, *Oribi* (who had been escorting SC127) joined late on 29 April. By that time the weather had worsened again and ONS5 was battling into a full gale. Station-keeping was virtually impossible and some ships became separated from the main body. Next day the weather eased slightly but the visibility deteriorated. *Oribi* tried to refuel and in so doing made such a mess of the oiler's gear that nobody else could fuel that day. This was to have serious implications for Gretton, the Escort Commander, whose own ship *Duncan* was the 'shortest-legged' of all short-legged pre-war destroyers.

That day, 30 April, passed quietly, so far as U-boats were concerned but another full gale blew up towards dusk. During the night *U–192* tried to close the convoy, was detected by H/F D/F, and driven off in a joint attack by *Sunflower* and *Snowflake*. These two were 'chummy' ships. The two captains had worked up an almost telepathic *rapport* with each other. Their ships were sometimes called *Sunflake* and *Snowflower*.

The U-boats still held off on 1 May because the weather had worsened into another full gale. By 2 May ONS5 had lost all cohesion and was no longer in any sort of convoy formation. The convoy had made only 20 miles' progress in 24 hours and most ships were at a virtual standstill, hove to as best they could manage. As ships lost the power to keep their stations in the convoy, they began to fan out, miles from one another. With ships spread over a distance of some 30 miles, it became impossible to tell which were the convoy and which were stragglers. One group of five stragglers, accompanied by *Pink*, were some miles astern. Two ships turned right round, fled before the wind and never rejoined.

The 3rd Support Group, commanded by Captain J. G. McCoy in *Offa*, with the Home Fleet destroyers *Impulsive*, *Penn* and *Panther*, joined late on 2 May, in visibility so bad that *Duncan* had to home them in with her radio signals. Gretton had tried to refuel *Duncan* during a lull, but the oiler had had to twist and turn to avoid ice floes and packs of small 'growlers' and by the time the ice had cleared, the full gale had returned and *Duncan* was not able to fuel. But, apart from *Duncan*'s fuel state, ONS5's situation was marginally improved on the day. The destroyers had arrived; most of the stragglers, except *Pink*'s little party and one or two others, had been rounded up; the convoy was once more roughly in its proper twelve columns and the aircraft were still flying. Gretton hoped that the weather, the aircraft and the escorts had persuaded BdU to leave ONS5 alone.

Sadly, such was not the case. The B-Dienst Service had located another convoy, SC128, on 29 April and BdU had formed the '*Amsel*' and '*Specht*' groups, a total of thirty-one U-boats, in a great semi-circle to intercept it. 'Do not hold back,' BdU signalled, 'something can and must be achieved by thirty-one boats.' The convoy's smoke was sighted by *U–628* on the evening of 1 May but the U-boats were lured away by flares fired by the escorts on the convoy's flank. The U-boats headed for the flares, thinking attacks were in progress. In spite of BdU's urgings, and his remarks about 'thirty-one boats', the U-boats had difficulty in staying in contact with the convoy in the bad weather and SC128 eventually steamed clear to the west of the U-boat line.

On 3 May the '*Amsel*' Group was augmented by a further thirteen U-boats and divided into four smaller groups, '*Amsel* 1', '2', '3' and '4', each of six boats, again spread out in a vast semi-circle east of Newfoundland, to await a north-east-bound convoy. The '*Specht*' and '*Star*' Groups were ordered to form reconnaissance lines to the north of the 'Amsel' Groups. By 2.50 p.m. on 3 May they were steering 205° at 4 knots, searching for the expected north- and north-east-bound convoy. But this convoy, actually SC128, was not sighted and once again passed clear to the west.

For ONS5 the night of 2–3 May passed quietly. The convoy was by then steering south-south-west and was in fairly good order, although *Pink* and *Northern Gem* were both still shepherding small parties of stragglers astern and the gale was still blowing from the convoy's starboard beam. By the morning of 3 May Gretton in *Duncan* was faced by a cruel dilemma. His ship was very low on fuel, but the enemy was clearly still in touch and he did not want to leave his Escort Group at such a time. But the weather forecast was very bad indeed and there was a possibility that *Duncan* might run out of fuel entirely and have to be towed.

The weather was too bad for boatwork or for transfer by jackstay. Gretton therefore reluctantly decided to leave the convoy and turn over command of the Group to Lieutenant-Commander R. E. Sherwood in *Tay*. Sherwood was a very experienced and capable officer and Gretton was confident of his ability. But Gretton himself was nevertheless very depressed at having to leave his convoy. *Impulsive* also had to leave for Iceland late on 3 May, and *Penn* and *Panther* had to return to St John's on the morning of the 4th. Replacements were needed: the 1st Support Group, of the sloop *Pelican* (Commander G. N. Brewer), with the frigates *Wear*, *Jed* and *Spey* and the US Coast Guard cutter *Sennen*, left St John's on 4 May to join ONS5.

BdU was also reorganizing his forces. The 'Specht' and 'Star' lines had not found the north-east-bound convoy, but, on the afternoon of 4 May, two 'Specht' boats, U–264 and U–628, both sighted destroyers, and U–264's destroyer was steering south. This was the forward screen of ONS5. These boats lost contact but just before 4 p.m. a third 'Specht' boat, U–260, also sighted a destroyer, steering south-west. These reports apparently decided BdU to search for a south-west-bound convoy, for at 1602 on 4 May twenty-seven U-boats from the 'Specht' and 'Star' Groups were formed in a new 'Fink' ('Finch') Group, spread out on a line running from north-west to south-east. They were warned to expect a convoy from 5 May onwards.

The 'Fink' line actually straddled ONS5's line of advance and at 1618 on the 4th U–358, one of the centre-forwards, reported a corvette approaching and immediately afterwards U–270, on the left wing, reported a destroyer. Finally, at 1817, U–628 reported the convoy crossing the centre of the line. BdU ordered the 'Fink' Group to operate on the basis of U–628's report and told them 'You are better placed than you ever were before'. BdU then ordered U–614 to join the 'Fink' line and encouraged them all with the signal: 'I am certain you will fight with everything you've got. Don't overestimate your opponent, but strike him dead!' By 2018 on the 4th another U-boat in the centre of the line, *U–707*, was in contact and shortly afterwards BdU ordered the '*Amsel* 1' and '2' Groups to operate against the south-west-bound convoy.

These twelve '*Amsel*' boats, with the '*Fink*' line, made a total of forty U-boats ordered to operate against ONS5. But, in fact, first blood went to the air escorts. As the convoy steamed towards the line, Canadian Cansos (Catalina flying boats) sighted *U–438* and *U–630*, the two most westerly boats of the '*Fink*' line, when they were still on their way to take up their patrol positions. *U–438* was damaged and *U–630* was sunk by an accurate clutch of depth-charges dropped by Catalina 9747, of No. 5 Squadron RCAF, just before 6 p.m. on 4 May, some two miles astern of the convoy.

The most ship losses were suffered that night. By midnight six U-boats reported being in contact. *U–125* mistakenly claimed one vessel sunk earlier, but probably sank the British *North Britain* a few minutes after midnight. At about 1 a.m. or shortly afterwards, the convoy lost the British *Harbury*, sunk by *U–628*, the US *West Maximus* and the British *Harperley* to *U–264*, and another British ship *Dolius* to *U–584*. *U–707* torpedoed the American *West Madaket* which sank the following afternoon. *U–952* later picked off the straggler *Lorient*. *U–358* sank the British steamers *Wentworth* and *Bristol City* in one attack just after 5 a.m. on 5 May. Four of the ships sunk were from Nos. 1 and 2 columns, on the convoy's port-hand easterly wing, and a fifth ship was one of *Pink*'s little flock.

Pink and *Northern Germ* were still bringing up the rear, but the main convoy of some thirty ships was defended by *Tay, Vidette, Sunflower, Snowflake, Loosestrife, Offa* and *Oribi* who counter-attacked vigorously and successfully. *Vidette* damaged *U–270* in one accurate attack. *Tay, Offa* and *Oribi* attacked in succession so effectively that *U–648, U–168* and *U–732* were depth-charged and had to retire, because of fuel shortage or damage. *U–662, U–514* and *U–707* were also heavily depth-charged and attacked by gunfire on the surface but remained operational.

By dawn on 5 May the U-boats reported five ships and one corvette sunk and five ships torpedoed. In fact, nine ships were lost though not all sank immediately. *U–514, U–531, U–260* and *U–270* were still in contact, although *U–270* was soon driven off, followed by *U–260*, who reported engine damage and claimed (wrongly) two torpedo hits. *U–413* aggrievedly reported being depth-charged by two corvettes which had pretended to be damaged and had then rounded on and attacked him (clearly, a joint *Snowflake/Sunflower* undertaking).

BdU now exhorted all U-boats operating against ONS5 to get ahead and make full use of daylight hours for submerged attack. The U-boats were to be as far ahead of the convoy as possible, because, BdU signalled, 'Immediately after onset of night the drum-roll must be timed to begin. Make haste, otherwise, as there are forty of you, there'll be nothing of the convoy left. The battles cannot last long as the sea space left is short, so use every chance to the full with all your might.'

That forenoon of 5 May seven U-boats reported ONS5 or its escorts, but their signals began to follow an ominously similar pattern: all reported contacts and went into attacks but all were almost at once repulsed, most of them with damage. In fact, by the end of the day, there were no longer forty U-boats as BdU supposed. There were not even thirty-nine, but thirty-eight. During the forenoon *Pink* obtained a very firm asdic contact, by far the clearest and sharpest they had ever heard, on a U-boat which had been sniffing around their little group, by that time some 80 miles astern of the main convoy.

Pink attacked with three charges, after which the U-boat went very deep and very quiet. The second attack shook the target 'like a rag doll in a puppy's mouth'. The U-boat tried to creep away on an opposite course but after the third attack it could be heard blowing tanks, and three huge bubbles broke surface, looking 'as if some giant soda-water syphon had been shaken up and exploded'; *U–192* was lost with all hands. *U–638* had been one of the seven U-boats which reported being in contact that morning. But its signal, 'Enemy in sight' at 9.50 a.m. was the last BdU heard from it. That night *U–638* was surprised by *Loosestrife* whilst attacking on the surface in poor visibility, driven down and briskly sunk with depth-charges at 11.30 p.m.

There were still eleven U-boats in contact that afternoon but one of them, *U–531*, transmitted its last signal at about 2 p.m. before giving up the chase. It was detected by *Oribi*'s radar just after midnight, forced down and sunk at 2.52 a.m. *U–628*, which had been shadowing almost continuously since the start, also gave up and reported that it had several defects and was proceeding to the supply U-boat. But BdU still expected much of those who were left. He ordered that from 11 p.m. radio beacon signals were to be broadcast from two boats when in contact so as to guide the others in. 'All are to make the most of the great chance tonight offers.'

Nine U-boats were in contact at dusk and another attack developed at about 8 p.m. *U–266* was the successful boat, sinking the British *Selviston* and *Gharinda* and the Norwegian *Bonde*, for a total tonnage, sunk in one attack, of over 12,000. In the falling darkness, the escorts braced themselves for another long night of strain and battle.

In fact, the worst was over. The convoy had had its last loss – thirteen ships in all – and the remaining battles were to be counter-attacks against the U-boats. Eight U-boats reported some contact during the night of 5–6 May. At one point *Tay* could see no less than seven U-boats on the surface close to her. *Sunflower* detected four U-boats in quick succession and damaged one, *U–267*, with gunfire. *Vidette* drove off three boats one after the other, and it was during this night that *Loosestrife* and *Oribi* had their successes, against *U–638* and *U–531*.

At about 3 a.m. on 6 May *U–125* reported it had been rammed (actually by *Oribi*). BdU ordered four U-boats to the rescue but *U–223* reported at 7 a.m. that it had found only a destroyer at the scene of the ramming and had been forced to dive and depth-charged enthusiastically for the next three hours. In fact, *Vidette* had already come across the disabled *U–125* just after 4 a.m. and dispatched it with depth-charges and gunfire.

The 1st Support Group, led by *Pelican*, had been closing ONS5 during the night and listening on the radio loudspeaker to the battles in progress. But at about 4 a.m. on 6 May, when *Pelican* was about ten miles from the convoy, a small contact was detected on her radar screen. Plotting showed that it was travelling at about 9 knots away from the convoy, 'probably a U-boat which had found things too hot for it'. Soon came the 'unmistakeable smell of diesel exhaust fumes' and then the U-boat itself, in the mist, on the surface, at a range of only about 200 yards, with men clearly visible in its conning tower. The U-boats' crew seemed to sight *Pelican* simultaneously – 'it must have been a ghastly shock' – and dived. But Brewer and his crew were far too experienced to miss such a gift of a chance. *Pelican* made two attacks and was rewarded by the sound of underwater 'breaking up' noises after the second. The U-boat was *U–438*, damaged by aircraft early on, and the sixth U-boat to be sunk around ONS5.

In the morning, 6 May, *Spey* discovered *U–634* on the surface, hit it three times with gunfire and, when it dived, attacked and damaged it with depth-charges. This was the twenty-fourth attempted U-boat attack made since the last merchantman was sunk. All U-boats were ordered to break off at 11.46 on 6 May. The twelve '*Amsel* 1' and '2' boats were to steer south, the rest to withdraw to the east. *U–631* then piped up for the first time, to report that it still had all its torpedoes left. BdU forebore to reply.

The statistics of the battle for ONS5 were impressive. Thirteen merchant ships had been sunk. Six U-boats had been sunk, and two more (*U–659* and *U–439*) lost in collision in the vicinity of the convoy.

141

Of the forty U-boats, all but four made some sort of signal during the battle. Five U-boats reported severe damage and twelve more reported lesser damage. The escorts had made some forty attacks and the U-boats had signalled that they were being driven off or forced to dive on twenty occasions. There were as many U-boats present as there were ships, and three and a half times as many U-boats as there were escorts.

ONS5 had therefore been a resounding victory for the escorts, especially in their tactical use of radar during the night of 5–6 May. Many U-boats had approached ONS5 on the surface, expecting to close their targets in poor visibility when the escorts would be blind. These were the tactics of 1940 and 1941. But times had changed. Almost all the escorts and many of the aircraft were now fitted with radar. It was the U-boats which had been blind.

In the convoy battles which followed ONS5 that May, the balance of profit and loss, of merchant ships sunk against U-boats sunk, began to tilt sharply against the U-boats. On 8 May Shark decrypts revealed U-boat movements in time for HX237 to be diverted. But the B-Dienst Service in turn revealed the diversion. BdU took the twelve 'Amsel 1' and '2' boats which had been waiting for ONS5 and formed a new 'Rhein' Group to operate against HX237.

The forty-six-ship HX237, escorted by C2 Escort Group, of eight escorts led by Captain Chavasse in the destroyer *Broadway*, was sighted by *U–359* on 9 May but the U-boat was driven off without making an attack. By the time HX237 reached the U-boat ambush line the escort had been strengthened by the 5th Support Group, with the escort carrier *Biter* and 811 Squadron's nine Swordfish and three Grumman Martlets. The Swordfish 'punched a hole' in the U-boats' line by forcing them down and harrying them so that they could not attack. In the actions against ONS5 BdU had instructed the U-boats to 'stay on the surface and fire when aircraft appear'. *U–403* did so, but was made to dive by approaching destroyers and lost contact.

All the 'Rhein' boats had now lost contact and dropped too far astern to take any further action. BdU formed another 'Drossel' ('Thrush') Group of eight U-boats which had been coming in from the east. *U–436* sighted HX237 in the evening of 11 May and called up *U–403* and *U–456* which together sank one straggler. *U–230* also shot down a Swordfish.

Convoys now had a variety of defences which could combine to attack U-boats. On 12 May *Broadway*, the frigate *Lagan* and a Swordfish from *Biter* together sank *U–89*. The next day a Liberator of 210 Squadron badly damaged *U–456* with an aerial Type XXIV mine; a Swordfish then called up the destroyer *Pathfinder* who sank the U-boat. Two stragglers from the convoy were sunk that day but in another combined enterprise a Sunderland of 423 Squadron, RCAF, assisted *Lagan* and the corvette *Drumheller* to sink *U–753*. Meanwhile the close escort were driving away the U-boats still in touch. On 14 May BdU gave up the operation as hopeless. The exchange rate for HX237 was three '*Drossel*' boats sunk for three stragglers.

While HX237's escort were inflicting this bruising loss on the U-boats, another convoy battle was taking place to the south, around the twenty-six-ship SC129, which was escorted by B2 Escort Group, led by Commander D. MacIntyre, a very old hand at the game, in the destroyer *Hesperus*. SC129's initial evasion course had been decoded by the B-Dienst Service and BdU had formed two more Groups, mostly of boats which had operated against ONS5, in '*Elbe* 1' of twelve boats, and '*Elbe* 2' of thirteen boats.

An '*Elbe* 2' boat, *U–504*, sighted SC129 on the evening of 11 May and reported it before being driven off. *U–402*, captained by one of the few remaining 'aces', von Forstner, closed the convoy just before dusk and sank two ships. But others were driven off by the destroyer *Whitehall* and the corvette *Clematis*, while MacIntyre himself in *Hesperus* badly damaged *U–223*, which managed to escape.

U-boats still made the fatal mistake of talking too much. Next morning *Hesperus* ran down the H/F D/F bearing of the shadower *U–186* and sank it. Eleven more U-boats reported contact during that day, 12 May, were all detected by H/F D/F and by nightfall had all been driven off without sinking any ships. The 5th Support Group had been steaming at full speed to reinforce SC129 and *Biter*'s Swordfish were flying around the convoy early on 13 May. They were joined that afternoon by Liberators of 86 Squadron RAF, one of whom sank *U–266* (which had attacked ONS5) astern of SC129 on 14 May. The final score for SC129 was therefore two ships sunk (both by von Forstner) for two U-boats.

On 11 and 12 May, acting on information from the B-Dienst Service, BdU formed three Groups, each of four U-boats and each picturesquely named after rivers, '*Isar*', '*Lech*' and '*Inn*', in a wide semi-circle south-east of Cape Farewell, to await ONS7. This forty-ship convoy was escorted by the B5 Group, of six escorts and the rescue ship *Copeland*. It was sighted on the night of 11–12 May by *U–640* which was actually on passage to join another group. Although repeatedly driven off, *U–640* shadowed for three days and its reports enabled a five-boat '*Iller*' Group to be formed. But *U–640* was then bombed and sunk by an American Catalina of VP–84 Squadron, and all the other boats lost contact.

BdU then formed two larger Groups, '*Donau* 1' of eleven U-boats and 'Donau 2' of twelve. One 'Donau 1' boat, U–657, sank the British ship Aymeric on the night of 16–17 May but was immediately counter-attacked and sunk by the frigate Swale. Two more boats, U–646 and U–273, were sunk by Hudsons of 269 Squadron RAF from Iceland on 17 and 19 May while they were on passage to take up their patrol stations. The grim exchange rate for BdU was four U-boats sunk around ONS7, for the 5196-ton Aymeric.

The boats which had been unsuccessful against ONS7 were redirected south, where the B-Dienst Service had located the forty-five ship convoy HX238. Twenty-two boats of the 'Donau' Group and another eight of the 'Oder' Group were deployed, but failed to find the convoy.

The next eastbound convoy was the forty-five-ship slow SC130, escorted by Gretton's B7 Group, with the same ships as with ONS5, plus the Canadian Kitchener, the rescue ship Zamalek and two trawlers. The action followed an increasingly familiar pattern: a U-boat sighting, cautious approach by its fellows and violent reaction by the escorts. The convoy was sighted on the night of 19 May by U–304, but the transmission was picked up by H/F D/F in three of the escorts and in Zamalek. The cross-bearings gave an excellent 'fix' of the U-boat's position and Gretton was able to turn the convoy sharply away, while giving an aircraft the U-boat's plotted position.

Air cover for SC130 was excellent. A Liberator of 120 Squadron RAF sank U–954 as it was trying to close the convoy on 19 May, and Liberators forced five other approaching U-boats to dive. Tay depth-charged and badly damaged U–952. Snowflake attacked U–381 and was somewhat disappointed not to sink it. The tip of the periscope was actually sighted in the middle of the exploding depth-charge pattern. But Duncan then came up and dispatched the U-boat with 'Hedgehog'.

The escort was reinforced at noon by the arrival of the 1st Escort Group, of the frigates Wear, Jed and Spey and the sloop Sennen. On their way to join from astern of the convoy the Group surprised two U-boats on the surface. U–209 dived and fired torpedoes but was sunk by Jed and Sennen. Escorts and aircraft combined for the rest of the day to drive off all the U-boats in contact except U–92 which made one fruitless attack. The last shadower was chased away by Jed and Spey just before sunset. BdU broke off the action the following morning, but all was not quite over. A Liberator pulled off one last coup by sinking U–258.

SC130 was an appalling result for BdU. Not one ship had been lost from the convoy, while four U-boats had been sunk. It meant that more U-boats than merchantmen were now being sunk during the average convoy's passage.

After this débâcle BdU formed the *'Moser'* Group of twenty-one U-boats on 19 May, to operate against HX239, whose course and details had been revealed by the B-Dienst Service. But, once again, the Shark Enigma decrypts had in turn revealed the U-boat deployments. HX239 made a large and timely diversion to the south and so it was the outward bound convoy ON184 which crossed the *'Moser'* line on 20 May.

ON184 was accompanied by the 6th Support Group, including *Bogue* whose Avengers attacked and damaged *U-231* and kept the other U-boats down until the convoy had passed over. *U-305* reported ON184 at midday on 22 May and BdU directed the nearest, most southerly U-boats in the *'Moser'* line towards it. But *Bogue*'s Avengers again drove the U-boats down and away and although *U-468* did beat off an attacking Avenger with gunfire, two Avengers sank *U-569*. No ships were lost from the convoy.

Meanwhile, to the south, the forty-two-ship HX239 was not quite out of danger. Its propeller noises had been detected by *U-218*'s hydrophones on the morning of 22 May and BdU ordered the U-boats to attack. But HX239 was formidably guarded, not only by B3 Escort Group, led by Commander Evans in the destroyer *Keppel*, with another destroyer *Escapade*, the frigate *Towey*, corvettes *Orchis*, *Narcissus* and the Free French *Roselys*, *Lobelia* and *Renoncule*, but also by the 4th Escort Group under Captain Scott-Moncrieff in the escort carrier *Archer* with four destroyers.

Archer's aircraft forced a gap in the U-boat line for HX239 just as *Bogue*'s had just done for ON184. Although *U-468*, who must have had an exceptionally talented anti-aircraft gunner on board, drove off an attacking Swordfish, on 23 May *U-752* was hit and badly damaged, as it was trying to dive, by rockets fired from another Swordfish. The wounded U-boat managed to defend itself against the Swordfish and a Martlet, but then had to scuttle when *Keppel* and *Escapade* approached. This was the first success by rockets in an anti-submarine role.

BdU had continued to urge the U-boats onwards: 'If there is anyone who thinks that combating convoys is no longer possible,' BdU signalled on 21 May, 'he is a weakling and no true U-boat captain. The battle of the Atlantic is getting harder but it is the determining element in the waging of the war.' The signal's sentiments were impeccable but words like 'weakling' would have been unthinkable in a signal from BdU only six months earlier. HX239, like ON184, had suffered no loss. Thus, four large convoys – SC130, HX238, ON184 and HX239, with a total of 161 ships – had crossed the Atlantic without losing a single ship, while their surface and air escorts had between them accounted for six U-boats.

In May, 1943, U-boats sank fifty ships of 264,852 tons. This was less than April and a big decrease on March. In the three weeks after the battle around ONS5, 468 ships in eleven convoys (HX236, ONS6, ON182, HX238, ON183, SC130, ON184, HX239, SC131, ONS8, and HX240) had all crossed the Atlantic without loss. Six ships were lost from three convoys (HX237, SC129 and ONS7). No ship had been lost in convoy since *Aymeric* from ONS7 on 17 May and no ship was lost from any convoy at any time when it had air cover. The total of U-boats sunk in May was forty-one from all causes, twenty-eight sunk by surface or air convoy escort.

For BdU and the U-boat arm, these statistics meant, in one word, defeat. On 23 May BdU decided to halt, at least temporarily, the U-boat offensive against the North Atlantic convoys. Sixteen U-boats who had most fuel remaining were sent south, to an area some 600 miles south-west of the Azores, from where BdU hoped they would be able to operate against more 'soft' targets and less fierce opposition on the convoy routes between the United States and Gibraltar. A few U-boats with less fuel were ordered to transmit frequent 'dummy' signals to conceal the withdrawal by giving the impression that the U-boat patrol lines were still in position and in force, and thus to make up in loquacity for what they lacked in numbers.

BdU also issued a series of signals, explaining the withdrawal and attributing it 'primarily to the present superiority of the enemy's location devices and the surprise from the air which these have made possible'. It was, BdU stressed, only a temporary withdrawal, while their own location devices, counter-measures against the enemy's location, and anti-aircraft flak armament were all improved. 'Wolfpack operations against convoys in the North Atlantic,' Dönitz wrote, 'the main theatre of operations and at the same time the theatre in which air cover was strongest, were no longer possible'. Unless the 'fighting power' of the U-boats could be 'radically' increased 'we had lost the battle of the Atlantic.'

Ironically, because the 'Shark' Enigma for 24 May was not broken for a week, it was the end of the month before the Allies realized their success. The series of great convoy battles fought in the North Atlantic in April and May, 1943, took place over hundreds of square miles of ocean, only identified by degrees of latitude and longitude. They had no physical features or circumstances to hang legends on, not even any names except the convoys' own designation letters and numbers. But the retreat of the Atlantic U-boats in May, 1943, in which ULTRA played a vital part, was a strategic victory for the Allies as important as Midway in the west and Stalingrad in the east.

13 | THE BAY OF BISCAY OFFENSIVE

Summer, 1943

An uncanny calm descended upon the North Atlantic in June, 1943. The weather was good, after the seemingly interminable gales of the winter and spring. As the sun climbed in the sky and day followed day, with no alarms or attacks, the men on watch in the convoys looked at each other in a wild surmise. There were thirty-two trans-Atlantic convoys, with 1,181 ships, in June. Not one ship was lost, not one convoy was even attacked.

July followed the same pattern, with no attack on any HX, SC or ON convoys. From the thirty-two ocean convoys in the month, not one of the 1,367 ships in convoy was lost. There were no losses from the 141 convoys, with 3,195 ships, around the coasts of the United Kingdom. Of the OS/SL convoys to and from Sierra Leone and the OG/HG convoys to and from Gibraltar, which sailed in conjunction with KMS convoys to North Africa, two convoys were attacked and two ships torpedoed. Both ships reached harbour.

There were no attacks on HX, SC and ON convoys in August. From another thirty-two ocean convoys during the month, with 1,209 ships, three ships were lost. OS53 to Sierra Leone had one ship sunk and another damaged by aircraft.

But this, as the OIC fully realized, was only a lull, while Dönitz reorganized and rearmed. In June, 1943, the OIC estimated that, despite recent losses, there were still 226 operational U-boats and another 208 working up in the Baltic. A decrypt of a telegram from the Japanese Embassy in Berlin revealed that Dönitz had said in an interview with the Japanese Ambassador that Germany expected to be able to resume effective U-boat warfare at the end of August.

On 1 June the sixteen U-boats sent to the Central Atlantic formed a new and aptly named '*Trutz*' ('Defiance') Group to operate against the Gibraltar–USA convoy GUS7A. The convoy was safely diverted to the south of the Group while aircraft from the carrier *Bogue* once more 'punched a hole' in the line by attacking three U-boats and forcing them to dive. Although one of the U-boats attacked, U–641, shot down an aircraft, two of *Bogue*'s aircraft sank U–217 on 5 June. Escorted by *Bogue*, the eastbound UGS9 also passed safely to the south of the U-boat line.

The '*Trutz*' Group reformed in three overlapping lines on 16 June, and on 2 July shifted again to form three new '*Geier*' ('Vulture') lines off Cape St Vincent, in the hope of finding convoys GUS8, UGS10 and GUS8A. But all three convoys were evasively routed around the U-boat lines, although U–572 sank the French tanker *Lot* from UGS10. None of the other '*Geier*' U-boats sighted any ships and three U-boats were sunk by aircraft. On 15 July U–135 sank one ship from OS51 but was then itself sunk by the convoy escort. The '*Geier*' Groups were disbanded. There were no more U-boat group attacks on convoys until September.

Until June, 1943, ULTRA had only been used defensively against the U-boats, to try and save convoys by timely rerouting. Because of the need to keep all available ships for close convoy protection, and, even more importantly, for fear of arousing the enemy's suspicions and endangering the ULTRA secret, the Allies had made no attempt to use ULTRA offensively by attacking the supply U-boat refuelling rendezvous. In fact, the Americans had pressed for such use of the intelligence from the 'Shark' Enigma in March, 1943, but Admiral Pound had resisted, fearing 'to risk what is so invaluable to us', as he told Fleet Admiral King, the US COMINCH. 'If our Z [Enigma] information failed us at the present time,' he signalled to King in April, at the height of the U-boat offensive, 'it would, I am sure, result in our shipping losses going up by anything from 50 to 100%.'

But on 12 June, 1943, *Bogue*'s aircraft, working from the Enigma and Direction Finding, chanced upon the Type XB minelayer-supply U-boat U–118 approaching a rendezvous and sank it. This had a quite unexpectedly dramatic effect upon the U-boat arm. Surface tankers could still be used to refuel U-boats in the Indian Ocean, but were quite out of the question in much of the Atlantic and BdU's long-range U-boat patrol plans for the Atlantic depended entirely upon the large 1,700 ton Type XB and Type XIV supply U-boats. After some delay, the Enigma decrypts began to show what drastic emergency arrangements for refuelling and changes of plan the loss of this one 'milch cow' U-boat had forced upon BdU. Some operational U-boats had to be recalled prematurely, others were delayed in reaching their operational areas. Another supply U-boat, the Type XIV U–488, with the help of four smaller Type VIIcs, carried out twenty-two refuellings in June, which partly retrieved the situation for BdU by enabling the

'*Geier*' Groups to continue operations. However, a full-scale US Navy offensive against the supply U-boats in the Central Atlantic was about to begin.

The US Navy formed Support Groups around CVE escort carriers, each with a typical air component of six Grumman F4F Wildcat fighters and twelve Grumman Avenger torpedo-bombers, normally armed with four 350-pound Torpex bombs or, latterly, the deadly little anti-submarine homing torpedo FIDO. A CVE group commander co-operated with a convoy escort commander but could act independently, and was not subject to the escort commander's orders. With a screen of four or five destroyers, the CVE group commander had a freer hand to range about the ocean wherever H/F D/F or ULTRA indicated targets. But the CVE Group was required to return to a threatened convoy before U-boats could attack it. Convoy defence was still the first object.

Operating in the calmer waters, lighter winds and generally better weather of the 'horse latitudes', the American CVE Groups were marvellously effective. Between 1 June and the end of 1943, the US CVEs *Bogue, Core, Santee, Card, Block Island* and their Groups between them sank twenty-three U-boats, including five large supply U-boats. *Card* was top scorer with eight kills. In mid-July *Core* and *Santee* together enjoyed a 'purple patch' in which they took it in turns to sink one U-boat a day for four consecutive days.

Such a high success rate, especially as several of the kills took place at or near fuelling rendezvous, might well have imperilled the ULTRA secret, but the fact that convoys regularly sailed in those areas on the routes between the USA and Gibraltar, the known or suspected presence of the CVEs, and last but most important, the very strenuous efforts the Germans made to improve their Enigma security, all helped to provide a 'cloak' of plausibility.

There were several breaks in the 'Shark' decrypts during this period. There was no 'Shark' Enigma at all for the first three weeks of July, 1943, when the Germans introduced modifications to the Enigma machine. They took further precautions, such as encoding all refuelling instructions in the '*Offizier*' setting, and making all U-boats keep radio silence when approaching a refuelling rendezvous. But BdU usually issued orders for refuelling up to a fortnight in advance of the date, which often gave enough time for the Enigma instruction to be broken or at least for a reasonable deduction to be made.

Although the Enigma might not reveal a precise rendezvous location, there was generally enough information on the numbers and types of the U-boats, the identity of the supply U-boat, the positions of favourite refuelling rendezvous, and the general movements and behaviour of U-boats on passage, to be able to send a CVE Group to the likeliest position. For example, early in July the Enigma revealed that a number of operational U-boats had recently sailed for patrols in distant areas, that they would require refuelling, that one favoured rendezvous was south-south-west of the Azores, and that the supply U-boat *U–487* (the Enigma even revealed her number and purpose) had been ordered to head for a position 35° N, 30° W. All this was more than enough for an estimate to be made of the approximate position and the date of the rendezvous. *Core*'s aircraft duly sank *U–487* on 13 July, and *Santee*'s aircraft sank *U–160*, an ocean-going Type IXC operational U-boat next day, while it was on its way to the rendezvous.

The Enigma occasionally revealed the mistaken conclusions BdU drew from events. On 8 June *U–758* was attacked on the surface by aircraft from *Bogue*. It did not dive but retaliated with spirited and accurate fire from its quadruple 2 cm flak guns, used operationally for the first time. Although *U–758* was damaged and eleven men were wounded, its fire kept eight of *Bogue*'s aircraft at bay and damaged two of them. After this misleading success, BdU ordered the U-boats to stay on the surface and fight it out. But this merely increased their losses. By August BdU was signalling to U-boat captains: 'Do not report too much bad news, so as not to depress the other boats; every radio message goes the rounds of the crew in every boat.'

The lull in the North Atlantic in the summer of 1943 allowed more attention to be paid to the offensive which Coastal Command had been conducting intermittently since the summer of 1942 against U-boats on transit passage through the Bay of Biscay from their bases in northern France to their patrol areas. In this 'Bay Offensive', as it was called, the battle had swung to and fro as one side or the other gained some temporary tactical or technological advantage.

RAF Wellingtons fitted with an early type of radar and Leigh lights (which brilliantly illuminated surfaced U-boats from the air at night) damaged three U-boats in the Bay in June, 1942, and went on to sink two in July. BdU suspected the use of some new location device by the Allies, and fitted U-boats with a rudimentary detector. The Bay Offensive slackened in October, 1942, when the U-boats were fitted with 'Metox', a more effective but still primitive form of radar detector.

In March, 1943, Coastal Command introduced Mark III (centrimetric) radar, and, as more aircraft became available, the Admiralty Submarine Tracking Room and Coastal Command together produced a systematic scheme of operations, using fixed systems of aircraft sweeps both by day and night, which could be moved around to cover the search area, as the latest information from ULTRA indicated;

two particular patterns of search operations were to be mounted, codenamed 'Musketry' and 'Seaslug'. Once ULTRA had provided a starting datum point it became practically certain that surfaced U-boats could be detected by radar. U-boat passage speeds varied very little and a patrol aircraft could easily cover the possible variations of distance run. Thus ULTRA enabled aircraft to concentrate their searches for U-boats, both outward- and inward-bound.

Too blatant a series of successes could once again jeopardize the ULTRA secret. But fortunately there were convenient 'covers': the Germans already suspected that the Allies were using new location devices effective by night and in poor visibility; secondly, it was no secret that there were U-boat bases in Northern France and that therefore U-boats had to transit through the comparatively restricted waters of the Bay to reach the open sea; and, finally, the Germans suspected the French Resistance in all the Atlantic seaboard towns of consistently betraying details of U-boat sailings to the Allies.

The 1943 campaign in the Bay began with the sinking of five U-boats in the first three months. Although only two U-boats were sunk in April, the circumstances surrounding the loss of one of them, U–356, sunk by Wellingtons of 172 Squadron, RAF, on 10 April, and reports from other U-boats attacked and damaged on passage in the Bay, convinced BdU that the Allies had some new mysterious form of detection gear. There certainly was a new radar: it, and the ULTRA-aided sweeps, and the fact that there were an unusual number of U-boats on passage in the transit area, many of them returning from the great convoy battles in April and the beginning of May, resulted in a dramatic increase in detection rate. The U-boats were forced to take new evasion tactics. Previously they had normally travelled on the surface by night. At the end of April they were ordered to stay submerged except for brief periods surfaced by day to recharge batteries. This slowed them down and thus allowed Coastal Command even more time for detection. Four U-boats were sunk and three more damaged in daylight attacks in the first week of May.

While the U-boat Command urgently set about arming the U-boats with quadruple 2 cm flak guns, BdU was forced to introduce more changes in tactics. From mid–May the U-boats were ordered not to dive if they were surprised on the surface, but to stay and fight it out. These tactics were as mistaken in the Bay as they had been in the Atlantic. In May six U-boats were sunk in the Bay and several more damaged so severely they had to turn back from their patrols.

At the end of May the U-boats were further ordered to make the passage of the Bay in groups, submerging at night but staying surfaced by day and staying close together so as to bring their combined fire-power to bear on an attacking aircraft. As soon as these new instructions were revealed by the Enigma at the beginning of June and a group of U-boats outward bound was actually sighted on 12 June, Coastal Command also changed tactics. An aircraft sighting a U-boat or a group of U-boats was not to attack at once, but to hold off, call up a second or even third aircraft and then make a joint attack.

By mid-June, when it had become clear beyond any doubt from the Enigma that BdU had withdrawn most U-boats from the North Atlantic and there was no longer the same threat to the convoys, Coastal Command was able to transfer many more aircraft to the Bay Offensive. The 'Musketry' and 'Seaslug' operations came into effect on 14 June; in these, search patterns by seven aircraft keeping on parallel courses were flown three times a day, over a wide area north-west of Cape Finisterre. On the same day a Whitley bomber of No. 10 Operational Training Unit RAF sank *U-564* which was accompanied by *U-185*. The German destroyers Z.24 and Z.32 came out to take off *U-564*'s survivors, leaving *U-185* to go on patrol alone.

Because of the constant harassment from the air, BdU cancelled all U-boat sailings across the Bay on 17 June and suspended group tactics until more U-boats were fitted with the quadruple 2 cm flak gun. Group sailings were resumed on 25 June, but by then the U-boats had a new foe in the Bay. On the 20th the 2nd Escort Group, under Captain 'Johnny' Walker in his sloop *Starling*, arrived to co-operate with the Coastal Command patrols. Walker's ships were covered by the cruiser *Scylla*, in case the six large German *Narvik* Class destroyers known to be at La Pallice came out to attack them.

Although Walker was unfamiliar with No. 19 Group Coastal command's patrol system, his Group had an early success on 24 June, when an aircraft sighting led them to an inward-bound trio of U-boats. *Starling* sank the Type XB minelayer-tanker supply boat *U-119* by depth-charge and finally by ramming. The rest of the Group, *Wren*, *Woodpecker*, *Kite* and *Wild Goose*, jointly dispatched *U-449* with depth-charges.

The main air offensive opened in July. USAAF and RAF Liberators, RAF and US Navy Catalinas, RAF and RAAF Sunderlands, RAF, RCAF, Polish and Czech Wellingtons, and RAF Fortresses and Halifaxes, using radar, depth-charges, Leigh lights, rockets and MAD (magnetic anomaly detectors, which picked up the magnetic disturbance of a submarine steel hull in the sea), sank sixteen U-boats in the month. Eleven more were damaged and some had to give up their patrols and return. One supply U-boat, *U-462*, was forced back twice.

The escort groups worked a five- to eight-day cycle of patrols. Besides Walker's 2nd Escort Group, EG 40, EG B5, the 5th Support

Group, including the carrier *Archer*, and with the cruisers *Bermuda* and *Glasgow* in the covering force, all took part in the Bay offensive. By 23 July Walker's 2nd Escort Group was on its third patrol in the Bay and a week later took part in one of the war's most successful attacks on U-boats, made possible by ULTRA.

The Home Waters '*Heimisch*' Enigma, which was being decrypted currently, had continued to give information on U-boat sailings and the provision of escorts for their departures. By 30 July the Enigma had revealed that U–461, U–462 and U–504 had sailed from French ports, that they were joining company to make the passage across the Bay in a group, and that U–461 and U–462 were two supply U-boats on their way to support the U-boat offensive in the Central Atlantic and eventually to assist in the revival of pack attacks in the North Atlantic. The Enigma also gave some indication of their route and estimated progress.

This was, of course, a target of the highest priority. On the morning of 30 July 2nd Escort Group and a large number of aircraft were patrolling the likeliest route of advance of the U-boats, which the Enigma had accurately revealed within narrow limits. Duly at 0937 on 30 July the three surfaced U-boats were sighted by a Liberator of No. 53 Squadron RAF, who called up other aircraft and Walker's ships. In a neat and clinical execution both supply U-boats were sunk by aircraft. (In a truly remarkable numerical coincidence, U–461 was sunk by Sunderland 'U' of 461 Squadron RAAF.) With the survivors of these two supply U-boats still in their dinghies, the 2nd Escort Group arrived and began to hunt for U–504, which had dived to try and escape. Asdic contact was soon gained and *Kite*, *Wren*, *Woodpecker* and *Wild Goose* made a series of depth-charge attacks. Wreckage and human remains were all of U–504 that ever came to the surface.

Since the beginning of June twenty-one U-boats had now been sunk in the Bay. Four more U-boats were lost to air attack in the first two days of August. In fact, by 2 August eighty-six U-boats had tried to transit the Bay: fifty-five of them had been sighted, seventeen (including three supply U-boats) had been sunk, eleven more damaged and six forced to turn back. These losses forced BdU early in August once again to change tactics. U-boats in groups on passage were told to disperse and proceed singly. Six U-boats which had just sailed were recalled and, from 5 August, sailings were suspended of all U-boats which had not been fitted with the quadruple flak gun and a new radar search receiver *Hagenuk*. Henceforth U-boats were routed further to the south, close to the Spanish coast, where they were marginally safer from radar detection under the shadow of the Pyrenees, staying dived in daylight and making the maximum use of Spanish territorial waters.

This new route, around the Spanish coast-line, was disclosed by the Enigma on 18 August, and by 23 August the Enigma had given details of the route and the fact that seven U-boats had so far used it safely. Coastal Command adjusted their patrols, had the first sighting of a U-boat in the new area on 22 August, and sank *U–134* close to the Spanish coast on the 24th.

Now, at last, the Luftwaffe began to make some effective contribution. The U-boats had been given very meagre air cover in the Bay, due to the long-standing vendetta between Dönitz and Göring, and Göring's own failure to grasp the importance of air power at sea. Junkers Ju.88Cs had been accompanying some U-boats but they were outclassed by the RAF's Beaufighters and Mosquitoes. The U-boat Arm complained, with some justification, that the U-boats themselves had shot down more enemy aircraft over the Bay than had the Luftwaffe. But on 25 August Heinkel He.177s flying from Cognac attacked the escort *Bideford* and scored a near-miss with an Hs 293 radio-guided missile – a new weapon not forecast or foreseen by the Enigma or any other Allied intelligence. On 27 August Heinkel He.177s, armed with the same weapons, sank the sloop *Egret* and damaged the Canadian destroyer *Athabaskan*.

Some idea of the scale of activity involved in the Bay Offensive may be gained from the figures: between 14 June and 21 September, for instance, the Bay Offensive had cost 576 ship-days and 3,981 Coastal Command sorties. The offensive slackened in September, but quickened again in November, until the end of 1943; thirty-two U-boats were sunk in the Bay between May and December. But, during that same period, 258 U-boats entered and 247 left the Bay, on transit to and from French ports. Therefore the ratio of U-boats sunk to U-boats present was not unduly high.

From May to December, 1943, 183 U-boats were sunk in areas other than the Bay of Biscay. Thus the Bay Offensive certainly did not show that it was better to leave the convoys and go out and search for U-boats. The main principle was unaltered, namely, that the most effective place to encounter and destroy U-boats was around their targets, the convoys. However, a very energetic sea and air offensive, coupled with vital information from ULTRA, did cause enough U-boat casualties to have a very powerful psychological impact upon the Germans, who did not discover until much later how or why they were losing so many U-boats in the Bay of Biscay.

The Bay Offensive probably had most effect in the long term and far afield. The losses of the supply U-boats forced BdU to order several Type IX operational boats to abandon their patrols and act as emergency tankers, while Type VIIs, unable to refuel, had to curtail their patrols, either stopping short of their designated areas, or having to return prematurely. By the end of August 1943, there were forty operational U-boats at sea, compared with seventy-one in July, and most of those forty boats were either on their way home for lack of fuel, or outward bound on patrols which had had to be shortened because there was no possibility of refuelling.

Meanwhile, the lull in the North Atlantic had continued. Early in September, 1943, the Naval Staff noted that 'this week, for the first time in the war, the U-boats have not sunk a merchant ship'. But this was no cause for complacency. Everybody involved knew that the main battle had to be in the North Atlantic. The U-boats must return there in force, sooner or later, or confess the war at sea lost.

By the end of August the signs were that the struggle was about to be renewed. Many U-boats had been fitted with much heavier anti-aircraft armament and the new radar search receiver. There was also a new weapon, on which BdU pinned high hopes: the 3,300 pound Zaunkonig (Wren) T5 acoustic torpedo, known to the Allies as the GNAT (German Naval Acoustic Torpedo). It had the modest range of 6,000 yards, and the very modest speed, for a torpedo, of 24 knots. Its acoustic range was also limited: ships moving at more than 19 knots or less than seven were generally immune to the GNAT, which also had a tendency to explode astern of its target in the turbulence of the wake. It was principally an anti-escort weapon, designed to enable a U-boat to draw aside and disable or sink an escort, and then attack the merchantmen unmolested.

Nine U-boats armed with GNAT and the supply boat *U–460*, all fitted with the new receiver sailed from the Biscay ports late in August. *U–669* was sunk by a Leigh Light-fitted Wellington in the Bay on 6 September but the others reached the Atlantic safely and five of them refuelled from *U–460*. Thirteen more U-boats sailed from Biscay ports and six from the Baltic early in September. None of these had GNAT.

On 15 September twenty-one of these U-boats were formed into the *'Leuthen'* Group. They were ordered to form a patrol line some 350 miles long, to the south of Iceland by 20 September. The B-Dienst Service was not now nearly so sharp, after the change in the Naval Cypher, but the U-boats were told to expect two westbound convoys. BdU's orders to the U-boats were to stay submerged the maximum amount and, when the convoy arrived, to go for the escorts.

The OIC had known since 6 September that another U-boat group operation was under way, but had no information about the destinations of the U-boats outward bound. BdU had taken special precautions over security. All positions in signals radioed to U-boats were in the form of reference points known only to the U-boat commanders concerned. By 13 September OIC's greatest problem was 'the where-abouts and intentions of some twenty U-boats which have recently left Biscay ports'. On 18 September OIC received the decrypts of the Shark Enigma instructions to the 'Leuthen' Group but because of the concealment of the reference points was still unable to decide where the line was to be established.

The Enigma also revealed details of the instructions given to the U-boats concerning their use of Hagenuk and the radar decoy balloon known as Aphrodite. U-boats were also instructed to shoot back at attacking aircraft. They were about to operate, in BdU's phrase, in 'the main battle area'. They would be engaged in 'the decisive struggle for the German race'. The Atlantic convoys, BdU forecast, would be weakly escorted. With the advantages of surprise, new weapons and installations, the U-boats were to 'decimate the escort for moral effect and to denude the convoy'. The first convoys involved in this new phase of the U-boat war were ON202 and ONS18.

ON202 was a convoy of thirty-eight ships, escorted by C2 Group, the Canadian destroyer Gatineau (Commander P. W. Burnett) and the destroyer Icarus, the frigate Lagan, and three corvettes, Polyanthus and the Canadians Drumheller and Kamloops. ONS18 was about 120 miles ahead and to the west of ON202, with twenty-seven ships escorted by B3 Group, the destroyers Keppel (Commander M. J. Evans) and Escapade, frigate Towey, corvettes Orchis, Narcissus and the Free French Roselys, Lobelia and Renoncule, and the trawler Northern Foam.

Among the ships in ONS18 was the Merchant Aircraft Carrier Empire MacAlpine. These MAC ships, as they were known, which first entered convoy service with ONS9 in May, 1943, were grain-ships or tankers converted into rudimentary but perfectly serviceable aircraft carriers by having flight decks, small island superstructures, arrester wires and crash barriers fitted on top of their hulls (the 'grainer' MAC ships even had a hangar) so that they could operate three or four Swordfish. MAC ships continued to carry up to 80 per cent of their usual cargoes. They flew the Red Ensign and were manned by their normal Merchant Navy personnel, with the addition of a small naval flight-deck party and aircrew. They were a 'cheap and cheerful' means whereby convoys could take their own defensive air component along with them.

A Liberator of 10 Squadron RCAF sank U–341, one of the most southerly of the 'Leuthen' boats, on 19 September. A last-minute attempt was made to divert ONS18 north of the 'Leuthen' line, but OIC's estimate proved to be some 100 miles south of the line's actual position and ONS18 ran over the 'Leuthen' line (to the surprise of the 'Leuthen' line) in the early hours of 20 September. Roselys depth-charged one contact, but *Escapade* suffered a serious accident, with twenty-one casualties, when a Hedgehog exploded prematurely on deck. But reinforcement was on its way. When the threat to ONS18 was realized the Canadian 9th Escort Group, the frigate *Itchen*, destroyers *St Croix* and *St Francis*, and corvettes *Chambly*, *Sackville* and *Morden*, was ordered to join ONS18's escort.

About 30 miles to the north-east ON202 had been reported by *U-270*, but *Lagan* ran down the H/F D/F bearing and attacked. The U-boat counter-attacked with a GNAT which blew off *Lagan*'s stern and killed twenty-nine of her ship's company. While *Gatineau* drove *U-270* off, *Polyanthus* attacked *U-238*. But this U-boat hung on and three hours later slipped through the screen and torpedoed two ships; one sank at once and the other was finished off by *U-645*.

The Liberators of 120 Squadron from Iceland arrived overhead at dawn on the 20th. 'U-boats stay on the surface for defence,' *U-338* signalled to the others, in accordance with the prearranged plan. The advice was unsound, particularly for *U-338*, which was sighted by a Liberator just after 10 a.m. and sunk with a FIDO homing torpedo.

By midday on the 20th the faster ON202 had almost caught up ONS18 and the two convoys were so close together that C-in-C Western Approaches ordered them to amalgamate under Commander Evans as Senior Officer in *Keppel*. But the signal to do so was received in a very badly garbled form, and the courses to steer were undecipherable. The convoys continued to close each other haphazardly and by that afternoon sixty-three ships and twenty-one escorts (the Canadian 9th E. G. having just caught up from astern) 'gyrated majestically about the ocean,' as Commander Evans said, 'never appearing to get much closer, and watched appreciatively by a growing swarm of U-boats'.

By that evening the swarm had grown to eight U-boats and the escorts were in for a hectic night. *Keppel* and *Roselys* ran down the H/F D/F bearing of the first shadower, *U-386*, and drove it off with depth-charges. But at about 8 p.m. *St Croix* was hit by a GNAT fired by *U-305* and finally sunk by another GNAT from the same boat an hour later. *Itchen* took off her survivors – and a GNAT exploded in her wake.

For the rest of that night the U-boats tried to shoot their way into the convoy, firing GNATs at any escort which approached them. *Icarus* had to jink violently to escape a GNAT fired by *U-229* and in so doing collided with the Canadian *Drumheller* (who signalled, rather plaintively, 'Having no U-boats?'). *Narcissus* was missed by a GNAT from *U-260*, but *U-952* hit and sank *Polyanthus*. For the second time that night *Itchen* took off survivors. *U-229*, *U-641*, *U-270*, *U-377* and

157

U–584 all fired at escorts, but their GNATs all missed or exploded in the wakes.

When the next dawn came, 21 September, both convoys were shrouded in thick fog. When it lifted, Commander Evans could see, *mirabile dictu*, the two convoys close together, ONS18 neatly in station to starboard of ON202, in a 'masterly manoeuvre', clearly 'organized by a Higher Authority'. But towards the evening the convoys were sighted by *U–584* and the escorts began on another busy night. *U–584* fired a GNAT at *Chambly*, missed and was damaged by return gunfire. The three Free French were repeatedly in action, attacking U-boats and driving them off. *Northern Foam* almost succeeded in ramming *U–952*. Finally, towards dawn, *Keppel* ran down a H/F D/F bearing astern of the convoy, surprised *U–229* still on the surface, rammed it and sank it.

Fog persisted until the afternoon of 22 September. When it lifted, *Empire MacAlpine* was able to fly off her Swordfish and air cover from shore also appeared, so that Commander Evans commented that the air all around 'was filled with Liberators'. The U-boats kept to their tactic of staying to shoot it out with aircraft. Some defended themselves very adequately but two were damaged.

After dark the U-boats went for their GNATs again. *U–952* missed *Renoncule* but when *Morden* sighted *U–666* ahead of the convoy and went into the attack, *U–666* fired two GNATs. One exploded astern of *Morden*, but the other ran on and hit *Itchen*, who blew up and sank. She had, of course, survivors on board her from *St Croix* and *Polyanthus*. Only three men survived from the three ship's companies.

Once again, much of the damage was done by a single determined U-boat commander. In the confusion after *Itchen*'s loss, *U–238* (Kapitan-Leutnant Hepp), who had torpedoed the two ships lost from ON202 on the 20th, penetrated the convoy's ranks a second time and sank three ships with one FAT salvo. The only other U-boat to score, *U–952*, which had so far had an eventful patrol, sank one ship and hit a second with a torpedo which did not explode. The Liberators were back when the sun came up and several U-boats again had to defend themselves against air attack. That morning, 23 September, BdU called off the operation.

The U-boat captains understandably overestimated their achievements. They claimed ten escorts and eight merchant ships sunk, for twenty-four T5s fired. Misled by this optimism, BdU considered the action 'very satisfactory'. In fact, during the five days' battle, nineteen U-boats – a high percentage of the total involved – had made contact with the two convoys. They had sunk three escorts (*Lagan* was eventually towed back) and six merchant ships, of 36,422 tons. This certainly was a major success, the best the U-boats had achieved since March – and their last of the war. But three U-boats had been lost and two seriously damaged.

The GNAT had not been operationally tested and BdU, naturally anxious for information on its behaviour at sea, ordered U-boats to transmit detailed reports at once. These reports were revealed through the 'Shark' Enigma and within days were being studied by the OIC who, from their own analyses, soon had a much better idea of the GNAT's true performance than BdU had from the exaggerated claims of the U-boat captains. It was clear that the GNAT was not quite the war-winning weapon BdU had hoped. The Allies had been expecting something of the sort for some time and a decoy device known as a 'Foxer', which made a loud rattling noise astern of the towing ship, was in service only sixteen days after the end of the attacks on ON202 and ONS18. No ship towing either a 'Foxer' or one of the later improved versions was ever hit by a GNAT. *Hagenuk*, the new radar search receiver, and *Aphrodite*, the new anti-radar decoy balloon were also ineffective.

With the advantage of the 'Shark' Enigma, now being read almost currently, the North Atlantic escorts went on in October and November, 1943, to inflict a second defeat on the U-boats. The next westbound convoy was the sixty-seven-ship ON203, with six close escorts and the Escort Group G.C4, with another seven escorts. On 27 September twenty-one U-boats of the '*Rossbach*' Group were spread out to intercept, but the 'Shark' Enigma revealed the U-boats' dispositions in ample time for the convoy to be diverted further to the north. It duly passed to the westward, unscathed, on 28 September. So, too, did the next convoy, ONS19, a day later.

The next eastbound convoy, HX258, was safely diverted to the south of the waiting U-boat line. Once the convoy had passed by, its air escort returned to the position of the U-boat line and in three days, 3–5 October, conducted a successful offensive in which several U-boats were attacked, three were badly damaged and three sunk. For good measure, another convoy, ONS204, crossed over safely to the west during this period.

From June, 1943, when the Naval cypher was changed, the B-Dienst Service was, except for a short period of very limited success at the end of 1943, effectively deprived of cryptanalysis as a source of information on convoy sailings and routes. There was still some information from agents, air reconnaissance, Traffic Analysis and Direction Finding, but, as the Germans themselves admitted, 'never again – not even for the shortest period – did we succeed in re-establishing the same standard of decryption that existed in 1942 and up to May, 1943'.

However, on 6 October, as a result of information from the B-Dienst Service, the seventeen surviving 'Rossbach' boats moved south to look for HX259 and SC143. HX259, with forty-eight ships and nine escorts, sailed from New York on 28 September. The thirty-nine-ship SC143, with six escorts and a MAC ship, had left Halifax the same day. Both convoys were routed to the north. But on 4 October the Enigma had revealed enough about the U-boats' lines to present OIC with a problem. It was unwise to allow both convoys to continue to the north. Both could now be routed to the south; or, one convoy could go north, the other south. If both were sent south and the U-boats also went south, the SC might be sighted first and the more important HX soon after, and a débâcle might ensue, as had happened to HX229 and SC122. It was therefore decided to route the SC to the north, where it would probably be sighted, and to reinforce its escort strongly. Meanwhile, the HX should have a clear passage to the south. This was an historic decision. It meant that, for the first time in the Battle of the Atlantic, the Admiralty had decided that a convoy's escort could be made strong enough to accept battle deliberately.

SC143 carried on to the north, with a small diversion even further to the north to avoid an area where U-boats were on passage, while HX259 was diverted to the south on 6 October. SC143 was strongly reinforced, by the 3rd Escort Group, by the 10th Escort Group from HX259 on 6 October, and the frigate *Duckworth* from ONS19 on 7th. Arrangements were also made to give SC143 the maximum air cover.

SC143 lost its formation for a time on 6 October, due to a mis-understanding of one of the Commodore's signals and was not properly reformed until about 3 p.m. on the 7th when the first U-boat was already in contact. By the evening eight U-boats were closing. The escorts had a strenuous time, running down H/F D/F bearings and attacking whenever they had the chance. At one stage 10th Escort Group misled the U-boats by staging a magnificent 'firework display' with starshell, searchlights and depth-charges, some 35 miles astern of the convoy. But, just after 6 a.m. *U-758*, which had already been driven off once by aircraft, returned and sank the Polish destroyer *Orkan*, of 10th Escort Group, with a GNAT.

Aircraft that day enjoyed an almost 100 per cent record; four sightings resulted in the sinkings of *U-419*, *U-643* and *U-610*, and damage to *U-762*. There was also the appearance of a very rare bird, a six-engined Blohm & Voss Bv.222 flying boat, used for the first time in the Atlantic. It actually sighted SC143 and broadcast homing signals, but no U-boat received them. That evening the convoy had yet another rare visitor – a Leigh Light Wellington which stayed with the convoy after dark, for the first time ever, and drove off *U-91* which was trying to close the convoy. But in the morning, after the aircraft had left, *U–645* came upon a scattered group of ships and sank the merchant ship *Yorkman*, the convoy's only casualty. A disappointed BdU called off the operation later that day. Thus, two large convoys had crossed over, losing just one 5,612-ton ship, and one escort, *Orkan*. Three U-boats had been sunk and others severely damaged. The Admiralty's decision to give battle had been amply justified.

Disappointed, but not deterred, at least for the time being, BdU formed the '*Schlieffen*' Group, of twelve U-boats, after convoy ON206 was reported by *U–844*, on the evening of 15 October. ONS20 was sighted by *U–964* early the next day. A five-day battle around both convoys began when *Duncan* and *Vanquisher* drove off the shadowing *U–844* from ON206 on the 15th. The sixty-five-ship ON206 was strongly escorted by B6 Group, with four escorts, reinforced on 13 October by the five ships of Gretton's B7 Group. ONS20 was escorted by the five destroyers of the 4th Escort Group.

Both convoys were very strongly escorted from the air. BdU had ordered the U-boats to fight their way through to the convoys on the surface. They did shoot down one Liberator and badly damaged another, but at a terrible cost to themselves: Liberators shared the kills of *U–844*, *U–964* and *U–470* between them, all on 16 October. But *U–426* closed the convoy that evening and sank *Essex Lance*.

Despite their losses, the U-boats made several attempts to get at ON206 during the night of 16–17 October, but the escorts frustrated them all and in the evening two Liberators sank *U–540* some way to the north of the convoy. By then B7 Group was already on its way to reinforce ONS20, about 150 miles to the north-east of ON206, which the Enigma had revealed was now threatened. On the way *Sunflower* (*Snowflake* was refitting) got a radar contact at 3,500 yards. The U-boat, *U–631*, dived but *Sunflower* soon had it in her sonar reach, and made two perfect depth-charge attacks. The first blew *U–631* to the surface. The second sank it.

ONS20 was reported by two U-boats during 17 October, but all the '*Schlieffen*' boats complained they could make no headway against the strength of the air escort. They shot one Sunderland down, but *U–448* and *U–281* reported many casualties among their gun-crews caused by aircraft gunfire. Finally, on 17 October, *U–841* was sunk by the destroyer *Byard*, of 4th Escort Group. BdU, once again disappointed, called off the operation the next day.

One ship had been sunk, from ON206, in exchange for six U-boats sunk. This, and other similar statistics from other convoys, showed how very fiercely the convoys were now being defended and how skilfully the precious information from the Enigma was being used.

ON207, ONS21, HX263 and ON208 were all completely untouched, although BdU deployed a new 'Siegfried' Group of twenty-one fresh U-boats against them.

Against ON207 the U-boats had a bruising reception. ON207 had air cover from Iceland and from the escort carrier Tracker, sailing with the convoy. The surface escort was provided by C1 Group as close escort, B7 Group in support, and Captain Johnnie Walker's 2nd Escort Group in the deep field. The U-boats were picked off, one by one. A Liberator of 224 Squadron shared U-274 with Duncan and Vidette on 23 October. A Sunderland of 10 Squadron RCAF sank U-420 on the 26th. Two days later Duncan, Vidette and Sunflower jointly sank U-282 with Hedgehogs.

From the beginning of September until the end of October, 1943, 2,468 merchant ships sailed in sixty-four North Atlantic convoys. Of those, only nine ships in convoy were sunk. In the same period, surface escorts sank five U-boats, aircraft operating around the convoys sank thirteen, and aircraft from American escort carriers another six – twenty-four U-boats in all. This was the second victory of the year against the U-boats, and it was won, like the first in May, around the convoys.

Towards the end of October, BdU had begun to comment upon air patrols apparently being flown from the Azores. An agreement between Great Britain and Portugal, Britain's oldest ally, had come into effect on 8 October, allowing the British to operate air bases on Fayal and Terceira in exchange for war materials and a guarantee against German retaliation. The first Fortresses flew on to the islands on the 18th and operations began the following day. This filled in the last of the infamous 'air gaps'. Air cover could now be given to the whole of the Atlantic north of 30° (but only after four years of war).

The new air cover could not have come at a more opportune time. After the losses around the North Atlantic convoys in September and October, BdU had once more moved the U-boats south, to operate against the convoys running between UK and Gibraltar, and the UK and Sierra Leone. For some of these convoy actions the U-boats themselves had an unprecedented degree of co-operation from the Luftwaffe, who provided a quite astonishing amount of air reconnaissance patrols, sighting reports and homing signals, and on one occasion, Heinkel He.177 bombers to attack a convoy with Hs 293 glider-bombs.

That convoy was the sixty-six-ship northbound SL139/MKS30 around which a fierce battle was fought off the Portuguese coast from 18 to 21 November. BdU had placed twenty-six U-boats in three patrol lines, 'Schill 1', '2' and '3', in positions where Luftwaffe reports had indicated the convoy would pass. But the convoy had a well-drilled close escort, the 40th Escort Group, of seven ships, later reinforced by five ships of the 7th Escort Group, two more destroyers, and the 5th Escort Group of seven ships. Overhead flew Liberators, Sunderlands, Hudsons, Catalinas and Fortresses by day, and Leigh Light Wellingtons by night. The Enigma had revealed the dispositions of the 'Schill' lines and the convoy was diverted to the west to avoid them.

The pattern of the battle followed that of so many in the North Atlantic. In the end three U-boats were sunk, and one damaged, while the convoy lost one straggler and one ship damaged. The U-boats shot down a Liberator and a Sunderland but the convoy's own anti-aircraft fire, greatly strengthened by the arrival on the 21st of the Canadian anti-aircraft ship *Prince Rupert*, destroyed three He.177s. Against that, the sloop *Chanticleer*'s stern was blown off by a GNAT.

More convoy battles on the route from Gibraltar to UK had shown by the end of the year that the U-boats were being defeated again, and by the same well-tried tactics as before, of convoy and escort. By December, 1943, the U-boats were withdrawn for the third time, in their third defeat of 1943, which was achieved, like the other two, around and over the convoys.

14 | ULTRA IN THE MEDITERRANEAN
1941–42

'Was information received in time to intercept these ships and if so with what result?' demanded the Admiralty signal of 21 April, 1941. 'Reply when W/T silence permits'. This was Mr Churchill, always itching to take the offensive and always ready to hasten events, enquiring of Admiral Cunningham, the C-in-C Mediterranean, whether any action had been taken on two ULTRA signals sent to him earlier in the month.

The signals referred to contained much detail. The first, of 17 April, said: 'A consignment of 400 tons of B4 and 250 tons of C3 aviation fuel is due to arrive Benghazi on or after 20/4', and the second, a day later, 'Further 150 tons petrol and 500 tons of bombs left Naples 16th April in two ships for Benghazi possibly calling at Tripoli en route'.

In fact, the signals had been too late. At that time the Italian naval codes were not being read and there was as yet no information from the German naval Enigma in the Mediterranean area. The main source was the Luftwaffe Enigma, which was being read, but which contained only occasional information about convoys and, as in this case, there were often delays in passing intelligence to those who could act on it.

British intelligence had been slow to realize German intentions in North Africa, but by April, 1941, it was clear that the Germans were rapidly building up their strength by passing convoys between Italian ports and Libya; 200,000 tons of Axis shipping was sent to Libya, mainly to Tripoli, from Italian ports in February and March, 1941. Between March and the middle of May, 1941, convoys for Tripoli were leaving Naples every three or four days, with individual ships sailing from Palermo and Trapani.

ULTRA was to play a part in attempts to cut off these supplies, but at this stage of the war neither the navy nor the RAF was strong enough in Malta – the crucial island lying across the Axis supply lines – to make the fullest use of the ULTRA available.

On 14 April Mr Churchill ordered that the highest priority should be given to operations against the enemy supply routes. Previously, on 7 April, the Admiralty had informed Cunningham by ULTRA signal that 'advanced elements of German 15th Armoured Division were embarking at Palermo on or after 9 April probably for Tripoli'. On 8 April Cunningham decided to station destroyers at Malta and sent Captain P. J. Mack with *Jervis*, *Nubian*, *Mohawk* and *Janus* of the 14th Destroyer Flotilla. When the destroyers arrived on 11 April air reconnaissance from Malta was stepped up at once. An enemy convoy was sighted that same day, and another on the 12th. Mack's ships sailed both times but were unable to intercept.

Admiral Cunningham was now under the strongest pressure from Mr Churchill to interrupt the flow of enemy supplies to Libya, and to bombard and blockade the port of Tripoli, using the battleship *Barham* as a block-ship. Cunningham was understandably reluctant to expend a capital ship for such a purpose and expressed his misgivings. But on 15 April Pound passed on to him a directive that 'every possible step must be taken by the Navy to prevent supplies reaching Libya from Italy and by coastwise traffic even if this results in serious loss or damage to H. M. Ships. . . . Failure by the Navy to concentrate on prevention of such movements [enemy supplies to Libya] to the exclusion of everything not absolutely vital will be considered as having let side down'. Cunningham replied crisply on 16 April that 'We are not idle in Libya and nobody out here will say the Navy has let them down'.

As it happened, reconnaissance aircraft from Malta reported a third convoy of five enemy ships, escorted by three destroyers, at about noon on 15 April. They were nearing Cape Bon, on the Tunisian coast, and steering south, clearly bound for Tripoli. Mack's destroyers sailed that evening, heading to intercept the enemy off the Kerkenah islands. The enemy ships were sighted in the early hours of 16 April and in a hectic gun and torpedo mêlée in the dark Mack's ships sank all five merchantmen (which were carrying units and supplies, including ammunition, of the 15th Panzer Division to Africa) and the destroyers *Tarigo*, *Lampo* and *Baleno*, for the loss of *Mohawk*, torpedoed by *Tarigo*.

But even with this brilliant success and Mr Churchill's continued urgings, the number of Axis ships sunk in April and May, 1941, was only twenty-one, certainly an increase on the ten sunk in the first three months of 1941, but still not enough to do serious damage to the enemy. The best intelligence information in the world is useless if the holder has not enough strength to act upon it.

By the autumn of 1941 the local situation had changed dramatically, both on the naval and the cryptanalytical fronts. Ironically, the Italians, whose naval cyphers had previously been secure, yielded to pressure from the Germans to change their cyphers. The Germans, whose naval Enigma key had been broken, claimed that the Italian cyphers were vulnerable. The cypher the Italians then began to use for most of their communications about shipping in the Mediterranean was a medium grade cypher, known as 'C 38 m', based on a Swedish coding machine called the 'C38'. GC & CS, who had previously made almost no headway against Italian cyphers, broke into the C 38 m in the summer of 1941.

The 6″ gun light cruisers *Aurora* (Captain W. R. Agnew) and *Penelope* arrived in Malta from the United Kingdom on 21 October and, with two destroyers from Force H, *Lance* and *Lively*, formed Force K. In two months, from October to December, 1941, this combination of high grade shipping intelligence from the C 38 m and Force K at Malta was to bring Axis supplies to Libya almost to a complete halt.

The C 38 m was decrypted at the GC & CS, transmitted to the Vice Admiral Malta, and from him sent in the form of operational orders to the Senior Officer Force K, Captain Agnew (who was not himself a recipient of ULTRA). Events then followed a regular pattern: advance information about the route and timing of an enemy convoy from the C 38 m; an aircraft sighting of the convoy, to provide a 'cover story'; a sortie by Force K; confirmation from the C 38 m of the damage done.

The first chance came on 25 October, but the C 38 m information did not arrive soon enough. Force K did sail but was unable to intercept a group of Italian destroyers carrying troops to North Africa. But on 8 November, the C 38 m decrypt was received in Malta in time for a Maryland reconnaissance aircraft of No. 69 Squadron to fly out and sight a large enemy convoy, some forty miles east of Cape Spartivento, in the afternoon.

The enemy convoy consisted of seven merchant ships, closely escorted by six destroyers, with a covering force of the heavy cruisers *Trieste* and *Trento* and four more destroyers. The convoy also had an air escort, and submarines were stationed off Malta to report the sailing of any Allied ships.

Force K sailed, unsighted by enemy submarines, that evening just before dark. Despite a failure of radio and radar in the Wellington which was supposed to guide Force K to the target, the nearest enemy ships were first sighted by *Aurora*, in the position where they were expected, just after midnight on the 9th.

The Captains of Force K had often discussed the action to be taken on attacking a convoy. All now knew what to do. After the first General Alarm bearing, Agnew had only to make two more signals

166

during the action: one to reduce speed, a second to avoid wasting ammunition. *Aurora* led the way round to the northward, to silhouette the enemy against the moon. The Italian ships were caught utterly by surprise and in yet another short, sharp and merciless night encounter with guns and torpedoes, all seven merchant ships, totalling 39,000 tons, and the destroyer *Fulmine*, were sunk. To complete a bad night for the Italian Navy, the submarine *Upholder* on patrol in the area torpedoed and sank a second destroyer, *Libeccio*.

Next day, when Force K returned triumphantly to Grand Harbour to well-earned praise and plaudits from all sides for what Cunningham rightly called 'a brilliant example of leadership and foresight', the C 38 m confirmed that the entire convoy had indeed been destroyed and that it had been carrying fuel for the Luftwaffe and badly needed equipment, including a large consignment of motor transport, for the *Afrika Korps*. (One ship with an obvious deck-load of vehicles was actually noticed during the action from *Penelope*'s bridge, where somebody described it as 'being lousy with charabancs'.) Meanwhile, the Italian Navy was badly shocked by the scale of the catastrophe inflicted upon such a heavily escorted convoy. On 9 November the Enigma revealed that Rommel had reported that transport to North Africa had completely stopped and, of 60,000 troops expected at Benghazi, only just over 8,000 had arrived.

By 15 November the C 38 m had revealed that another large enemy convoy, of four large supply ships and seven destroyers, with a covering force of three heavy and two light cruisers and another seven destroyers, was to sail for Tripoli on the 20th, which was two days after the new Allied offensive in North Africa, Operation CRUSADER, was due to be launched. By 18 November GC & CS had even managed to establish the convoy's exact route.

The convoy was duly sighted by a Sunderland as it emerged from the Straits of Messina on 21 November and it was attacked that evening by RAF Wellingtons, Swordfish of 830 and Albacores of 828 Squadrons of the Fleet Air Arm from Malta. One cruiser, *Duca degli Abruzzi*, was torpedoed and had to return. During the night the submarine HMS/M *Utmost* torpedoed *Trieste* which also had to turn back. The whole convoy (as revealed by the C 38 m the following day) was then recalled to Taranto, clearly for fear of another attack by Force K.

Force K's turn came again two days later, when the four ships sailed for what its sailors were now calling 'another Club Run'. The targets were two German ships, *Maritza* carrying ammunition and *Procida* carrying high octane fuel for the Luftwaffe to Benghazi. Obviously, these ships' cargoes were vital to Rommel and Mr Churchill pressed unusually hard, even for him, for them to be sunk, going so far as to ask whether Cunningham had seen the decrypts which described their safe arrival as 'decisive'.

The two German ships were escorted by two Italian torpedo boats, *Lupo* and *Cassiopaea*, but the escort was of no avail. Both ships were intercepted and sunk by Force K, although the two torpedo boats did their gallant best to protect their charges, only leaving the scene when it was quite clear both ships were doomed. On 25 November Luftwaffe Enigma revealed that the loss of these two ships had placed German operations in North Africa in 'real danger'. Fuel now had to be ferried across in all available aircraft and in Italian destroyers. Indeed by the end of November the C 38 m revealed that Italian destroyers were transporting petrol in drums on deck and floating them ashore at Derna, so as to shorten their time in harbour and reduce the risk of air attack.

But the successes were not wholly on one side. When the C 38 m had revealed the passage of *Maritza* and *Procida*, Force B, of the cruisers *Ajax, Neptune, Naiad, Euryalus* and *Galatea*, and four destroyers, all under Rear Admiral Rawlings, had sailed from Alexandria very early on the morning of 24 November to support Force K. Cunningham himself sailed later the same day with his battle squadron of *Queen Elizabeth, Valiant* and *Barham*, and eight destroyers, to support the cruisers if Italian heavy ships appeared.

The following afternoon, at about teatime, when Cunningham's ships were cruising between Crete and Cyrenaica, some 60 miles north of Sollum, *U–331* penetrated the destroyer screen and hit *Barham* with three torpedoes. *Barham* made a great slow circle to port, quickly heeling inwards as she did so, and then blew up with an appalling detonation which sent a great column of grey and black smoke hundreds of feet into the air. When the smoke cleared, all that remained were the dots of her survivors' heads on the surface of the sea. *Barham*'s Captain and over 800 of her people were lost. Although the C 38 m revealed that the enemy was unaware of *Barham*'s loss, and the news could therefore be kept secret for some time, thus to some extent mitigating the effect by preventing the enemy taking heart from the news, the implications of this attack were grave for Cunningham and his fleet. A few days earlier, on 13 November, off Gibraltar, *U–81* had hit the carrier *Ark Royal* with one torpedo, from which she sank the next day. Clearly these newly arrived German U-boats introduced a new and very threatening dimension to the Mediterranean sea war.

Nevertheless, the efforts of Malta-based surface ships, submarines and aircraft, assisted by advance warning from the C 38 m, were preventing reinforcements reaching North Africa. Between June and

October, 1941, only about 16 per cent of the cargo failed to arrive. But in November this figure soared to 62 per cent, and there were further delays caused by ships turning back or hesitating to sail, and by mining and bombing of the convoy ports.

Towards the end of November the C 38 m gave details of the next convoy and its covering force which, for the first time, was to include battleships. Force B, of *Ajax* and *Neptune*, with the destroyers *Kimberley* and *Kingston*, again under Admiral Rawlings, sailed from Alexandria for Malta on 27 November. The Axis convoy sailed in two sections, for Benghazi and Tripoli on 29 November, with a covering force of four cruisers, nine destroyers and a battleship. But, forewarned by the C 38 m, the convoy was first sighted on 1 December by a Sunderland and then attacked by RAF Blenheims from Malta who sank the merchant ship *Capo Faro* and damaged a destroyer and a tanker carrying troops and petrol. Meanwhile Force K, with Force B in support, first headed for Benghazi to catch and sink the Italian defensively-armed auxiliary cruiser *Adriatico*, and then steamed back across the Gulf of Sirte at high speed to dispatch the tanker *Iridio Mantovani* and the destroyer *Da Mosto*, both previously damaged by the Blenheims. Once again, Force K returned to Malta with enemy feathers in their caps.

On 5 December and again on the 8th the C 38 m revealed that the Italians were not only using destroyers but also cruisers to transport fuel to North Africa: the two 6″ gun cruisers *Alberto di Giussano* and *Alberico da Barbiano*, both with large deck loads of fuel, accompanied by the torpedo boat *Cigno*, would sail from Palermo at 6 p.m. on 12 December, bound for Tripoli at 22 knots, arriving on the afternoon of the 13th. They were due to pass Cape Bon at about 2 a.m. on 13 December. An RAF Wellington confirmed the signal by making the now obligatory sighting of the enemy ships on the 12th.

Clearly this was another task for Force K. But there was a snag. The monthly C 38 m settings were changed on the 1st of the month and, while the settings for December were being worked out, Pound had ordered air reconnaissance from Malta and sailings by Force K to be maintained at the previous intensity, so that Italian suspicions would not be aroused by a sudden lull.

Thus recent excursions by Force K had seriously depleted Malta's fuel stocks, and in the event Force K was to take no part on this occasion. But it so happened that four destroyers, *Sikh* (Commander G. H. Stokes), *Legion*, *Maori* and the Dutch *Isaac Sweers*, had sailed from Gibraltar on the 11th, bound for Alexandria to reinforce Cunningham's destroyer flotillas. The four were not a flotilla but were merely taking passage together, with mail, passengers and stores for Malta and then Alexandria.

All four destroyers had deck loads of stores, although Stokes had prevented the dockyard at Gibraltar loading as much as they wanted, for fear his ships would be unable to fight if called upon. Stokes' initial orders were to 'stay out of trouble' and on no account to become involved with superior forces. A signal from Vice Admiral Malta on 12 December had informed Stokes of the Italian ships and warned him that torpedo bombers from Malta were going to attack. Stokes' four ships had themselves been sighted by an Italian reconnaissance aircraft during the day, but the Italians had calculated that even if Stokes' ships increased speed, their two cruisers would still be ahead of them.

Stokes had also calculated that he too could be off Cape Bon at about the same time as the enemy. Just after midnight his four ships, in the order *Sikh, Legion, Maori, Isaac Sweers*, were rounding Cape Bon at 30 knots. Stokes ordered his ships to slow down, so that their large phosphorescent bow-waves would not betray them. Radar and visual contact with the enemy was made at about 2 a.m. To Stokes' surprise, the enemy ships had turned right round and were steering back towards him, having apparently been alarmed by the sound of aircraft engines overhead and fearing a torpedo attack.

Stokes led his ships inshore, where they were hidden by the darkness of the land close to starboard, and from that landward side, where the enemy could not see them and had never expected them to be, Stokes' ships opened fire with guns and torpedoes. In a brief, crushing action, lasting less than five minutes, the two Italian cruisers, caught utterly by surprise, were both sunk, with the loss of some 900 lives. The torpedo boat escaped with slight damage.

The four destroyers were cheered into Malta and, among the many signals Stokes received, was one from 830 Swordfish Squadron, whom he had robbed of their target: 'Many congratulations. Your attention is drawn to St John, Ch. 10, v. 1.' ('He that entereth not by the door into the sheepfold, but climbeth up some other way, the same is a thief and a robber.')

Stokes' destroyers had no sooner entered harbour and fuelled than they had to sail again. The C 38 m had already revealed that the Italians were going to try again to pass ships across to Tripoli on 12 December. A convoy of several ships, including some which had turned back on 22 November, was to sail from Taranto in three groups, each with battleship cover, and the battleship *Littorio* giving further cover to the whole operation.

Admiral Cunningham ordered the 15th Cruiser Squadron, of *Naiad, Galatea* and *Euryalus*, under Rear Admiral Philip Vian, with nine destroyers, to sail from Alexandria to intercept, and ordered Force K, Force B and Stokes' four destroyers to sail from Malta to support

170

them. Cunningham could not take *Queen Elizabeth* and *Valiant* to sea for lack of destroyers to escort them. Instead he had to resort to a trick. The C 38 m decrypts had given plenty of insight into the way the Italians studied British W/T procedures and what their reactions were likely to be. While strict radio silence was imposed at Alexandria, the minelayer *Abdiel* put to sea to broadcast radio traffic simulating the battle squadron on its way towards Tripoli.

The ruse worked. The Italian convoys and covering forces were recalled on the evening of 13 December, but, during their return voyage to Taranto, the battleship *Vittorio Veneto* was badly damaged by a torpedo from the submarine HMS/M *Urge*, and two merchantmen were sunk by the submarine *Upright*. Two more merchantmen were damaged in a collision. However, as the cruiser *Galatea* returned through the swept channel some 30 miles west of Alexandria on 15 December she was torpedoed and sunk by *U–557*.

Malta was now perilously short of fuel. The supply ship *Breconshire* sailed with fuel and other stores from Alexandria late on 15 December, accompanied by Vian's two remaining cruisers, *Naiad* and *Euryalus*, the anti-aircraft cruiser *Carlisle*, and eight destroyers. The plan was for Vian's force to be met off the 'bulge' of Benghazi on 17 December by the cruisers of Force K and four destroyers from Malta, who would remain with *Breconshire* and escort her into Malta, while Vian turned back to Alexandria after dark on the 17th.

Meanwhile, on 16 December the C 38 m and the Luftwaffe Enigma had both revealed that the enemy was going to try yet again to pass over his convoys, with battleship support, between 16 and 19 December. Cunningham now decided that Vian's main object would still be the protection of *Breconshire* but that he should also try to attack the Italian convoy that night, while Force K took *Breconshire* to Malta. Having sent back *Carlisle* because of her lack of speed, Vian himself pressed on with *Breconshire*, hoping to cross ahead of the main Italian force and deliver his charge into the hands of Force K.

Force K, of *Aurora*, *Penelope* and four destroyers, joined Vian on the morning of 17 December. Air reconnaissance reported the enemy ships at 1025 that morning: two battleships, two cruisers and seven destroyers, some 150 miles to the north-north-west of Vian's force. Actually this was *Littorio*, flying the flag of Admiral Iachino, with two more battleships, *Andrea Doria* and *Giulio Cesare*, two heavy cruisers and ten destroyers. Some 60 miles to the west of Iachino, but not located by the aircraft, was the convoy, with yet another battleship *Caio Duilio*, three cruisers and eleven destroyers.

Iachino also learned of Vian's force from reconnaissance aircraft (which first identified *Breconshire* as a battleship and continued to report her as such) and steamed south-west at 24 knots, his two older battleships' maximum speed, hoping to intercept the British ships before sunset. Vian's ships were attacked by Italian bombers and torpedo-bombers more than twenty times that day but survived untouched. The C 38 m gave some information about *Littorio*'s course and speed, but not her position, and air reconnaissance could not provide continuous information about the Italian fleet throughout that day. However, Vian knew enough about the enemy's whereabouts to be able to keep *Breconshire*, his main responsibility, out of danger until he turned her over to Force K, who delivered her safely into Malta.

Vian's cruisers and destroyers met the main Italian fleet at sunset on 17 December. It should have been a great chance for Iachino but, as always, the Italians were reluctant to take risks with their ships and now knew themselves to be very much inferior at night fighting. When Vian's destroyers raced forward to deliver a torpedo attack, Iachino turned away and this brief engagement, known as the First Battle of Sirte, was soon over. Contact was lost in the darkness, Iachino being content to go back to covering the convoy.

The Italian convoy had turned back for a time but now resumed its course. Vian still hoped to engage it. After losing contact with the Italian fleet, Vian patrolled for a few hours either side of midnight across what he had previously been informed by ULTRA was the route for the Benghazi-bound section of the convoy. However, by that time Iachino had changed the arrangements; the Benghazi secion, with the valuable merchant ship *Ankara*, carrying tanks, was not detached until late on 18 December. Vian was not aware of this. He had only an ULTRA signal, received late on 17 December, informing him that Iachino had been allowed to alter the convoy's route. It was this news which probably made Vian decide that it was not now coming his way; he broke off the search soon after midnight.

When Vian was halfway back to Alexandria, the C 38 m revealed the positions of the enemy convoys and the news that the Italians had decided to send their main naval force back to Taranto at 1400 on 18 December. This changed the situation completely. The enemy convoy, having enjoyed a night of most unexpected peace and quiet, arrived at Tripoli after dark on 18 December to find itself under torpedo attack by Albacores of 828 Squadron from Malta, who hit and disabled the merchantman *Napoli*, which had to be towed in, and in the midst of an air-raid by Wellingtons laying magnetic mines in their path. The convoy anchored off for the night and entered Tripoli on 19 December. It was the safe arrival of this convoy, with 300 vehicles, large stocks of 88 mm ammunition, fuel and other stores, which enabled Rommel to launch his counter-attack on 21 January, 1942.

Meanwhile, when the information from the C 38 m had been confirmed by aircraft sightings, Force K, who had only just arrived in Malta with *Breconshire*, sailed again at 1830 on 18 December to try and intercept the four ships of the convoy's Tripoli section. But at about 1 a.m. on 19 December Force K ran into a minefield some 20 miles east of Tripoli. *Neptune* struck two mines, which disabled her. *Aurora* and *Penelope* both struck mines and *Aurora* was badly damaged, although she was able to reach Malta under her own power. *Penelope* stayed to help *Neptune* who struck a third mine. *Kandahar* entered the minefield to give assistance but she too struck a mine which blew off her stern. Finally, *Neptune* hit a fourth mine and sank; she had only one survivor. Admiral Ford sent out the destroyer *Jaguar* which found the crippled *Kandahar* some 36 hours later and rescued most of her ship's company. But the ship herself had to be sunk.

Indications of this minefield, which effectively destroyed Force K in a matter of hours, had been given by the C 38 m which had disclosed in October that the Italians had laid a minefield (Operation 'B') off Benghazi, and another, Operation 'T', during June. But the C 38 m had given no other details about the lays. Captain Agnew, the Senior Officer Force K, was not himself an ULTRA recipient and received ULTRA information transmuted and rephrased through signals and orders from Vice Admiral Malta. He may never have been told of the possibility of the minefield, or its existence might even have been discounted by the staffs in Malta and Alexandria. It was laid close to the 100-fathom line, a depth of water in which the Royal Navy had considered it was impossible to lay moored mines.

This disaster was quickly followed by another. At about 9 p.m. on the evening of 18 December the Italian submarine *Scire* surfaced off Alexandria, about $1\frac{1}{2}$ miles from Ras el Tin lighthouse, where the submarine launched three two-man submersible 'chariots', or 'pigs' as they were called. It was a very dark night, with a calm sea and a clear sky – perfect for their enterprise. The three 'chariots', with their helmeted, rubber-suited and goggled crews sitting astride, set off in the darkness towards Alexandria. Their objective was to penetrate the harbour entrance and, if possible, to lay explosive charges under major units of the Mediterranean Fleet.

The C 38 m had been giving cryptic warnings of some form of raid. By 17 December Cunningham had been warned by GC & CS of C 38 m signals showing the Supreme Command of the Italian Navy's interest in some undertaking at Alexandria. A message on 17 December informed Cunningham that an Italian reconnaissance sortie that day had revealed two British battleships at their usual berths and – an odd and possibly significant detail – that the sea was calm. The next day the C 38 m revealed that that reconnaissance sortie had been regarded by the Italians as 'urgent'.

Clearly something was about to happen. It could be an air-raid, in greater strength than usual, or it could even be a desperate 'suicide' attack by some other weapon, to disable the Mediterranean fleet and prevent it interfering with Rommel's supply convoys. The position would have been clearer had GC & CS been able to read the Italian naval book cyphers during the previous year. Unforeseen and previously unknown to British intelligence, the Italian 10th Light Flotilla, as it was called, had already undertaken other operations in the Mediterranean, including successful 'chariot' attacks on shipping at Gibraltar, the sinking by one-man explosive motorboats (EMBs) of the cruiser *York* at Suda Bay in Crete in March, 1941, and an abortive EMB attack on Malta in July.

Lacking precise intelligence information, Cunningham issued a general warning at 1025 on 18 December: 'Attacks on Alexandria by air, boat or human torpedo may be expected when calm weather prevails. Look-outs and patrols should be warned accordingly.' But, despite the increased vigilance, the extra patrols, and the charges exploded in the water to deter just such attacks as their own, the charioteers took advantage of a moment when the anti-torpedo nets were drawn aside to permit Vian's destroyers to return to harbour, and succeeded in penetrating the main anchorage in the early hours of 19 December. Explosive charges were laid under *Queen Elizabeth* and *Valiant* and the large tanker *Sagona* (which the attacking charioteers mistook for an aircraft carrier). When the mines duly detonated, *Sagona*'s stern was blown off and both battleships were severely damaged. In one sublimely brave exploit by the Italian Navy, Cunningham's entire battle squadron had been rendered *hors de combat*.

In the next few days the C 38 m revealed that, fortunately for the Allies, enemy reconnaissance did not show at once how well the charioteers had succeeded. Both battleships had settled more or less on an even keel, so that it was possible to conceal the true extent of the damage done to them. Daily life and ceremonial carried on more ostentatiously than normal in both ships. Bold pictures appeared in the press at home of an unruffled Admiral Cunningham standing at the salute on *Queen Elizabeth*'s apparently undamaged quarterdeck while colours were hoisted in the morning. It took a keen eye to discern that the flagship was several feet lower in the water than usual.

The damage to the battle squadron reduced Cunningham's effective strength to three cruisers, *Naiad*, *Euryalus* and *Dido*, under Vian, with *Carlisle* and some destroyers at Alexandria, and two cruisers, *Penelope* and the damaged *Aurora*, at Malta. However, for a time, air escort from Malta and from the airfields in Cyrenaica enabled Cunningham to compensate for his weakness at sea. In the first week of January, 1942, under fighter protection and escorted by Vian's cruisers, the fleet auxiliary HMS *Glengyle* was run into Malta with fuel and other stores and the empty *Breconshire* brought safely out.

Admiral Cunningham intended to run one convoy of four or five ships to Malta every month. The first convoy, of four ships, sailed from Alexandria on 16 January, closely escorted by *Carlisle* and eight destroyers, with Vian's cruisers as a covering force. One merchant ship, *Thermopylae*, developed engine defects, turned back, was bombed and set on fire and had to be sunk. The destroyer *Gurkha* was torpedoed by *U–133* and later sank. But the remainder, effectively escorted by Beaufighters of No. 201 Naval Cooperation Group RAF and by Hurricanes from Malta, arrived safely. Between 24 and 28 January *Breconshire* made another run to Malta and *Glengyle* and a second ship were brought out.

The Italians did not learn (actually from a prisoner-of-war) of their success in Alexandria harbour until 30 January. But from 29 December onwards, the C 38 m had showed that the Italians were getting ready to sail another convoy to Tripoli under battleship escort and gave details of the convoy's size – nine merchant vessels of 10,000 tons – and its exact route.

But this was to be yet another example where ULTRA information was ineffective without sufficient force to make use of it in the field. Force K was now reduced to *Penelope* and three destroyers. Between 30 December and 5 January, as a necessary preliminary to the convoy's sailing, massive air-raids by more than 400 aircraft of Fliegerkorps II from Sicily rendered Malta's airfields largely unusable. Lack of reconnaissance from Malta meant that the convoy was not sighted until it was nearing Tripoli. An air strike was launched but failed to find the convoy. On 5 January the C 38 m reported the convoy's safe arrival in Tripoli (but did not vouchsafe the information that it had also included fifty-four tanks).

Fliegerkorps II continued its efforts against Malta throughout January, 1942, when not a single day and only eight nights passed without a raid; there were 262 raids during the month, seventy-three of them by night. Thus, Malta's Swordfish, Wellington and Blenheim squadrons had been reduced to only a few serviceable aircraft when, on 22 January, the Italians sailed another convoy with battleship cover. Again the C 38 m disclosed the convoy's sailing, its movements, the strength of its covering forces, and the fact that it would be carrying a large quantity of motor transport. The C 38 m did not reveal whether or not this convoy was carrying tanks, but a previous C 38 m decrypt of 14 January, enquiring whether the port facilities in Tripoli could handle tanks weighing 25 tons, strongly suggested that it was. In fact, it had seventy-three.

The convoy, codenamed Operation T. 18, sailed in two sections: four merchantmen, escorted by six destroyers and two torpedo-boats, left Messina on the morning of the 22nd, with a covering force of three cruisers and another four destroyers. The 13,000 ton former Lloyd-Triestino liner *Victoria*, described in Count Ciano's diary as 'the pearl of the Italian merchant fleet' but now a troopship and carrying some 1,600 men of a Panzer division, sailed from Taranto, escorted by the battleship *Caio Duilio* and four destroyers, at 5 p.m. the same day.

The three cruisers were sighted by a reconnaissance aircraft from Malta early on 23 January. The *Duilio* group was also sighted shortly afterwards and, at 11 a.m., the three merchantmen (one having already turned back) and their escort. The two convoy sections joined up at 1 p.m. that afternoon and were shadowed, despite their escort of eight Junker Ju.88s, which was later increased to twelve, until 4.15.

Then, and for the next hour and half, there began a series of attacks by Flying Fortresses, Wellingtons, Blenheims and torpedo-carrying Beauforts (making their operational debut in the Mediterranean), involving fifty-three aircraft in all, by No. 201 Naval Co-operation Group, flying from Cyrenaica and Egypt. But for all the effort, only one ship was lost. At sunset *Victoria* was hit and brought to a standstill by a torpedo from a Beaufort. In the gathering darkness, as the troops were getting into the lifeboats, two out of a strike of five Albacores of 826 Squadron Fleet Air Arm, flying from an airfield near Benghazi, attacked with torpedoes. The CO of 826, Lieutenant-Commander J. W. S. Corbett, was shot down and, with his crew, became a PoW, but the torpedo from the second Albacore, piloted by Lieutenant H. M. Ellis, hit and finally sank 'the pearl'. The C 38 m later revealed that over 1,000 of the troops on board *Victoria* survived and reached Tripoli, as did the rest of the convoy on 24 January, despite very persistent attempts by 830 Squadron from Malta, determinedly led by their CO, Lieutenant-Commander F. H. E. Hopkins. The Swordfish flew two sorties through a full gale during the night to make torpedo attacks, but without success.

Within a few days the airfields of Cyrenaica were once more in Axis hands and the situation changed again very much to the Allies' detriment. The February convoy, codenamed Operation MF.5, sailed from Alexandria on the evening of the 12th in two sections, a short interval apart: in Convoy MW.9A, the fast merchantmen *Clan Chattan* and *Clan Campbell*, escorted by *Carlisle* and four destroyers, and in convoy MW.9B, a third fast transport, *Rowallan Castle*, with another four destroyers. Next day the convoy came under heavy air attack despite fighter cover from shore. *Clan Campbell* was hit, her speed was reduced, and she was diverted to Tobruk. Vian's cruisers, *Naiad*, *Dido* and *Euryalus*, with eight destroyers, joined on 14 February, the critical day, when the convoy would be beyond fighter cover. By that time anti-aircraft ammunition was already being rationed. High level and dive bombers made a series of attacks in which *Clan Chattan* was hit and caught fire. Ammunition on board her began to explode. Her crew and service personnel were taken off and she was sunk by the destroyers.

That afternoon the convoy met Force K, of *Penelope* and six destroyers, escorting convoy ME.10 of four empty ships from Malta. Vian turned back for Alexandria with the 'empties', while *Penelope* and her destroyers took *Rowallan Castle* on towards Malta. But she too was bombed and disabled. The destroyer *Zulu* took her in tow but when it became clear that she could not reach the 'umbrella' of Malta's Hurricanes by daylight she was sunk, on the orders of Admiral Cunningham. *Penelope* and her two accompanying destroyers, *Lance* and *Legion*, reached Malta on 15 February.

The enemy might not have the benefit of ULTRA, but they did have agents in Alexandria and intensive air reconnaissance and, most important of all, the certain knowledge that every Allied convoy had to be going to Malta. The Italians knew of the sailing of the MW convoys and a powerful force, of the battleship *Caio Duilio*, four cruisers, and eleven destroyers sailed from Taranto to intercept. They lay in wait for a time to the north-east of Malta but eventually returned to Taranto on 15 February. Their objective, the convoy, had simply ceased to exist.

By contrast, a week later, in Operation K.7, the Italians passed across two convoys of three ships, from Corfu and Messina, with battleship and cruiser cover. The convoy sailings and details of the covering force were revealed by the C 38 m and some ships were located by a radar-equipped Wellington on the night of 21 February. Next day and during the following night attacks were mounted by Flying Fortresses, Beauforts, Blenheims, Wellingtons and Albacores. But the Albacores failed because of a navigational error of 100 miles in the locating report, and of the others, some turned back, some had engine troubles or radio failures, and some failed to find the target. Only one Fortress and one Wellington found and bombed the convoy. Both missed. The entire convoy reached Tripoli unscathed.

It seemed that the enemy was also running a monthly replenishment routine, for in the first week of March the C 38 m gave details of more Italian convoys. The operation, codenamed V.5, involved three convoys to Tripoli, sailing from Brindisi, Messina and Naples, and two return convoys. The whole undertaking, which lasted from 7 to 9 March, was covered by cruisers, destroyers and torpedo boats. All the convoys reached their destinations without mishap. Vian's cruisers and destroyers sailed from Alexandria on 9 March, but did not encounter the enemy. They did, however, rendezvous with the cruiser *Cleopatra* and the damaged destroyer *Kingston* from Malta. Vian's ships beat off attacks by Italian torpedo bombers and German bombers on 10 March but Vian's flagship *Naiad* was torpedoed and sunk by U–565, about sixty miles north-east of Sollum on the 11th.

It was now time for the monthly convoy, codenamed MW.10, to Malta. *Breconshire*, *Clan Campbell*, *Pampas* and the Norwegian *Talabot* sailed from Alexandria on 29 March, escorted by *Carlisle* and six destroyers. The close escort was to be joined at sea by six *Hunt* Class destroyers who, however, were first sent on a submarine 'hunter-killer' operation along the North African coast towards Tobruk. They found one submarine, U–652, which sank *Heythrop*. Vian, now flying his flag in *Cleopatra*, with *Dido* and *Euryalus*, and four destroyers, sailed a day later. On the same day Force H, under Vice Admiral Syfret, flying his flag in the battleship *Malaya*, sailed from Gibraltar with the cruiser *Hermione*, nine destroyers and the carriers *Eagle* and *Argus*, to fly in more Spitfires to Malta.

The convoy was sighted and reported by the Italian submarines *Onice* and *Platino*, and attacked by German aircraft late on 21 March. Just after midnight on the 22nd three cruisers and four destroyers sailed from Messina, and the battleship *Littorio*, wearing the flag of Iachino, and six destroyers (two of which soon turned back), sailed from Taranto. *Littorio*'s sailing was revealed in a C 38 m decrypt, and reported by the submarine HMS/M *P.36*, on patrol in the Gulf of Taranto, in the early hours of the 22nd.

Early on the morning of 22 March *Penelope* and *Legion* joined Vian from Malta. Vian by then had *P.36*'s report and the ULTRA decrypt and knew that he was likely to encounter heavy enemy ships later that day. It was *Euryalus* who first made the signal 'Enemy in sight' at 2.27 p.m. that afternoon. (As Captain E. W. Bush, commanding *Euryalus*, later recalled, it was the frigate *Euryalus* who first sighted the combined French and Spanish fleets before Trafalgar.) Superbly led by Vian himself in a brilliant action known as the Second Battle of Sirte, Vian's covering cruisers and destroyers defeated a vastly superior force. Making judicious use of skilfully laid smoke screens, advancing to threaten with guns and torpedoes, then retreating as though to lead their adversaries into a trap, and advancing again, they frustrated and fought off first the Italian heavy cruisers and then *Littorio* herself.

At dusk Iachino was persuaded to break off the action and retire, although only one of his cruisers had suffered slight damage. To complete the Italians' sense of defeat and despondency, two of their destroyers foundered in a gale during the return to harbour. Of Vian's ships, two destroyers had been damaged: *Cleopatra* had been hit by a 15″ shell, and *Euryalus* had suffered a near-miss which swept her upper deck with splinters. The convoy, with the *Hunts* in close company, had wheeled away to the south and then to the west, unharmed. Bush later wrote, 'Had the roles been reversed it is difficult to imagine that anything of either convoy or escort would have survived.'

Unfortunately the action had delayed the convoy so that it was still at sea when enemy aircraft found it at daylight the next day. *Breconshire* was bombed and disabled eight miles from Malta. She reached Marsaxlokk on the 25th, where she was bombed again and finally beached as a wreck two days later. *Clan Campbell* was bombed twenty miles from Malta and sank at once. Only *Pampas* and *Talabot* entered harbour, to the cheers of the people of Malta. The cheers were premature. Both ships were bombed and sunk while alongside. In the event only some 5,000 of the 26,000 tons of cargo in the convoy were safely unloaded.

The position of the people and garrison of Malta was now desperate. The bombing raids were at their height, whereas the island's resources on the ground and in the air were at their lowest. Figures from the Luftwaffe Enigma showed the tonnage of bombs dropped on Malta rising from 750 in February, 1942, to 2,000 in March, and to 5,500 in April. Submarines were having to lie submerged on the bottom in harbour during daylight to escape air attack. *Penelope* was hit so often by bomb splinters while in dock that she was aptly called HMS *Pepperpot*.

Ominously, the C 38 m began to reveal the outlines of an Axis plan, codenamed Operation Herkules, to invade Malta itself. The invasion was never attempted. By May, 1942, Luftwaffe strength in Sicily was being reduced as units were transferred to the Russian front. The Axis failure to seize Malta, at a time when it would have been feasible to do so, was one of their greatest strategic errors of the war. In many ways Malta was the key to the Mediterranean campaign. The main convoy routes of the two sides ran roughly at right angles, with Malta as their nodal crossing point; the Allies ran ships to and from Gibraltar and Alexandria, passing Malta, east and west, while the Axis ran supply convoys between Italy and North Africa, passing Malta, north and south.

Malta's fortunes and the progress of the land campaigns in North

179

Africa were very closely linked in a tight circle of cause and effect. If Malta had enough air and sea power to disrupt the Axis supply convoys, then the Allied offensive on land prospered and Malta's own position became more secure. The converse was true: if Malta lacked the resources to interrupt Axis supplies, then the Allies were forced back on land and Malta's own situation became more perilous.

In June two more convoys were sailed, HARPOON of six merchant ships from the west, and VIGOROUS of eleven from the east. Both were fiercely attacked; VIGOROUS was threatened, as Vian himself said, 'with all known forms of surface attack', including the battleships *Littorio* and *Vittoria Veneto*, and had to turn back to Alexandria. Only two HARPOON ships reached Malta, at the cost of the cruiser *Hermione*, five destroyers – *Bedouin*, *Hasty*, *Airedale*, the Australian *Nestor* and the Polish *Kujawiak* – two minesweepers and six merchant ships.

In August all other allied naval priorities were temporarily set aside for the PEDESTAL convoy of fourteen merchant ships, escorted by two battleships, three aircraft carriers, seven cruisers and thirty-two destroyers. Five merchant ships, including the tanker *Ohio*, reached Malta, at the cost of the aircraft carrier *Eagle*, the cruisers *Cairo* and *Manchester*, the destroyer *Foresight* and nine merchant ships; the aircraft carrier *Indomitable*, the cruisers *Nigeria* and *Kenya*, and three merchantmen were damaged. Two U-boats were sunk, and about forty Axis aircraft destroyed. But Malta was only reprieved, not relieved. Not until the PORTCULLIS convoy of December, 1942, was the siege of Malta finally and properly lifted.

During this bleak period, ULTRA had little effect. There were still small local successes, as on 5 May, when the C 38 m revealed precise details of another attack by Italian human torpedoes on Alexandria, which was fully frustrated when it took place, as expected, on 14–15 May. But on the broader front ULTRA could not compensate for the weakness of the Allied forces. It was not until the opening of the battle of El Alamein in October, 1942, and the successful Allied TORCH landings in North Africa in November that ULTRA was able to contribute to a winning strength in the air, on land, and at sea.

15 | HOW ULTRA WAS NEARLY LOST

It seems that what the German Navy really needed most in the Second World War was a good bookmaker. In the war at sea, and especially in the war against the U-boats, it was as though too many horses lost which should have won, or won when they should have had no chance. All those fortunate sightings claimed by Allied aircraft and submarines, the searches ostensibly carried out on the evidence of D/F bearings, the betrayals blamed on the French Resistance, all those convoys diverted out of danger in the very nick of time, all those seemingly providential arrivals of escorts or aircraft at remote rendezvous could not *all* be due to chance or the fortunes of war. Over a period of years, from the summer of 1941 when GC & CS first broke the German naval Enigma, a statistician or actuary should have been able to detect a bias in the pattern of events. Certainly by the end of 1943, any reasonably competent bookmaker or his clerk could have warned the Kriegsmarine that there was something suspicious about the odds being shouted in the ring.

It is, of course, possible, even probable, that somewhere at some time some German intelligence officer did become convinced that the Enigma had been broken by the Allies. But in the intellectual climate of Nazi Germany, and more particularly in the Byzantine atmosphere of intrigue and jealousy in Hitler's court, it would have been an exceptionally bold man who went to the Führer Bunker and, like he who drew aside Praim's tent curtain at dead of night and told him half Troy was burned, informed Hitler that the Third Reich's communications system for all three services, world-wide, must now be considered insecure and should be entirely reconstituted, from the basic essentials upwards, with fresh codes and procedures. In any case, the protestations of one man, or even of a group of men, would not have been enough. It would have needed a gross breach of security by the Allies to convince Hitler and the many intelligence officers whose

181

careers (to say nothing of their lives) depended upon the continuing belief that the Enigma was invulnerable.

Ironically, such gross breaches of security were committed by the Allies, not once but many times. The Royal Navy alone, on several occasions, compromised the ULTRA secret through faulty procedures, carelessness, ignorance or an excess of zeal. All the B-Dienst Service had to do, on those occasions, was to read the signals actually available to it, and draw the correct conclusions.

The ULTRA secret was put at risk by the Royal Navy almost at once when, between 7 May and 11 July, 1941, fifteen German supply or weather-reporting ships were sunk in the Atlantic. Eight of these sinkings, beginning with the weather ship *Muenchen* on 7 May, were a direct result of information from the Enigma. Pound had decided that, to safeguard the ULTRA secret, two of these ships should not be attacked, but by chance both were sighted and sunk. The Germans were indeed made suspicious by this 'holocaust' of their ships and mounted an investigation. But, for the first time, though not for the last, they decided that the Enigma must be inviolate.

Meanwhile, Mr Churchill was pressing for more and quicker operational use to be made of ULTRA (or BONIFACE, as he called it, using an earlier code-name). He appeared to be under the impression that Admiral Cunningham, C-in-C Mediterranean, was dragging his feet over the use of this priceless information. In July, 1941, Churchill minuted to the First Sea Lord, Admiral Pound, 'I wish I knew what he [Cunningham] *did* when he received these messages'.

Unknown to Churchill or to Cunningham, information from the Enigma was already being used in the Mediterranean in such a manner as to jeopardize the ULTRA secret. On 16 July, 1941, an ULTRA signal informed Vice Admiral (Malta) and other addressees: 'S.S. "Bosforo" leaves Naples shortly for Benghazi, passing through position 33° 06′ N, 20° 16′ E. at 0330Z 19 July, where she will be met by a torpedo-boat which will carry out A/S search of Benghazi area p.m. 18 July. A./S search along line of approach will be carried out by aircraft a.m. 18 July and A/S and fighter patrols will be flown from dawn 19 July. Due Benghazi 0900Z 19 July'.

Captain (Submarines) in Malta at once informed a submarine on patrol by W/T: 'Italian m/v "Bosforo" 3,567 tons length 347 feet, draught 21 feet poop forecastle and long bridge, *leaves Naples shortly and will pass through 033° 06′ N, 020° 16′ E repetition 033° 06′ N. 020° 16′ E at 0630C 19th repetition 0630C/19th to arrive Benghazi 1200C 19th.*

'Torpedo-boat will make A/S search off Benghazi p.m. 18th and rendezvous with "Bosforo" in above position.

'There will be A/S air search along line of approach a.m. 18th and

A/S and fighter patrols from dawn 19th.'

Except for the substitution of 'm/v' for 'S/S', Captain (S)'s signal was an almost direct quote of the ULTRA, with exact repetitions of the ship's name, signalled position, destination, time of arrival, and the details of torpedo-boat and air patrols. Had this signal been captured by the enemy or broken by enemy cryptanalysis, ULTRA would certainly have been compromised. As the sharp Admiralty reproof pointed out, what Captain (S) should have done was to have ordered the submarine, which was already on patrol, to move to a new area 'if not already in contact with the enemy' where she would have had a good chance of sighting *Bosforo* at a time and in a place favourable for evading any possible anti-submarine patrols.

Three days later, on 20 July, C-in-C South Atlantic received an ULTRA signal: 'At 0119 and 0157B/20 two U-boats were operating in positions 07° 48' – 08° 42' N. 14° 30' – 15° 24' W. and 19° 30' – 20° 24' N. 20° 48' – 21° 42' W. respectively'. C-in-C S.A. warned the armed merchant cruiser HMS *Moreton Bay* to divert out of danger; 'Immediate' by W/T: Submarine reported in area 019° 30' N. to 20° 24' N., 20° 48' W. to 21° 42' W. Alter to westward as required then resume route'. The positions given repeated exactly those in the ULTRA and, furthermore, they were the positions of the corners of a secret German naval grid square and if the message had become known to the enemy would certainly have compromised the ULTRA source.

In November, 1941, Flag Officer North Atlantic, at Gibraltar, informed ships and authorities in the North Atlantic area of three German U-boats in 'the following positions' – giving an exact repeat of ULTRA information. In the same month, C-in-C Mediterranean passed to the Naval Attaché in Ankara the contents of an Enigma decrypt revealing that the enemy knew of an Allied plan to pass Russian tankers into the Mediterranean from the Black Sea. The Naval Attaché in Ankara was not an authorized ULTRA recipient. Turkey was a neutral country with a famous reputation as a hot-bed of espionage.

Thus it was not surprising that the Admiralty broadcast some swingeing reprimands which everybody took to heart. There were no more lapses for nearly a year, when it was the Army who were at fault. In September, 1942, the enemy learned that General Montgomery had had foreknowledge of Rommel's attack at Alam el Halfa in August, and also that Montgomery knew of Rommel's illness. Mr Churchill himself rebuked Montgomery.

Early in December, 1942, there were indications from the C 38 m that the enemy was planning some kind of special operation against a North African port, probably Bône. The information was first promulgated in an ULTRA of 5 December: 'Midday 5th, high Italian naval authorities required Italian naval command in Tunisia to provide 24 hours notice of date on which an operation (unspecified) was to take place, so that air force authorities could be informed. Personnel were being sent in destroyer 512, due Bizerta 5th'.

Further information was given in two ULTRAs of 11 December. At 0234Z/11, 'Germans require recent recce photos of Bône harbour sent to strong indications Bizerta by 1500 hours 11th and if possible visual recce before 1600 hours 11th. Strong indications concerned with projected motor torpedo-boat operations'. A second ULTRA at 1816Z/11, 'An operation, nature unknown, which necessitates suspension of air attacks on an unspecified port was being planned on 11th. Bizerta authorities interested.' This ULTRA commented that the two previous ULTRAs of 5th and 11th, 'may refer. The matter appeared to be of great urgency'.

Clearly the operation planned was to be a MAS (torpedo-boat) attack, mounted from Bizerta, on the harbour of Bône during the night of 11 December. The information and the conclusions to be drawn from the ULTRA signals had to be given to the Naval Officer in Charge, Bône. But NOIC Bône was not an ULTRA recipient and the information must have been given to him in a raw and unparaphrased form, and with no special instructions as to how ULTRA material had to be handled.

It was a fundamental breach of ULTRA procedure to pass ULTRA information to NOIC Bône, a non–ULTRA recipient, in such a way. But worse was to follow. Lacking any such guidance, and any knowledge of ULTRA, NOIC Bône at once broadcast a warning to the destroyer HMS *Velox*, escorting a convoy to Philippeville, repeating the signal to a wide circle of interested addressees, including Admiral Cunningham, who was now Naval Commander of the Expeditionary Force (N.C.X.F.) for the TORCH landings in North Africa, NOIC Philippeville, Commodore Algiers, and the Air Officer Commanding Eastern Air command: 'Emergency. E-boat attack on Bône is expected tonight. Delay your advance to arrive off Philippeville at dawn. Bône 1300/12. Fighter protection between Philippeville and Bône arranged. N.C.X.F. pass to A.O.C. Eastern Air Command.'

Worse still, NOIC Bône's signal was in Naval Cypher No. 3, a code which the Italians were suspected of having had some success in breaking. Indeed they had: on 18 December a signal was decrypted, from the Italian Communications staff in Bizerta to the German Naval Command Tunisia: 'According to W/T Intelligence on 11/12 an authority in Bône broadcast the following W/T message addressed to a

184

vessel or a Senior Officer of a convoy: "Attack by enemy S-boat is to be expected. Adjust speed so as to be off Philippeville at first light and to reach Bône at 1300. Bomber [sic] protection wll be provided between Philippeville and Bône".'

From this it was clear to the OIC that the enemy had the text of NOIC Bône's signal which was in an unparaphrased form very close to that in the original raw ULTRA. It followed that ULTRA was now perilously close to being compromised. The danger emerged even more starkly later the same day, when another signal was decrypted, from the German Naval Command Italy to the German Naval Command Tunisia: 'Italian Navy informs us that according to a reliable source the enemy had knowledge of the planned M.A.S. attack against Bône on the night of 11/12 to 12/12. Arrival of a convoy of 7 steamships, escorted by Aurora group, was postponed (on that account) until the afternoon'.

On 19 December, the Admiralty signalled to Cunningham by ULTRA: 'Italians were aware on 18th December that the arrival of a British convoy was postponed owing to knowledge of the planned M.A.S. attack for the night of 11–12 December. (Comment: This information was passed in the Admiralty Message of 1816/11, NOIC Bône unnecessarily disclosed our knowledge of enemy intentions to a wide circle and probably led to this leakage. The fact that the attack did not take place may lead the enemy to suspect the real source of our information).'

Cunningham replied promptly: 'This danger was realized and the matter taken up in the appropriate quarter immediately on receipt of NOIC Bône's signal. Error is regretted.' This was not much consolation to the watchers in the OIC who, this time, could do no more than cross their fingers and hope. They knew that the enemy now had enough information to discover the ULTRA secret and it seemed it would only be a question of time before the enemy tumbled to the solution.

But, miraculously, nothing happened – not even after a further series of hair-raising security lapses. NOIC Bône had unwittingly imperilled the ULTRA secret by disclosing an unnecessary amount of information. On 3 January, 1943, Captain 10th Submarine Flotilla at Malta made basically the same error in a signal by W/T to the submarine *P.42* on patrol: 'Immediate. *Three merchant ships one destroyer* at 1100A in position *037° 29' N. 010° 24' E.* Course 065°, speed 14 knots,' in which the words and figures in italics exactly repeated the text of an ULTRA signal. This was the same error as the Captain (Submarines) at Malta had committed in 1941. But, after a further ULTRA message, that the three ships' sailings had been cancelled, Captain S/M 10

185

signalled again to *P.42*, 'Cancel my last. Proceed to Malta as previously ordered'. Pound later criticized Captain S/M 10's handling of this in a message to Vice Admiral (Malta), in which he pointed out that 'the object of Captain S/M 10's first signal could have been achieved, together with security of the source of intelligence, by ordering submarine *P.42* to an intercepting patrol position without further details.' 'This is a matter,' Pound added, 'over which we cannot afford to have any, repeat *any* slips.'

On occasions Flag officers and their staffs abroad could be excused for asking themselves, why does the Admiralty send us this Special Intelligence if it does not want us to act upon it? In the far-flung naval commands all around the world, the sinking of even one U-boat was a rare and joyful event. Only the Admiralty could oversee the whole position world-wide and assess the effect of a single incident. But ULTRA was more than once imperilled by over-hasty reaction and by including too much information in the operational signals.

At 1608A on 9 January, 1943, the Admiralty sent to Flag Officer West Africa and the C-in-C South Atlantic the ULTRA message: 'Important. A German supply U-boat has been ordered to rendezvous with and fuel Italian U-boat "Cagni" at 1200/12 or if possible sooner in 01° 03′ N. 23° 57′ W. At 1700/6 this U-boat was in 15° 00′ N. 34° 20′ W. Comment: Information is being passed to COMINCH. There are indications that the supply U-boat is intended after this rendezvous to proceed further south.'

Flag Officer West Africa disposed forces to intercept the U-boat and told the Admiralty what he had done in a signal at 0933Z on 10 January: 'Have ordered HMS *Ilex* and *Holcombe* to hunt submarine in position 01° 03′ N. 23° 57″ W from day 12th January. Aircraft will be cooperating'. The U-boat was not found but Flag Officer West Africa must have felt he had done all he could and must therefore have been very shocked to receive a sharp reprimand from the Admiralty on 12 January: 'Your signal 0933Z/10 January contains *exact* position and date given in Admiralty Message 1608A/9 January.

'Your personal attention is called to the necessity for careful consideration of what action can be taken. On many occasions it will not be possible to make direct operational use of this information without prejudicing the source which it is vital to preserve.

'The presence of a combined destroyer and air hunting force at a rendezvous probably chosen for its remoteness would undoubtedly arouse the enemy's suspicions.'

In fact the enemy's suspicions were aroused. Even the supply U-boat, the Type XV *U–459*, noticed something amiss. At 1849 on 12 January *U–459* reported 'two waiting destroyers' in the rendezvous square. BdU ordered the rendezvous to be moved to another grid square. This too was revealed by the Enigma but no further action was taken. (*U–459* survived only for another six months, being sunk by aircraft in the Bay of Biscay offensive on 24 July, 1943.)

In March, 1943, there were two sequences of events in the Mediterranean, one on land and the other at sea, which endangered ULTRA to such an extent as to call down further severe Whitehall reprimands upon the heads of the area commanders. Early on the morning of 6 March the Afrika Korps attacked the Eighth Army at Medenine in Tunisia, to begin the battles for the Mareth Line. Rommel attacked believing that he had caught Montgomery by surprise. In fact the Enigma had revealed so much of Rommel's preparations and intentions beforehand that there was a danger that the very completeness of Montgomery's defensive positions would betray how much he must have known in advance. Mr Churchill warned Montgomery to 'safeguard our previous secret so far as possible in your dispositions'.

The Afrika Korps attack was repulsed with heavy losses. By the evening three Panzer divisions were in retreat, having lost fifty out of 140 tanks. Afterwards the Enigma revealed that the Germans had concluded, from PoWs and captured documents, that Montgomery not only knew in advance that Rommel was going to attack, but when, where and in what strength. The Germans did not in fact suspect the Enigma, but it had been a near enough shave to put ULTRA at risk. In the opinion of Whitehall there had been 'an alarming lack of security' which 'might well produce German cypher security countermeasures which would deny us all use of ULTRA'. Montgomery was again rebuked, as he had been after Alam el Halfa.

At sea the C 38 m and the Luftwaffe Enigma had given full details of an operation in which the enemy was going to sail two convoys to Bizerta, on 11 and 12 March, of four merchant vessels and a tanker, with cargoes which Kesselring called 'decisive for the future conduct of operations'. An attack on the convoys by air and surface forces was planned and duly carried out. Two merchant ships and the tanker were sunk. Unfortunately, there was a failure to carry out the necessary air sightings to give ULTRA a 'cover story'. Unknown to the Allies, the enemy convoy was delayed and some of the British forces were then sighted by the Luftwaffe at the point on the route *where the convoy would have been* had it not been delayed.

The enemy's suspicions were now thoroughly aroused. In a situation report made on the evening of 11 March German Naval Command Tunisia informed German Naval Command Italy that 'air attack on R-boats at 0940, 15 miles north of Zembretta, carried out by 12 Lockheeds and 30 Lightnings, like that on the R-boats at 1400/4/3, would lead to the conclusion that convoy intentions have become known to the enemy'. A message to Luftwaffe Command in Italy from Fliegerkorps Tunisia on 13 March put it in even stronger terms: 'The enemy activity of today in the air and on the sea must, in the view of Fliegerkorps Tunis, lead to the conclusion that the courses envisaged for convoys C and D were betrayed to the enemy. At 0845 a comparatively strong four-engined aircraft formation was N.E. of Bizerta. Also a warship formation consisting of light cruisers and destroyers lay N. of Bizerta, although no enemy warships had been sighted in this sea area for weeks.'

Reading the decrypts of these exchanges, the watchers in Whitehall, still nervous over events at Medenine, became increasingly alarmed. Pound and Churchill both reprimanded Cunningham, N.C.X.F. and naval C-in-C for the area of the Mediterranean. Churchill went so far as to threaten to withhold ULTRA altogether unless it was 'used only on great occasions or when thoroughly camouflaged'.

On 14 March Pound sent a personal message to Cunningham, repeated to the C-in-C Levant, who was responsible for the eastern end of the Mediterranean, and to Vice Admiral (Malta): 'As a result of an attack at 0840Z/11 March by 12 Lockheeds and 30 Lightnings on R-boats 15 miles north of Zembretta Germans suspected that the route of a convoy mentioned was known to British. This convoy which had been routed through this area was in fact delayed.

2. Luftwaffe authority at Tunis reported that at 0845/13 March a comparatively strong force of 4-engined bombers was to the N.E. of Bizerta also that a warship formation consisting of cruisers and destroyers had been to the north of Bizerta although no enemy war-ships had been sighted in this area for weeks.

3. From the British sea and air activity he appreciated that the courses planned for convoys C and D must have been betrayed to the enemy.

Comment: I am sure you appreciate when planning operations based on Special Intelligence the necessity for giving cover to the source by air recce or other means. Particular care is necessary where our air or sea forces seldom operate. German suspicions are now aroused and great care will be required until these are allayed.'

Cunningham replied on 15 March that 'care was taken to arrange air reconnaissance in vicinity of both convoys. Reconnaissance could not in fact reach northernmost convoy, but arrangements were made for dummy enemy reports to be made from vicinity. The convoy along north Sicilian coast was sighted by ASV aircraft at frequent intervals and the information provided was more accurate than that of Special Intelligence.

2. As regards movement of warships, there have been warships in vicinity of Skerki Bank on average every other day for the past fortnight. *Abdiel* [minelayer] has done 3 lays in this period accompanied part way by destroyers; 2 destroyers have gone through to Malta; and Force Q has operated. Enemy was aware of at least a proportion of these moves and reports of them.

3. While not minimising seriousness of arousing enemy misgivings, I consider his statement comes as much from a desire to cover his failure in protecting the convoy as from real base of suspicion. He did the same thing in excusing the recent failure against 8 Army [i.e. the defeat at Medenine].

4. The arrival of the convoy was of vital importance to the enemy and Tedder and I realize the equal importance of attacking it and concealing the source of the information. Short of failing to make proper effort against the convoy which I suggest would have been inadvisable, there appears to be no other action that could have been taken. I share your anxiety in this matter which is extremely difficult one to handle, but I assure you it received the closest attention.'

However, the enemy's suspicions did soon subside. Neither after Medenine, nor after the Bizerta convoy, nor when suspicions were raised a third time after the land battles at El Guettar and Maknassy at the end of March, did the enemy follow up their suspicions. Once again, they were confident of the Enigma; instead, they blamed interrogation of PoWs, the cutting of ground lines by the Allies, Allied air and ground reconnaissance, intelligence derived by the Allies from the use of plain language or careless signal procedures by their own forces – anything and everything except the Enigma.

For the rest of 1943 the ULTRA secret was unthreatened; but early in 1944 there was another sequence of events which showed how easy it might be to betray ULTRA, even when the correct procedures and safeguards were employed. Three naval operations involving ULTRA followed close upon each other. Each, taken by itself, seemed innocuous. Each had a satisfactory 'cover story' and none seemed to pose a threat to ULTRA. But when the circumstances of all three were considered together they placed ULTRA in great danger, perhaps the greatest of the whole war at sea.

After the first defeat of the U-boats in the Atlantic in May, 1943, BdU began to send more U-boats to remoter areas, in the Indian Ocean and around the Cape of Good Hope, where the enemy escorts were fewer and where refuelling from surface ships could still take place in comparative safety. In June, 1943, seven German U-boats operating near the Cape of Good Hope sank ten ships. They refuelled from the tanker *Charlotte Schliemann* at the end of June and, operating in the Mozambique channel, sank twenty-five more ships in July and August. At the end of August one U-boat went on to Penang, while the rest began their return voyages to Europe.

These U-boats were to have been replaced by eleven Type IX U-boats in Operation *Monsun*. The *Monsun* boats sailed at the end of June, 1943, to operate in the Indian Ocean between Bombay and the Persian Gulf. They should have had their own supply boat, *U–462*, but it was sunk in the Bay of Biscay on 30 July (on what was its third attempt to get out across the Bay). Of the eleven *Monsun* boats, only five arrived on station. The rest were either sunk or forced to turn back.

Refuelling was the key to long-range U-boat operations in the Indian Ocean, as it had been in the Atlantic. The Enigma had revealed the June refuelling by *Charlotte Schliemann*, at a rendezvous off Madagascar, but only after it had taken place. But in August the Enigma began to disclose the activities of a second tanker, *Brake*, which had enough fuel, supplied by the Japanese, to replenish ten U-boats. On 13 September the Enigma revealed that *Brake* had refuelled the *Monsun* boats on the 8th at a rendezvous which was probably about 450 miles south of Mauritius. However, the *Monsun* boats accomplished very little – they claimed to have sunk only three ships and one *Monsun* boat had been sunk – before making for Penang at the end of October.

In January, 1944, the *Monsun* boats from Penang began patrols in the area from Ceylon across to the Gulf of Aden and down to Mauritius. Here, they enjoyed a rare and brief period of success. In January, February and March, 1944, thirty Allied merchant ships of 195,880 tons were sunk (the highest shipping losses anywhere in the world at that time) and seventeen of those ships, of 94,520 tons, were sunk by the *Monsun* boats. They could have achieved more, in an operational area where there was a severe shortage of escorts, had the Enigma not made it possible to lay ambushes for their tankers.

The first target was *Charlotte Schliemann*. She had refuelled two U-boats on 27 January. Enigma decrypts had revealed that the fuelling was to take place, but the rendezvous position could not be fixed precisely enough and the operation to intercept her failed. However, early in February, the Enigma again disclosed that *Charlotte Schliemann* was to refuel four U-boats on 11/12 February. But the German system of disguising the rendezvous areas made it difficult to choose between three possible positions: (a) 840 miles, (b) 440 miles and (c) 680 miles respectively from Mauritius. The time of the rendezvous was to be 1200 on 11 February.

The C-in-C Eastern Fleet, Admiral Sir James Somerville, mounted an operation involving Catalina flying boat searches from 9–14 Feb-

ruary of areas within 120 miles of all three rendezvous possibilities
The destroyer HMS *Relentless* was ready in support if the rendezvous
proved to be at (a), and the cruiser HMS *Newcastle* was available if it
were (c). Meanwhile, as a precaution, Somerville ordered surface ships
to keep clear of all the rendezvous points on 11 Feburary.

No flying was possible on 9th and 10th February. But at 1450 on
11th, a Catalina sighted *Charlotte Schliemann*, with a U-boat actually
alongside her, at a position about 35 miles to the south-south-east of
rendezvous (a). *Relentless* duly intercepted *Charlotte Schliemann* at 0040
on 12 February, approximately 120 miles south-east of the rendezvous,
and the tanker scuttled herself. The U-boat later reported that it had
seen the aircraft, but did not know of any attack on the tanker.

As *Charlotte Schliemann* had been sunk before she had been able to
refuel all the U-boats, *Brake* was summoned up to take her place. It
was the circumstances of the interception of *Brake*, so soon after the
sinking of *Charlotte Schliemann*, which was seriously to compromise
ULTRA.

Somerville signalled by ULTRA to the Admiralty on 21 February
that he estimated the enemy would assume *Charlotte Schliemann* had
been lost by 22 February and that *Brake* would sail from Batavia to
replace her on the 22nd or 23rd. He proposed to mount Operation
SLEUTH, with the cruiser HMS *Gambia*, the aircraft carrier HMS
Illustrious and two destroyers, to intercept *Brake* in an area south-west
of the Cocos Islands on her way to the U-boat rendezvous.

The Admiralty approved the plan but warned that the enemy
was still apparently unaware that surface ships had been used against
Charlotte Schliemann and that if the enemy ever did become aware of
it, the appearance of surface ships at *Brake*'s refuelling rendezvous
would seriously compromise ULTRA. Any operation with surface
ships must have D/F bearings as a 'cover story'. Catalina patrols should
be flown but the aircraft must avoid *Charlotte Schliemann*'s rendezvous
area, which it was assumed *Brake* would also use. (The Admiralty's
anxiety lest ULTRA be imperilled by some precipitate minor action
in a remote ocean can almost be felt.)

On 23 February the Admiralty informed Somerville that the Enigma
had disclosed a waiting area for U-boats south of Mauritius, between
latitudes 28° 20′ and 31° 00′ S. and longitudes 66° 00′ and 70° 00′ E.
Brake was due to arrive in this area on or about 8 March. Somerville
planned to intercept her on 29 February, south-west of the Cocos
Islands, with *Newcastle*, a second cruiser *Suffolk*, the escort carrier *Battler*
and the destroyer HMS *Quadrant*. The Admiralty told Somerville that
U-boat W/T signals had been intercepted and D/F'd and could be used
as cover for an anti-U-boat operation by *Battler* and *Quadrant*. But the

191

Admiralty warned, once again, of the dangers of approaching *Brake*'s rendezvous before she had been sighted from the air or had broken W/T silence.

Somerville's ships had sailed, and on 1 March he informed the Admiralty that in order to avoid premature disclosure to the U-boats of air and surface patrols, he intended to destroy *Brake* on her way to the rendezvous area. But the situation was changing. On 29 February an ULTRA informed Somerville that *Brake* had left Batavia and would arrive in the refuelling area on 11 March. The possible location of the rendezvous had also been changed, to one of two positions further to the south, at 32° S. and at longitude either 62° 12' or 73° E. Always fearful of compromising ULTRA, the Admiralty informed Somerville that he should not try to intercept *Brake* on her way to the refuelling area.

The dialogue between Colombo and Whitehall as to where, when and at whose hands *Brake* would meet her fate continued, with the Enigma acting as a kind of sinister, prompting fugleman. Somerville, while conceding the need to preserve ULTRA, was determined to destroy *Brake*. The Admiralty, just as concerned over *Brake*, was nevertheless determined to safeguard ULTRA. Somerville cancelled his original plan and instead planned to search the area 300 miles northeast of the rendezvous on 9, 10 and 11 March with *Newcastle*, *Suffolk*, *Battler* and two destroyers. He also proposed that Catalinas from Mauritius search the more westerly of the two rendezvous alternatives and asked whether, if D/F bearings showed U-boats near either of the two, he could send *Battler* and the two destroyers to search after a decent interval had elapsed. The Admiralty agreed, but, cautious as ever, insisted that the Catalinas could only search the western alternative after definite D/F bearings had been obtained.

On 9 March the situation changed again. The Admiralty informed Somerville that D/F bearings had been obtained, which would cover a search for a surface vessel or a U-boat at either of the two rendezvous, but, on the day of the rendezvous neither ships nor aircraft were to approach within a hundred miles of the position unless contact had already been made. The Admiralty also gave permission for Catalinas to search the western rendezvous without previous D/F cover, and commented that the easternmost rendezvous was still considered the most likely.

So it proved. On 12 March a Swordfish of 834 Sq. from *Battler* sighted *Brake* with two U-boats alongside. *Battler*'s Meteorological Officer had studied the weather conditions in the area for some months and was popularly supposed to have predicted the most likely time and place for a U-boat rendezvous. *Battler*'s ship's company were

192

delighted by their Met. Officer's expertise, but surprised and annoyed when their aircraft returned as ordered without making an attack and no strike was mounted against the enemy. In fact, as they later heard, the destroyer HMS *Roebuck* closed and sank *Brake* in a position some thirty miles from the more easterly rendezvous. The two U-boats escaped and one of them signalled that it had sighted two flying-boats and carrier-borne aircraft during the day. It presumed that 'refuelling had been basically compromised'.

This was truer than the U-boat captain knew. The ex-Italian U-boat *UIt–22*, on passage from Europe to the Far East with cargo, had been ordered to rendezvous at 1200 on 11 March with the homeward bound *U–178*, about 400 miles south of Cape Town, and transfer some radar gear. When this was revealed by the Enigma, the details were sent to C-in-C South Atlantic who laid on an air search (Operation WICKETKEEPER). *UIt–22* was duly sunk by aircraft at 0722 on 11 March as the U-boat was approaching the rendezvous from the northeast and a few miles away from it. Next day *U–178* signalled: 'On 11th owing to constant patrol by fast land aircraft for the most part under water, R/V has not come off. At R/V point this morning saw large oil patches. Persistent day air. Boat not met up to evening. Request orders.'

Battler's ship's company might credit their Met. Officer with almost supernatural powers, but the OIC had no illusions that ULTRA was now under its gravest threat of the war so far. None of these three rendezvous incidents had been dangerous in itself. In none was the risk greater than had been accepted successfully many times before. *Charlotte Schliemann* had been sighted first by a Catalina 35 miles from her rendezvous, on the date of the rendezvous, and had been sunk by *Relentless* 120 miles from the rendezvous ten hours after the air sighting. *Brake* had been sighted by *Battler*'s Swordfish 30 miles from the rendezvous on the day after the signalled date of the rendezvous, and sunk by *Roebuck*, after ample 'cover' had been given by enemy W/T. *UIt–22* had been sunk by aircraft very near the rendezvous, and on the signalled date, but the position was one where air patrols were not unlikely.

It was not the incidents individually but their combination that imperilled ULTRA. Surely the coincidences were too great even for German intelligence to gloss over? Despite all the care and the precautions taken, the fact remained that three Axis warships had been sighted and then sunk, over a comparatively short period, in rendezvous positions specially chosen for their remoteness, either on the very day of the rendezvous or (as in *Brake*'s case) the day after.

The Germans did suspect that their rendezvous positions had been betrayed and that their cyphers were insecure. On 13 March, the day after the *Brake* sinking, they introduced emergency procedures for modifying the Enigma settings after compromise had been suspected. These modifications did not delay GC & CS for long and in fact by 16 March the OIC had the decrypt of an Enigma of 14th, giving details of two rendezvous to be kept by the only remaining supply U-boat, *U–488*, on 19 and 23 March, in an area west of the Cape Verde islands.

But first it was imperative to have a period of calm, to allow enemy suspicions the chance to subside. The Admiralty sent ULTRAs to the operating authorities in West and South Africa, informing them of *U–488*'s rendezvous but ordering them to keep all their forces clear of the area. On 17 March the Admiralty sent a general signal informing ULTRA recipients worldwide (all thirty-one of them) of the new modifications to the German Enigma settings and instructing them to take action to make sure that none of their forces made contact with the enemy at or near any of the known rendezvous, or anywhere outside their normal operating areas.

The OIC must then have fervently hoped and prayed that nobody would now stumble across an enemy by chance, as in the cases of *Gedania* and *Gonzerheim* in June, 1941. In fact, as it happened, aircraft from the American escort carrier *Block Island* and the US destroyer escorts *Corry* and *Bronstein* had already sunk *U–801* as it approached one of the rendezvous points, west of the Cape Verdes, on 16 March. Three days later *Block Island*'s aircraft sank a second U-boat *U–1059*, also west of the Cape Verdes.

As a result of these sinkings there was an exchange of signals between Pound and the US COMINCH, Admiral King, who had, of course, received the Admiralty's general signal of 17 March concerning the new modifications to the Enigma settings and the need to leave the rendezvous areas unmolested. To the implication that *Block Island*'s recent activities might have endangered the ULTRA secret, King retorted sharply that it was the *Charlotte Schliemann* and *Brake* incidents which had aroused the enemy's suspicions; that it was likely that the enemy suspected that only current Enigma settings had been compromised, by capture; that *Block Island* had been nowhere near either of the rendezvous areas but had been carrying out a normal search and destroy operation, of a kind and in an area which could only confirm the enemy's belief that the Atlantic was a dangerous place to be; that enemy suspicions would in fact be strengthened if the Allies suddenly stopped attacking U-boats in the refuelling areas; and, furthermore, in King's opinion, diverting so many convoys away from waiting U-boat wolfpacks over the years had probably aroused the

194

enemy's suspicions much more than the attacks in the rendezvous areas. To all this Pound tactfully replied that he agreed that the German Navy very probably had not yet decided that the Enigma was generally insecure. Nevertheless Pound pointed out that *Block Island* had been operating near rendezvous positions given in signals which had the modified Enigma settings introduced on 13 March.

To cap it all, with the help of the Enigma, the US destroyers *Frost*, *Inch*, *Snowden* and *Barber*, screening the escort carrier *Croatan*, sank *U–488* at one of the rendezvous points west of Cape Verde on 26 April. The watchers in Whitehall, and in Washington, waited anxiously for the German Navy at last to awake and to introduce some radical changes in their general cryptographic security, including fundamental reform of their Enigma procedures. But BdU merely attributed losses in the central Atlantic to the fact that, as Admiral King rightly remarked, the Atlantic was now dangerous, too dangerous even for occasional refuelling. Refuellings would now only be carried out in urgent cases, from combatant boats. This situation was likely to continue until the introduction of submerged refuelling.

With hindsight, it now seems scarcely believable that the German Navy did not realize that the Enigma had been consistently broken over a long period of time. Instead, they continued to suspect treachery, careless talk, the French Resistance, or the American Special Operations Executive. They assumed that cyphers or contents of messages must have fallen into Allied hands, or that the Allies were succeeding through what the Germans termed 'external observations'. They continued to place sublime trust in the Enigma. Even so able and wily an officer as Karl Dönitz could not bring himself in his conversation or his memoirs to believe, even years after the war, that the German Enigma had been broken.

Thus, happily for the Allies, the secret of ULTRA remained secure. But, as an official British naval staff appreciation of the use of ULTRA over the whole course of the war admitted, this security was only achieved through 'luck and the amazing stupidity – amounting almost to "pigheadedness" – of the German Intelligence as regards the unbreakability of their cyphers'.

This 'pigheadedness' allowed the Allies, over the years, to consolidate the knowledge derived from the Enigma, and to perfect their techniques in using such knowledge, to the point where major operations were conducted with complete insight into the enemy's plans. A post-war survey of the value and use of Special Intelligence in J.I.S. work concluded that during Operation TORCH, for example, the Allied landings in North Africa in November, 1942, 'the U [Ultra] cover was so detailed and complete that we had advance notice of every intention and move of the German Forces in Africa and Italy, and of the many moves and intentions of such Italian forces as fell into the Italo-German programme'.

By the end of the war, so detailed, so complete, so wide-ranging and so continuous was the information Special Intelligence was providing about the Third Reich – not merely its naval and military strength and intentions, but also its political and economic state – that, the same survey of J.I.S. work concedes, 'without Special Intelligence the war would have been much longer, and more costly, and indeed might never have been won'.

GLOSSARY

BdU: *Befehlshaber der U-boote*, Head of the U-boat Arm

Break: to establish the plain language equivalents of the groups of a code book, or, to reduce a cypher to plain language; to reconstruct any code or cypher system

C 38 m: Swedish encyphering machine used by the Italian Navy

Code: a substitution system having groups (usually of a fixed number, e.g. 3, 4, or 5, of letters, figures, or letters and figures) as the equivalents of phrases, words, syllables, letters, numbers, punctuation marks, etc., common phrases, and even whole sentences of plain language

Code Word: word which serves to convey a previously arranged meaning, e.g. that an expected situation has arisen, or that a particular procedure is to be put into operation, or that a particular situation or operation has been completed or achieved

Cryptanalysis: art or science of ascertaining the essential nature of codes and cyphers and reconstructing the systems and operations used by the encoders and encypherers, or enough of these, to enable the messages to be read

Cypher: any system whereby the individual letters, figures, punctuation marks, etc., of plain language, or the individual letters, figures or other symbols of an encoded message, are rearranged among themselves (transposition) or with an admixture of other figures or letters (dummies) or replaced by different letters, figures etc., (substitution), with a view to making the message unintelligible to anyone not in authorized possession of the knowledge or apparatus necessary to reverse the systematic process and so restore the order of letters, figures etc., of the original plain language or encoded message.

Decrypt: a foreign communication which has passed through the stages of cryptanalysis and decryption and is in its original language prior to translation

Decypher: to convert a cypher text into the original plain language by reversing the operations of encyphering

D/F: Direction Finding

D/F Fix: approximate position of transmitting station, obtained by

197

plotting the bearings of two or more D/F stations on its transmission, the position being the area in which the bearings intersect

'Dolphin': GC & CS name for 'Heimisch' (q.v.) Enigma key

Dummy: cypher or code message sent merely as practice, or to produce an impression of activity where real traffic is rare or non-existent, or to complicate the work of the cryptanalyst

Enigma: electro-mechanical wired enciphering machine, with a series of drums or wheels, first put on the market commercially in Europe in the 1920s, adopted by the German Navy in 1926, the German Army in 1929, and the German air Force in 1934; the arrangements and settings of the drums or wheels could be changed frequently and for every setting a would-be decrypter had to choose from one hundred and fifty million, million, million solutions

Fleet code: British low-grade 3-letter code, changed monthly, used always unrecoded and purely for tactical purposes and during exercises

GC & CS: Government Code and Cypher School, Bletchley Park

'Heimisch': German naval Enigma key, used by ships and authorities in home waters and the Baltic from September, 1939, until the end of the war and by U-boats until February, 1942, and read by GC & CS (who named it 'Dolphin') virtually currently from 1 August, 1941

High-Grade: code or cypher systems designed to provide long-term security, i.e. to resist breaking indefinitely, or for a comparatively long period

'Hydra': name used for 'Heimisch' (q.v.) after January, 1943

HYDRO: prefix used for certain messages in the Flag Officers' Cypher which, in January, 1940, the Admiralty informed selected flag officers would contain intelligence from a particularly sensitive and absolutely reliable source. Prefix and procedures changed to ULTRA in June, 1941

JIS: Joint Intelligence Staff

Key: series of figures, numbers or letters which are used in the encypherment and decypherment of messages in a given cypher system

Low-Grade: code or cypher system not expected to resist attempts to break it for long, especially if used to any great extent; usually employing only one encoding or enciphering process, and that a fairly simple one, e.g. simple substitution, periodic substitution with a short period, simple transposition, uncyphered code

Machine cypher: cypher system in which the enciphering and decyphering are performed by means of a machine

NID: Naval Intelligence Department

OIC: Operational Intelligence Centre, in the Admiralty, where operational intelligence from all sources was gathered and analysed in one centre, and from where findings were transmitted to the operational staff within the Admiralty and to overseas commands

One-time pad: an additive table used once only and then destroyed; a demonstrably secure cypher, provided the additives are random, because it gives no depth

PR; Photographic Reconnaissance

RFP: Radio Finger Printing, a process which filmed the type and peculiarities of a transmitter

Setting: used especially of a cypher, meaning the position (usually denoted by page, line and column numbers) on a cyphering key or subtractor, especially a long subtractor, where the cyphering of an encoded message begins

'Shark': GC & CS name for 'Triton' (q.v.) Enigma key

Sig Int: Signal Intelligence derived from the comprehensive study, including cryptanalysis, of communications systems

Special Intelligence: short title ULTRA (q.v.)

Subtractor: series of figures or letters (or a group or signal unit of such) which is added, non-carrying figure by figure, or letter by letter, to the figures or letters of code-groups or to the letters of plain language in the process of encyphering. Similarly, they are subtracted from the cypher in the processes of stripping and decyphering. An adder, or an additive

TA: Traffic Analysis, the study of communications networks, and of procedure signals, call-signs, low-grade codes and plain language, together with DF and other technical aids

TINA: the study of morse characteristics of individual wireless operators

Tracking Room: Admiralty centre where movements, whereabouts and intentions of enemy U-boats, known or estimated, were plotted and displayed

'Triton': Enigma key, with a fourth wheel, used by U-boats in the Atlantic (other than in the far north) from 1 February, 1942, until 24 May, 1943; broken by GC & CS (who named it 'Shark') in December, 1942

Type X or **Typex**: British cypher machine, basically similar to the German Enigma machine

ULTRA: short title, and message prefix, for Special Intelligence, and for messages containing Special Intelligence, i.e., intelligence from a particularly sensitive and absolutely reliable source, available as the result of the solution of high-grade codes and cyphers, (or those codes and cyphers placed for security reasons in this category), and distributed to specially selected and severely restricted numbers of recipients by means of one-time pad cyphers

Y Service: the interception of signals, including DF.

INDEX

Manchester, HMS, 26, 27, 180
Mansfield, HMS, 123, 129
Manxman, HMS, 43
Maori, HMS, 169, 170
Marconi, 102
Mareth Line, 187
Maritza, ss, 167
Marsdale, HMS, 35, 36
MASCOT, Operation, 91
Matabele, HMS, 57
Matthew Luckenbach, ss, 129
McCoy, Capt. J. C., RN, 137
McKeesport, ss, 136
Medenine, battle of, 187
Metox receiver, 150
MF 5, Operation, 176
Milwaukee, USS, 87
Modoc, USCG Cutter, 28
Mohawk, HMS, 17, 165
Montbretia, HMS, 107
Monte Gargano, 12
Montgomery, Gen Sir B., 183, 187
Moonstone, HMS, 10
Moore, V-A Sir H., 87, 88, 89
Moosejaw, HMCS, 99
Morden, HMCS, 157, 158
Moreton Bay, HMS, 183
Morosini, 100
Muenchen, 23, 24, 33, 36, 37, 39, 182
'Musketry', Operation, 151, 152

Nabob, HMS, 91
Naiad, HMS, 168, 170, 171, 174, 177, 178
Napoli, ss, 172
Narcissus, HMS, 120, 145, 156, 157
Nariya, ss. 126
Nasturtium, HMS, 97
Naval Cyphers, No. 1, No. 2, No. 3, No. 4, 103, 105, 110
Nelson, HMS, 35
Neptune, HMS, 35, 168, 169, 173
Nestor, HMAS, 100, 180
Newcastle, HMS, 191, 192
Newfoundland Escort Force, 95
Nigeria, HMS, 36, 62, 180
Noble, Ad. Sir P., 100
Norfolk, HMS, 24, 26–29, 62, 80, 83
North Cape, battle of, 79–84
Northern Foam, HMS, 156, 158
Northern Gem, HMS, 135, 138, 139
Northern Spray, HMS, 135
Norwegian Campaign, 7
Nubian, HMS, 17, 165

Nurnberg, 53, 54, 73

Obdurate, HMS, 73, 74
Obedient, HMS, 73
OBVIATE, Operation, 73
Offa, HMS, 136, 137, 139
Ohio, ss. 180
Oliver, Capt. R. D., RN, 38
'One Time' Pads, 199
Onice, 173
Onslaught, HMS, 86
Onslow, HMS, 73, 75
Orchis, HMS, 120,145, 156
Oribi, HMS, 136, 139, 140, 141
Orion, HMS, 17
Orkan, PS, 160, 161
Orwell, HMS, 73
Osmond-Ingram, USS, 120
OSTFRONT, Operation, 82
Ottawa, HMCS, 107

P.36, HMS/M, 26, 178
P.42, HMS/M, 185, 186
P.54, HMS/M, 70
Pampas, ss, 178, 179
Panther, HMS, 136, 137, 138
PARAVANE, Operation, 92
Pathfinder, HMS, 142
Paul Jacobi, 57
PEARL, 2
Pedestal, Operation, 180
Pelican, HMS, 138, 141
Penelope, HMS, 166, 171, 173–175, 177–179
Penn, HMS, 136, 137, 138
Pennywort, HMS, 129
Perth, HMAS, 17
Pimpernel, HMS, 110, 112, 123
Pinguin, 7
Pink, HMS, 135, 137–140
Pizey, Capt. C. T. M., RN, 50
PLANET, Operation, 90
Platino, 178
Pola, 20, 21
Polyanthus, HMS, 156–158
Polyphemus, 38
Port Auckland, ss, 129
PORTCULLIS, Operation, 180
Pound, Ad. Sir D., 34, 44, 65, 66, 67, 70, 71, 109, 130, 148, 182, 186, 188, 194, 195
Power, Cdr. M., RN, 19
Pridham-Wippell, V-A, H. D., 16, 17, 20

205

Prien, Kap. Lt. G., 5
Prince of Wales, HMS, 26, 28
Prince Rupert, HMCS, 163
Prinz Eugen, 24, 26, 33–36, 39, 40–52, 56, 57, 61, 73, 76
Precida, ss. 167
Proudfoot, Lt. Cdr, RN, 114, 116
Pursuer, HMS, 87, 88
Python, 38

Quadrant, HMS, 191
Queen Elizabeth, HMS, 168, 171, 174

R. 121, 81
Raeder, Ad. E., 52, 54, 70, 76
Ramsay, Ad. Sir B., 47, 48, 49
Ranger, USS, 78, 79
Rawalpindi, HMS, 5
Rawlings, R-A H. R., 168, 169
Relentless, HMS, 191, 193
Renoncule, FS, 120, 145, 156, 158
Renown, HMS, 44, 58
Repulse, HMS, 26, 27
REP, 29, 30, 199
RHEINEUBUNG, Operation, 38, 39
Riccardi, Ad., 11
Richard Beitzen, 57
Roberts, Capt. G., RN, 116
Rodney, HMS, 30, 31, 44
Roebuck, HMS, 193
Rommel, Gen. E., 183, 187
Roselys, FS, 120, 145, 156, 157
Rosthern, HMCS, 119
Rotherhamm, Cdr. G. E., RN, 27
Rowallan Castle, ss. 176
Royal Air Force: Bomber Command, 44, 51, 52, 56, 91; Coastal Command, 44, 46, 47, 49, 86, 150, 152; Fighter Command, 44, 46, 47, 48, 49; Naval Co-Operation Group, No. 201, 175, 176; No. 10 O.T.U., 152; Patrols: 'Habo', 46, 'Jim Crow', 44, 46, 'Line SE', 46, 'Stopper', 46; Squadrons: No. 9 Sq., 92: No. 22 Sq., 41; No. 42 Sq., 43; No. 53 Sq., 153; No. 69 Sq., 166; No. 72 Sq., 48; No. 84 Sq., 21; No. 86 Sq., 43, 133, 143; No. 91 Sq., 47; No. 120 Sq., 144, 157; No. 172 Sq., 151; No. 201 Sq., 130; No. 210 Sq., 142; No. 217 Sq., 43; No. 223 Sq., 46; No. 224 Sq., 46, 162; No. 269 Sq., 98, 107, 144; No. 617 Sq., 92
Royal Australian Air Force: No. 461 Squadron, 153
Royal Canadian Air Force: No. 5 Sq., 139;

No. 10 Sq., 156, 162; No. 401 Sq., 48; No. 411 Sq., 48; No. 423 Sq., 143
Royalist, HMS, 87
Royal Oak, HMS, 5
Rudloff, Korv. Kap., 115, 118

Sachsenwald, 31
Sackville, HMCS, 157
Sagona, ss, 174
Santee, USS, 149, 150
Saxifrage, HMS, 110, 123
Scharnhorst, 5, 6, 7, 40–52, 58, 73, 76, 77, 79–84
Schenk, USS, 116
Schniewind, Ad., 65
Schultze, Korv. Kap., H., 112
Scimitar, HMS, 98
Scire, 173
Scott-Moncrieff, Capt., RN, 145
Scylla, HMS, 71, 152
Sealion, HMS/M, 44, 45, 46
Searcher, HMS, 87, 88
'Seaslug', Operation, 151, 152
Seawolf, HMS/M, 58
Selviston, ss, 140
Sennen, USCG Cutter, 138, 144
'Shark' Code, 24, 105, 108, 109, 110, 119, 124, 134, 159, 199
Sheffield, HMS, 31, 35, 73–76, 80, 83
Sherwood, Lt. Cdr. R. E., RNR, 138
Sherbrooke, Capt. R. St. V., RN, 73–77
Sikh, HMS, 169, 170
Sirte, First Battle of, 171–172
Sirte, Second Battle of, 178–179
Skeena, HMCS, 98, 99
Slayden, Cdr. G. M., RN, 57
SLEUTH, Operation, 191
Snowden, USS, 195
Snowflake, HMS, 135, 136, 139, 144
Somali, HMS, 23
Somerville, Ad. Sir J., 12, 14, 15, 190, 191, 192
SOURCE, Operation, 77
Southern Princess, ss, 126
Sparrowhawk, HMS, 27
Spencer, USCG Cutter, 118, 119
Spey, HMS, 138, 141, 144
Spichern, 33
Springbank, HMS, 101
Stannard, Lt. R. B., VC RNR, 114, 115
Starling, HMS, 87, 152
St. Croix, HMCS, 157, 158
St. Francis, HMCS, 157
Stockport, ss, 119
Stokes, Cdr. G. H., RN, 169, 170

206